RUSSIA'S CONSTITUTIONAL REVOLUTION

R OBERT B. A HDIEH

RUSSIA'S CONSTITUTIONAL REVOLUTION

LEGAL CONSCIOUSNESS AND THE TRANSITION TO DEMOCRACY

1985–1996

The Pennsylvania State University Press
University Park, Pennsylvania

Library of Congress Cataloging-in-Publication Data

Ahdieh, Robert B., 1971–
   Russia's constitutional revolution :
legal consciousness and the transition to democracy,
1985–1996 / by Robert B. Ahdieh.

      p.   cm.
   Includes bibliographical references and index.
   ISBN 0-271-01609-4 (cloth : alk. paper)
   ISBN 0-271-01610-8 (paper : alk. paper)
   1. Russia—Constitutional history.   2. Law reform—Russia.
I. Title.
KLA2110.A93   1997
342.47′029—dc20
[344.70229]   96-6116
                                                    CIP

It is the policy of The Pennsylvania State University Press to use acid-free paper for
the first printing of all clothbound books. Publications on uncoated stock satisfy the
minimum requirements of American National Standard for Information Sciences—
Permanence of Paper for Printed Library Materials, ANSI Z39.48-1992.

CONTENTS

Preface   vii

Introduction   1

PART I: DEVELOPMENT   11

1. The Gorbachev Years   13

2. The Russian Federation   47

PART II: AN EMERGING PARADIGM   91

3. Principles   95

4. Practice   115

Conclusion   197

Epilogue   219

Bibliography   229

Index   245

To my father,
whose enthusiasm for excellence
has been contagious

PREFACE

No work of this sort rests on the shoulders of the author alone. A first book, almost by definition, requires guidance and assistance galore. Completing it while being a full-time student demands yet further support. More specifically, in grappling with events of such recent vintage, whose full significance is still unclear, the combined wisdom of many holds the best promise for success. My only hope is that I have drawn together well the contributions of all those who have been a part of this effort.

First, to a group of my professors, both within the classroom and without, who have guided the development of my ideas on Russia and the place of the law therein, I owe my deepest thanks: Stephen Cohen, whose love for Russia taught me what a true Sovietologist is; Stanley Katz, who captured my attention and my life with a love for the law; Richard Ullman, whose encouragement brought these efforts to fruition; and Richard Falk, whose vision of law has helped shape my own. My immense gratitude is likewise due Robert Sharlet, Peter Juviler, and Zbigniew Brzezinski, whose patience with my ideas, my prose, and my occasional ignorance, together with their generous encouragement, helped turn a thesis into a scholarly work. And, for putting up with my recurring absences in Russia and still managing to teach me the language, thanks to my many Russian professors. I hope you're finally proud of me.

The list of those to thank in Russia is too lengthy to include, but let me note a few of the most generous. My thanks to Mikhail Gorbachev, who allowed me to conduct much of my research from the offices of the Gorbachev Foundation; to those at the Moscow State Institute of International Relations, especially Yuri Melville and Nikolai Topornin, for both educating me in Russia's unique legal culture and setting my field work in motion; to the Lopez family and Misha Mossin, without whom I would not have survived in Russia; and especially to those who took the time to speak with me, often at great length and on multiple occasions, on these challenging and difficult questions—you have made this work what it is. Finally, I wish to note especially Avgust Mishin, who enthusiastically spent more than three hours discussing his hopes for constitutionalism in Russia only days before he passed away.

The willingness of many individuals, including Harold Berman, Erik Hoffmann, Eugene Huskey, and Donald Barry, as well as David Remnick, to take the time to look at various incarnations of this work and to generously comment on it not only improved the final product but inspired me to pursue its refinement with heightened vigor. Thank you to you all. For their editorial reviews of the manuscript, I am likewise grateful to Charles Lynch and Juliette Soderberg.

To Sandy Thatcher, Cherene Holland, and Lisa Bayer of Penn State Press, who have helped at every stage, my gratitude. Thank you, most of all, for giving me a chance.

The extensive research, writing, and revision of this book would have been impossible without the constant and loving support of my entire family—my parents and grandparents, as well as my beloved sister, Linda, and my wife, Krista, who have all been far too patient with me. Yet to them, I owe not this book, but my life.

Finally, to the many Baha'is in Russia and throughout the world who have inspired in me a love for and fascination with all of humanity, thank you for turning my face to the East.

INTRODUCTION

We, the multinational people of the Russian Federation, united by a common destiny on our land, affirming human rights and liberties, civil peace and concord, preserving the historically evolved unity of the state, proceeding from generally recognized principles of the equality and self-determination of peoples, honoring the memory of our forebears, who handed down to us love and respect for the fatherland and faith in goodness and justice, revitalizing the sovereign statehood of Russia and affirming the unshakable nature of its democratic foundations, striving to ensure the well-being and prosperity of Russia, proceeding from our responsibility for our homeland to present and future generations, recognizing ourselves as part of the world community, adopt the Constitution of the Russian Federation.

—Preamble to the Constitution of the Russian Federation, adopted on 12 December 1993[1]

The constitution must show us how we ought to live.

—Valery Zorkin, former chairman, Constitutional Court of the Russian Federation[2]

In the eyes of many, the law is not among the critical concerns facing Russia at this juncture in its history. Even less so, constitutionalism. Such matters do not share the limelight with crime, inflation, and political conflict, in either mass or elite psychology. "It used to be—and probably still is—the tacit knowledge of any Soviet or Russian law professional that he is not in the

1. *Izvestiia*, 10 November 1993, 3–5. Translation available in *Current Digest of the Post-Soviet Press* 45 (8 December 1993): 4–16.
2. Valery Zorkin, member, Russian Constitutional Court, 2 February 1994 (hereafter Zorkin, interview of 2 February 1994). All interviews were conducted in Moscow and translated by the author, unless otherwise indicated. Professional titles are given as of interview date.

mainstream of things."[3] Yet constitutionalism is among the first principles of both democracy and the free market; it lies at the heart of Russia's future development. Absent legal stability and constitutional order, no political or economic reform will survive, let alone succeed. The development of constitutionalism is thus a matter of urgent public policy.

The study of constitutionalism's development in Russia is compelling at a theoretical level as well. Its emergence represents an ongoing case study, a work in progress, without precedent or parallel in history. The chaotic milieu and unpredictable character of this transformation sharply distinguish it from any previous endeavor to reconstitute a nation. Most often, the constitutional project involves the acceptance and adoption of somewhat alien governing structures by a discrete sociopolitical grouping. The challenge of developing constitutionalism in such cases is to bring an already existing legal culture to coalesce around new institutions. The eighteenth-century American colonies exemplify this scenario with their preexisting legal consciousness, upon which a new constitutional structure was simply draped. In Russia, quite to the contrary, constitutionalism and the law "do not have much immediate appeal."[4]

"Throughout Russian history, peasant and *intelligent* [sic] alike have looked askance at law, which has traditionally been associated not with justice but with *proizvol,* or tyranny."[5] Thus, the obstacles to constitutionalism do not lie in the logistics of its creation but in Russian culture itself.

Traditional western scholarship generally characterizes constitutionalism as the principles and practices of limited government, including the separation of powers and judicial review.[6] In this view, it is simply a set of structural guidelines designed to temper democracy and majoritarian rule. Yet this definition is only helpful in describing constitutionalism in its developed form, as it overemphasizes one strand of the thread of constitutionalism and

---

3. Alexander Blankenagel, "Toward Constitutionalism in Russia," *East European Constitutional Review* 1 (Summer 1992): 28.

4. Nikolai Biryukov, professor of philosophy, Moscow State Institute of International Relations. Presentation in English at Princeton University, 15 November 1993. Hereafter Biryukov, presentation of 15 November 1993.

5. Eugene Huskey, "From Legal Nihilism to *Pravovoe Gosudarstvo:* Soviet Legal Development, 1917–1990," in Donald D. Barry, ed., *Toward the "Rule of Law" in Russia? Political and Legal Reform in the Transition Period* (Armonk, N.Y.: M. E. Sharpe, 1992), 38.

6. See Walter F. Murphy, "Constitutions, Constitutionalism, and Democracy," in Douglas Greenberg, Stanley N. Katz, Melanie Beth Oliviero, and Steven C. Wheatley, eds., *Constitutionalism and Democracy: Transitions in the Contemporary World* (New York: Oxford University Press, 1993), 3–25.

ignores the other. Focusing on constitutionalism's institutional component of constitutional structures (*konstitutsionnyi stroi*), it ignores the a priori element of constitutionalism most often absent in transitional legal cultures: namely, its psychological underpinning—a developed legal consciousness (*pravovoe soznaniye*). Together, these are the basic girders that make possible and uphold constitutionalism. In constructing the foundations of a new constitutional and political order, one might see constitutionalism as the mortar comprising its substance. The strength of the mortar requires both sand and water in the right proportions, the absence of either leaving it without resilience.[7]

In attempting to assess the development of constitutionalism in modern Russia, use of this broader definition is both necessary and appropriate. We must diverge from the narrower western view in order to evaluate progress in what essentially remains an "unconstitutional" society, where western terms of reference continue to mean relatively little.[8] Yet the constitutional process in Russia during the last decade has ignored the development of legal consciousness. What, then, has all the talk of constitutional reform amounted to? Often to little more than rhetoric and pious hope.

While acknowledging their mutual dependence, the effective construction of constitutionalism in Russia requires that we not conflate legal consciousness with constitutional structures. This mistake is represented by the translation of *constitutionalism* into Russian as *konstitutsionnyi stroi*—constitutional structure.[9] The tendency of Russia's constitutional reformers to adopt and apply this limited definition during the last decade, and their resulting failure to address legal consciousness and its development in their frenetic drive to build new constitutional structures, lay behind many of the political and economic failures of recent years.

Constitutionalism, I will argue herein, is not a set of government institutions but an entire process of governing. Since the selection of Mikhail Gorbachev as general secretary of the Soviet Communist Party in 1985, the Soviet Union and Russia have had a rich constitutional and legal history.

7. For an insightful commentary on the broader scope and significance of constitutionalism, see Julio Faundez, "Constitutionalism: A Timely Revival," in Greenberg, 354–55, 357–58.

8. For an analogous discussion of the alien character of democracy to Russia, see Viktor Sergeyev and Nikolai Biryukov, *Russia's Road to Democracy: Parliament, Communism and Traditional Culture* (Hants, England: Edward Elgar, 1993), 1–3.

9. Use of this translation declined as *konstitutsionnalizm* entered the Russian lexicon in 1992 and 1993.

This period witnessed the rise and fall of various institutions, the appearance and disappearance of divergent models of governance, and a perpetual ebb and flow in legal consciousness. Yet a decade later constitutionalism still remains largely absent from Russia. This unfortunate reality is the result of a narrow focus on constitutional structures in disregard of, and often at the expense of, legal consciousness. Structures alone, without a supportive legal culture, inevitably collapsed. Ten years of development have thus left Russia with neither the structures nor the consciousness necessary for effective constitutionalism. A new paradigm of constitutionalism, grounded in a new set of underlying principles, must therefore guide Russia's future constitutional development.

Appropriate to this view of the emergence of constitutionalism in Russia, I have divided this book into two basic parts. Part I is essentially descriptive and attempts to present, in all its controversy and complexity, the development of constitutionalism in the Soviet Union and Russia from 1985 to 1993—from Gorbachev's initial reforms to the adoption of the new Russian Constitution and the birth of the Second Russian Republic in 1993. What progress, I will ask, has been made toward constitutionalism in Russia? What factors have encouraged this process? And which have stood in its way? Following a chronological line, Part I notes the major events in the constitutional and legal history of this period and focuses on their impact on the legal consciousness of the Russian masses and elites. Particular developments and events are highlighted insofar as they shed light on the transformation of attitudes toward the law. The outward face of Russia may have changed abruptly, I will suggest, but underlying attitudes often remain the same. The recent history of constitutional structures has been quite fluid, while that of legal consciousness has only grudgingly moved ahead.

The limited growth of legal consciousness and the often destructive relationship of institution and consciousness building, the themes of Part I, are the backdrop for Part II. More prescriptive in intent, this section picks up where Part I left off. Moving beyond the narrow, instrumental view of constitutionalism that defined the latter period, Part II considers the future pattern of constitutional and legal development in Russia. It integrates various issues beyond the confines of traditional constitutional scholarship and suggests the changes necessary in these areas if constitutionalism is to become a reality. The Second Russian Republic, to begin with, must imbue its legal and political processes with certain principles that have been given inadequate attention in the past. Part II begins with a consideration of these basic principles. Revolving around the aforesaid dialectic of structures and consciousness, and the necessary prioritization of the latter, these principles involve the source of increasingly amorphous groups of masses and elites, the pace of constitutional change, and the relationship of such change.

These guiding principles are then systematically applied in the context of the critical issues facing Russia today. Constitutionalism, it will be argued, is at the heart of these challenges, providing both "a common framework for analysis and . . . a guide for the difficult task of building or rebuilding the political order."[10] The second half of Part II thus examines the various factors that will impact upon the development of constitutionalism, asking how their constructive potential can be maximized. Yet the relationship of constitutionalism and Russia's political, economic, and social situation is a symbiotic one. A better understanding of constitutionalism may thus suggest new approaches to Russian reform more generally or, at the very least, new guiding principles for these reforms. In this view, constitutionalism is as critical to the process of economic and political reform as the progress of such reform is to the effective development of constitutionalism.

It would be overly simplistic to label particular events of the last decade as discrete positive or negative influences on the development of constitutionalism. In unstable environments, all events play upon the creation of constitutionalism.[11] Moreover, the events that appear most relevant are not always the most influential. Thus, while an analysis of the politics of constitution drafting in Russia during the last few years might be enlightening, the formal process of constitution making was probably one of the least important factors in the development of the legal consciousness, and even the constitutional structures, of modern Russia.

Valery Pisigin, a member of President Boris Yeltsin's Council of Economic Advisers and a liberal political activist, once described the Central Bank's confiscation of old rouble notes in July 1993 as the most significant factor in the development of Russian constitutionalism in recent years. This act, he suggested, effectively undermined any sense of a law-ruled state that had haltingly developed since 1985.[12] It "destroyed the emerging public confidence in the rouble, in Yeltsin, and in democracy."[13]

10. Faundez, 356.
11. Igor Klamkin, director, Public Opinion Foundation, 4 February 1994. Hereafter Klamkin, interview of 4 February 1994.
12. Valery Pisigin, president, Society and Politics Association and former adviser to President Yeltsin, 27 July 1993. Hereafter Pisigin, interview of 27 July 1993.
13. Dwight Semler, "Summer in Russia Brings No Real Political Progress; Federative Issues

Accordingly, the development of constitutionalism must be seen as part and parcel of the entire complex history of the period extending from 1985 into the mid-1990s. Constitutionalism's maturation lies not in a closed and empirical formula, but is based "on several phenomena: the emergence of democratic forces in society; the effort to restructure the economy and to provide a legal basis for the new arrangements; and the striving of territories and ethnic groups to assert their autonomy from the center."[14]

Robert Sharlet, a leading scholar of Soviet and Russian constitutional history, powerfully conveys this view of constitutional development as caught up in broader political, economic, and social processes. Looking back at the final years of the Soviet Union, he writes:

> In the political theater of the Soviet Union in the early 1990s, constitutional rhetoric had become two-dimensional. Beneath the everyday exchanges in the press, the executive suites, and in the parliaments over tactical political issues, a constitutional convention *writ large,* addressing strategic questions on the future shape of the political system, had been under way for several years. I am not referring to a discrete, organized meeting such as the American Constitutional Convention in Philadelphia; the Soviet convention was quite different, and in fact probably unique in world constitutional annals as it was riven by ambivalences. It was both planned and spontaneous, and occurred over time in multiple venues; the quiet of constitutional deliberation was occasionally punctuated by gunfire and violence; negotiation was both continuous and episodic, operating on several levels simultaneously at different tempos and with varying degrees of intensity; and essential compromise, so vital to constitution-making, advanced and receded as circumstances constantly changed and inveterate antagonisms welled up to block the prospect of peaceful union and, in the end, the process of orderly dissolution of the union.[15]

The chaotic and conflictual picture of the constitutional debate and development process that emerges from our consideration of the past in Part I is

Dominate Constitutional Discussions," *East European Constitutional Review* 2 (Summer 1993): 22.

14. Donald D. Barry, introduction to Barry, *Toward the "Rule of Law" in Russia?* xvi.

15. Robert Sharlet, "Citizen and State Under Gorbachev and Yeltsin," in Stephen White, Alex Pravda, and Zvi Gitelman, eds., *Developments in Russian and Post-Soviet Politics* (Durham, N.C.: Duke University Press, 1994), 109.

consonant with Sharlet's view of recent years. Instability may be the most significant feature of this period and, in an optimistic view, the best evidence that *positive* change and progress remain possible.

The attempt to capture this panorama of recent Russian history in our study of constitutionalism will, at times, take us beyond those events and decisions that directly involve constitutional issues. Yet often, such apparent irrelevancies are critical to constitutional and legal developments, both in the abstract and in the concrete.[16] A juridical test of materiality would thus be quite pointless. Yeltsin's health, for instance, is important to students of constitutionalism such as Vyacheslav Nikonov, who points out that the accession of a Vladimir Zhirinovsky to the Russian presidency will leave "no further questions of constitutionalism."[17]

Part I will thus progress from Mikhail Gorbachev's initial political rhetoric to his efforts at constitutional restructuring, and from the August 1991 coup attempt to the sudden demise of the Soviet Union. Turning to independent Russia, I will examine the circumstances leading up to President Boris Yeltsin's 1993 Constitutional Conference and the chain of events in its aftermath, from the attack on the parliament to the adoption of the new constitution in December 1993. Finally, I will consider the Russian Constitutional Court (1991–93), a constitutionally mandated institution whose emergence and stormy first-term career suggest important lessons for the future development of constitutionalism in Russia.

While the broadest factors in the development of constitutionalism are not addressed, their influence, usually for the worse, should always be remembered. Stemming from the economic and political collapse of the Soviet state, they include the dramatic rise in crime, unemployment, and poverty. The attitudes and psychology of a nation in transformation are bound to be influenced by the widespread failure of whole industries and by the gradual breakdown of state institutions and already weak social welfare regimes. This wholesale chaos is the frustration of committed legal reformers in Russia, who point to the Napoleonic or Justinian codes as legal frameworks that, unlike their own, emerged not at moments of upheaval, but at moments of stability.[18]

16. Avgust Mishin, professor of constitutional law, Moscow State University, 14 August 1993. Hereafter Mishin, interview of 14 August 1993.

17. Vyacheslav Nikonov, member of Federal Assembly (Duma) and former legal expert at the International Reform Foundation. Interview in English at Moscow Pizza Hut, 3 February 1994. Hereafter Nikonov, interview of 3 February 1994.

18. Giorgi Satarov, senior adviser to President Yeltsin, 4 February 1994. Hereafter Satarov, interview of 4 February 1994.

These elements of decline and collapse are the background for the consideration in Part I of more specific factors and events, and they appear again in Part II as I attempt to outline a future scenario for constitutionalism's development. Even where unmentioned, they must be borne in mind, as they are the basis for all modern analysis of the former soviet republics. One might even view these regressive developments and the creation of stable constitutionalism as twin, yet opposing, processes that have defined the character of recent Russian history.[19]

Consideration in Part I of the development of constitutionalism to date will help us to understand the latter as "a work in progress . . . not a ready-made doll house, but a do-it-yourself kit."[20] Part II will thus argue that constitutionalism's full scope as "a cultural, institutional, socioeconomic, and political as well as a legal and technical challenge" has not been faced up to.[21] I will suggest that the historical analysis of Part I reveals Russian reformers' extreme emphasis on the creation of constitutional structures rather than on the transformation of legal consciousness, a practice that resulted in the repeated collapse of institutions founded on a public and elite psychology lagging in its evolution.

Russian reformers attempted, as had many before, to simply impose the principles of western constitutionalism (as well as democracy and the market) on a society ill-prepared for them. Yet in the Soviet Union's and Eastern Europe's unique "post-totalitarian phase . . . the standard political and economic recipes based on intent to restructure and reorganize these societies by implanting in them 'the basic achievements of world civilization' fail to work." This involves no failure of the principles themselves. Rather, "years of totalitarianism have transformed the society. They have created a type of mentality, as well as institutional structures and social groups, that resist the transformation."[22] Intimately related to the reformers' disdain for the transformation of Russian legal consciousness, I will argue in Part II, has been the tendency of change—whether political, economic, social, or constitutional—to run from the top down. This preference for reform from

19. Vladimir Kudriavtsev, vice president, Russian Academy of Sciences, and academician of law, 31 January 1994. Hereafter Kudriavtsev, interview of 31 January 1994.

20. Nikolai Biryukov, professor of philosophy, Moscow State Institute of International Relations. Interview at Princeton University, 18 November 1993. Hereafter Biryukov, interview of 18 November 1993.

21. Erik P. Hoffmann, "Challenges to Viable Constitutionalism in Post-Soviet Russia," *Harriman Review* 7 (November 1994): 23. Hereafter Hoffmann.

22. Sergeyev and Biryukov, *Russia's Road to Democracy*, vii.

above, finally, is tied to Russia's "revolutionary consciousness" and a desire to do too much too quickly, and to reject gradual, more effective methods of reform.

The traditional model of Russian development has been one of "revolution from above." This was applied in the legal arena on several occasions in Russian history, most comprehensively during the last decade. Yet it has consistently proven inadequate. While its efficacy in economics and other areas may still be unclear, with regard to the development of constitutionalism, it may now be judged a failed model. In its place, I suggest in Part II, Russia must choose a path of "evolution from below," focusing on local institutions, individual rights, and other elements of legal culture. While this approach may be alien to Russia at the broadest level of abstraction, its application to particular issue areas in the latter half of Part II—from political corruption to judicial development, and from federalism to economic reform—will suggest concrete policies that can strengthen legal consciousness at the grass roots. This is the key to the creation of a Russian civil society and the emergence of a new constitutional order.

What, then, does this book contribute to the debate on Russian constitutional issues? To begin with, it attempts to shed light on the often overlooked question of Russian legal consciousness. As nearly twenty years have passed since a full-length monograph considered this theme,[23] a treatment of this dimension of Russia's constitutional development is long overdue.

Equally significant, if not more so, is the methodology of this assessment. The complex, multi-factored character of constitutionalism's development limits the value of traditional scholarship in its analysis. Any attempt to better understand constitutionalism must acknowledge this complexity. My personal observations of the former Soviet Union and Russia will thus figure prominently in my discussion. Since 1989, during several visits to the Soviet Union and Russia ranging in length from several weeks to nearly one year, I have been privileged to observe closely the transformations I analyze.

I have attempted to meet as wide a cross section of Russian society as possible, interviewing everyone from cab drivers to former President Mikhail Gorbachev, for whom I worked as a research associate. I have lived with Russian students and families, attempting to adopt (sometimes too successfully) the thinking of the Russian man in the street. In addition to my studies

---

23. Richard E. Wortman, *The Development of Russian Legal Consciousness* (Chicago: University of Chicago Press, 1976).

at a previously closed Communist Party school, the Moscow State Institute of International Relations, I have had extensive contact with the Soviet Peace Committee, formerly a KGB front organization but now an independent think tank; with CNN's Moscow bureau; with the Academy of Sciences' Institute of State and Law; and with the International Monetary Fund. Together, these experiences provided me with a wealth of perspectives on recent developments.

This exposure has been augmented by a set of wide-ranging interviews, some formal and recorded herein, others impromptu and held on late nights around various kitchen tables. These interviews included talks with many of the major players involved in instigating the changes I examine, but also with many less powerful individuals who have been intimately affected by them. No other approach, I believe, could effectively capture a sense of Russian legal consciousness and its transformation during the late twentieth century. The spectrum of opinions and positions these interviews generated go to the heart of Russia's latter-day reconstitutionalization. They present not an *ex post* history of what has been but a realistic portrait of what still is; hence, the medium truly is the message.

Eyewitness reportage does, of course, have its limitations. But, as perfected by Alexis de Tocqueville and the Marquis de Custine in their respective analyses of early America and tsarist Russia, it can provide valuable insights into transitional cultures. It is my hope that this endeavor may parallel such works, with even a small measure of their beneficial impact. If so, it will have well served its purpose.

PART I

DEVELOPMENT

There was a happy possibility—step by step, in an evolutionary manner—to move onto the path of constitutionalism. Sadly, that chance was lost.

—Valery Zorkin, former chairman,
Constitutional Court of the Russian Federation,
interview of 2 February 1994

CHAPTER ONE

THE GORBACHEV YEARS

A CONSTITUTIONAL HERITAGE

Contrary to western public opinion, Mikhail Gorbachev, for all his talents, was not a magician. The legal reforms and spirit of *pravovoe gosudarstvo* (law-based state) that Gorbachev brought to the Soviet Union, though hardly rooted in Russian culture, did have some history within it. In Gorbachev's own view, these had "always existed in the nation. We were never without law, though often we chose to ignore it."[1] While not readily apparent, some sense of constitutionalism did exist. Yet its relative weakness characterizes it as a precursor to rather than as the source of Gorbachev's legal reforms.

Some argue that the history of constitutionalism in Russia dates back centuries to the quasi-representative *sobori* of the early tsarist period. More commonly, however, scholars cite 1864 and Tsar Aleksandr II's reforms as the birth of constitutionalism in Russia.[2] While these reforms never reached fruition because of Aleksandr's growing conservatism and the return to repression that followed his assassination in 1881, they did leave a significant mark in the legal field. The 1864 reforms introduced jury trials, professionalized the defense bar, and expanded law faculties. From them

1. Mikhail Gorbachev, interview of 17 August 1993.
2. The 1864 reforms, in fact, had roots in the early 1800s and the reign of Aleksandr I. It was to him that the renowned Mikhail Speransky presented, in 1809, a draft of what could have been Russia's first constitution, setting out a semi-constitutional monarchy. Yet this was rejected by the tsar, who instead established a consultative Council of State to serve him in an advisory capacity. It is interesting to note that the several movements for legal reform in Russian history all emerged at moments of national weakness—Aleksandr I's in the face of setbacks in the Napoleonic Wars, Aleksandr II's in the aftermath of Russia's defeat in the Crimean War, and Nicholas II's in the wake of his defeat in the Russo-Japanese War. This may suggest interesting questions about Gorbachev's own legal reforms and their timing.

emerged an increasing dependence of the urban population on everyday courts that would survive until the collapse of Imperial Russia.

It is significant, moreover, that the theme of *pravovoe gosudarstvo* became a prominent feature of scholarly discourse following Aleksandr's reforms, easing "the way for its reception in the Soviet Union when the political atmosphere of *perestroika* permitted it" a century later.[3] The liberal legal scholarship of this period, which emerged in the 1860s and survived into the early 1900s—especially that of Boris Nikolaevich Chicherin (1828–1904), a prominent legal reformer and one-time mayor of Moscow—can be favorably compared with contemporaneous western legal thought. The actual practices of the tsarist legal system, meanwhile, were comparable with those of Germany or Japan at the time. In the legal arena, Russia had come quite far.

This set the stage for Tsar Nicholas II's liberalizing Manifesto of 17 October 1905, which was quickly followed by the Fundamental Law of 1906, Russia's first constitution.[4] This charter emerged in the wake of Russia's defeat in the Russo-Japanese War and the public upheavals that followed in 1905. But without a favorable climate of liberal legal thought, its promulgation would have been impossible.

The 1906 constitution was limited both in its substance and in its actual application by the tsar but was clearly a new step in constitutionalism's development. It included a relatively comprehensive bill of rights and explicitly declared the supremacy of laws in article 84. It hedged such liberalism, of course, with clauses such as article 86, requiring the tsar's sanction for all laws, and articles 96 and 97, which placed certain issues under the tsar's sole jurisdiction. Most important, however, the constitution established Russia's first elected parliamentary body—the Duma. Though at best only "semi-constitutional and semi-responsible," the 1906 constitution thus outlined a positive trajectory for Russian constitutionalism that could have produced a very different nation from the Russia we know today.[5] The exceedingly liberal program of political and legal reform the Provisional Government introduced after the monarchy's collapse in February 1917 supports this conclusion.

On the eve of the October 1917 Bolshevik Revolution, then, a strong legal

---

3. Donald D. Barry, introduction to Donald D. Barry, ed., *Toward the "Rule of Law" in Russia?* (Armonk, N.Y.: M. E. Sharpe, 1992), xv.

4. Adopted on 23 April 1906.

5. T. H. Rigby, "The Government in the Soviet Political System," in Eugene Huskey, ed., *Executive Power and Soviet Politics: The Rise and Decline of the Soviet State* (Armonk, N.Y.: M. E. Sharpe, 1992), 6.

culture had emerged and begun to take root. Noting as much, T. H. Rigby expresses hope that in modern Russia, "the relevant antecedents of contemporary politics and government will be found less and less in the last seventy years and more and more in the decades and centuries that went before."[6] For while communist rule may not have been entirely lawless, its primary constitutional legacy is very different from that of late Imperial Russia.

In Chapter 3, the lawlessness strand of Soviet legal history will be considered and its negative impact on Russian legal consciousness assessed. Here I will, consequently, highlight the legalist aspects of Soviet history that Gorbachev also inherited. The Bolsheviks, notwithstanding their ideological vision of a withering state, were exceedingly practical ideologues who saw the law as a valuable tool in their arsenal of authority. Decree no. 1, "On the Courts," was thus issued immediately after the revolution; the RSFSR[7] Family Code in October 1918; and, by November 1918, their decree on "strict observance" of the law. This formal legalism, however, initially coexisted with a strong tendency toward legal nihilism.[8]

The latter school, represented by E. Pashukanis, head of the State and Law section of the Communist Academy, idealistically postulated, as had Marx, that the law would wither away with the state. Instead, this utopian commitment to following Marx's writings, and to his principle that the inherently bourgeois law had no role in communist society, itself withered away with Stalin's decisions to appoint Andrei Vyshinsky, the consummate legal instrumentalist, as chief prosecutor, and to adopt the highly formalized 1936 constitution.

With these decisions the law came to play a prominent, if sometimes nominal, role in the Soviet Union. This was a legalism of a particular character. "Lenin himself, in his struggle to regain control over society [after the civil war of 1918–21], emphasized the importance of socialist legality." For him, however, this consisted of the "uniform countrywide application of the central commands."[9] Further characteristics of the Soviet Union's pecu-

---

6. Rigby, "The Government," 7.

7. Russian Socialist Federation of Soviet Republics (RSFSR).

8. This is especially interesting in light of Marx's early faith in the law and its efficacy as an instrument of change, which he renounced in his later writings. See M. D. A. Freeman, "The Rule of Law—Conservative, Liberal, Marxist and Neo-Marxist: Wherein Lies the Attraction?" in W. E. Butler, ed., *Perestroika and the Rule of Law: Anglo-American and Soviet Perspectives* (London: I. B. Tauris, 1991), 47–49.

9. Andras Sajo and Vera Losonci, "Rule by Law in East Central Europe: Is the Emperor's New Suit a Straightjacket?" in Douglas Greenberg, Stanley N. Katz, Melanie Beth Oliviero, and

liar legalism were its prioritization of public law over private law; the place of the tsarist institution of the procurator—a hybrid prosecutor, court agent, and body of judicial review—as the most powerful actor in Soviet law; the co-opting of attorneys through their training and the structure of their working collectives; the preemption of a purported judicial independence by the political bureaucratization of the judiciary; and a vision of the law "as instrumental to social and economic planning."

Especially on account of this final characteristic, Soviet law was painfully inconsistent. Thus, in some areas, "the law was hair-splittingly keen on precise details; in many others one cannot find any reasonable rule." The latter result was often a conscious one, however, as such abstraction would allow those charged with the law's application the discretion to execute their masters' political will. Functionaries of the law thus had an understanding of the appropriate "sources of law" on any given issue. "The system created for itself the advantage of keeping most of its participants (including the decision makers) in a dependent position. This dependence resulted from imprecision and the insecurity stemming from it."[10]

Yet increasingly, form became reality. The courts began to consistently apply the elaborate codes of law that stood on the books. In the realm of family law, for example, divorce and custody cases received fair trials before impartial judges. This neutral adjudication process had no place in political cases, but otherwise became increasingly available to the populace, especially with Stalin's death. "With the abandonment of terror, Stalin's successors increasingly relied on law to govern an ever more complex and differentiated society."[11] This quiet judicial activity helps explain the often ignored promulgation and amendment of detailed codifications of law in the USSR, including various codifications of family law and the 1958 Fundamental Principles of Criminal Prosecution, one of the cornerstones of de-Stalinization.[12]

The growing role of law in Soviet society became even more apparent with the elaborate public discussions surrounding the drafting and adoption of

Steven C. Wheatley, eds., *Constitutionalism and Democracy: Transitions in the Contemporary World* (New York: Oxford University Press, 1993), 324.

10. Sajo and Losonci, "Rule by Law," 324–25.

11. Robert Sharlet, *Soviet Constitutional Crisis: From De-Stalinization to Disintegration* (Armonk, N.Y.: M. E. Sharpe, 1992), 63.

12. For more on the Soviet legal order, see Harold J. Berman, *Justice in the USSR* (Cambridge, Mass.: Harvard University Press, 1963); Peter H. Juviler, *Revolutionary Justice and Order: Politics and Social Change in the USSR* (New York: Free Press, 1976); and various works of John N. Hazard.

Leonid Brezhnev's 1977 constitution. Though not entirely substantive, these exchanges drew in the general public and evidenced their great interest in the law. Finally, under Yuri Andropov,[13] the law took on a form immediately meaningful and real in its impact on the common man. Andropov's campaign for discipline strove to encourage obedience to the law and to reduce corruption at all levels of Russian society. "For him, the discipline campaign was a way of signaling that the Soviet constitution, and especially the policies and laws underpinning it, were to be taken seriously by all involved."[14]

It is evidence of Mikhail Gorbachev's connection to this tradition of Soviet legalism that, when Andropov's former protégé himself became general secretary in March 1985, he revived the latter's emphasis on legal discipline, which had fallen by the wayside during Konstantin Chernenko's brief interregnum as general secretary. Gorbachev's early campaigns against absenteeism and alcoholism can thus be seen as direct descendants of Andropov's endeavors.

Russian and Soviet history, then, while not leading inexorably to Gorbachev's rhetoric of constitutionalism and *pravovoe gosudarstvo*, did provide him a ripe ground for it. In fits and starts over more than a century, it had "sequentially laid the foundation for Gorbachev's proposal for a law-based state."[15] It was for Gorbachev, however, to seize this opportunity.

RHETORIC

When Peter Barenboim, a reform-oriented Soviet attorney, began writing of the separation of powers in 1980, "it was greeted," he remembers, "by absolute silence. . . . No one yet knew the meaning of impeachment, constitutional review, and other such concepts. These were, in the minds of most, mere technicalities of little concern or consequence in the USSR."[16] At the height of Brezhnev's stagnation, few imagined that such bourgeois concepts would be the watchwords of Soviet jurisprudence only a few years later. But few imagined any part of what lay ahead.

---

13. Andropov served as general secretary from 1982 to 1984.

14. Sharlet, *Soviet Constitutional Crisis,* 62.

15. Sharlet, *Soviet Constitutional Crisis,* 87.

16. Peter Barenboim, vice president, Union of Advocates of the Commonwealth of Independent States, 3 February 1994. Hereafter Barenboim, interview of 3 February 1994.

With his appointment as general secretary of the Communist Party on 11 March 1985, Mikhail Gorbachev brought a new rhetoric and a new vocabulary to Soviet politics. In speeches both within the Soviet Union and abroad, he echoed an increasingly coherent set of themes under the umbrella of *perestroika,* restructuring. By the Twenty-Seventh Party Congress in 1986, *perestroika* took on concrete form in Gorbachev's call for four broad categories of reform: "*glasnost,* or a new, more open information policy; democratization, or greater public participation in the policy process; a deep economic reform to stimulate the stagnant economy; and 'new thinking,' or a process of reevaluation, especially in foreign policy."[17] Added to these by 1987 was the theme of *pravovoe gosudarstvo,* the law-based state, which Gorbachev described as essential to the stability of the Soviet Union.

Gorbachev's motivations in calling for the creation of a law-based state are difficult to discern and appear conflictual. While he suggests he desired to use the law as "an instrument of progress," his consistent linkage of *pravovoe gosudarstvo* with his primary interest—economic reform—may support different conclusions.[18]

At one extreme is Nina Belyaeva's view of Gorbachev's aspirations as empty of real substance. His goals, she suggests, were "to refurbish the system with a fresh coat of paint, to instill more enthusiasm in the people, and to put some more fuel into the old machine."[19] However, the character of his closest advisers—legal experts who have long been committed to the principles of the rule of law—suggests that Gorbachev may have had higher motives. Vladimir Kudriavtsev, one of these advisers, describes their goal as the "introduction of the law as the supreme arbiter of government-citizen relations of every sort."[20] Yet this assessment of Gorbachev's goals, at the other extreme from Belyaeva's, may give Gorbachev too much credit.

Rather, Gorbachev's primary concern appears to have been power—not in the crudest sense, but power nonetheless. From the start,[21] he knew he lacked a sufficient power base to implement the radical economic reforms he

---

17. Sharlet, *Soviet Constitutional Crisis,* 11. While most constitutional histories of the Gorbachev period begin in 1987, with his rhetoric of the law-based state, or in 1988, with his actual legal reforms, it is my assertion that *glasnost* and *demokratizatsiya* were as relevant to legal consciousness as was his legal rhetoric. Therefore, I begin at the beginning.

18. Mikhail Gorbachev, interview of 17 August 1993.

19. Nina Belyaeva, "Russian Democracy," *Washington Quarterly* 16 (Spring 1993): 6.

20. Kudriavtsev, interview of 31 January 1994.

21. Conventional wisdom has it that Gorbachev's selection as general secretary was highly contested and was only sustained by a narrow margin in the Politburo's final vote.

saw as critical to the survival of the country. Only this clear and present reality could have driven him and his circle to so radically reconfigure the equation of power and risk destruction of the order that had put them where they were. His central goal was thus "to awaken a dormant society and energize and mobilize a more activist citizenry on behalf of his economic program."[22]

For him, *pravovoe gosudarstvo,* as well as *glasnost* and *demokratizatsiya,* were essentially leverages for economic reform. While of some intrinsic value, their worth was largely instrumental. They would allow him to shift the locus of power away from conservative elements in the Communist Party and thereby act notwithstanding the resistance of the lethargic Party bureaucracy. An alternative source of legitimacy was necessary to justify this power shift, and Gorbachev, a lawyer by training, chose the law as this instrument. As the Brezhnev years had seen the law become "the single most important instrument available for transforming Soviet society into a more acceptable pattern of life,"[23] this choice was an appropriate one. Gorbachev could now legitimate his reform program not only with Marxist ideology but with arguments of legality and constitutionalism as well. Yet Gorbachev's view of constitutionalism was not the broad one advocated herein. Legal consciousness was not high on his agenda.

While Gorbachev and his advisers, among them both academics and politicians, spoke of the need for a *pravovoe gosudarstvo,* this did not mean, as Harold J. Berman has noted, the rule of law. Rather, their more limited aspiration was rule *by* law.[24] Closest to the German *Rechtsstaat,* their concept of *pravovoe gosudarstvo* did not extend so far as *verkhovenstvo prava,* the supremacy of law. While use of the more limited term of *pravovoe gosudarstvo* may have simply been a matter of functional semantics, it may also suggest a lack of serious concern with the weakness of Russian constitutional values and traditions that scholars see as the "very core of Russia's problem."[25] Yet this broader vision was out of the reach of Gorbachev's circle.

22. Sharlet, "Citizen and State," 113.
23. W. E. Butler, introduction to Butler, *Perestroika and the Rule of Law,* 2.
24. See Harold J. Berman, "The Rule of Law and the Law-Based State (*Rechtsstaat*)," in Barry, *Toward the "Rule of Law" in Russia?* 43–60. Accepting Berman's distinction, I would argue that Russia must now adopt the principles of constitutionalism and universal human rights, making its goal the more challenging rule of law and not the more limited aspiration to rule by it. See Sajo and Losonci, "Rule by Law."
25. Vasiili Vlasihin, director, Department of Comparative Law, Institute of U.S. and

They also appeared to lack a full grasp of the process they had set in motion. Thus does Andrannik Migranyan, a political scientist now advising President Yeltsin, see *pravovoe gosudarstvo* as "a term they [Gorbachev's circle] invented, not really understanding what it means."[26] Gorbachev seemed to have little sense of what was involved in the transformation of which he spoke. What institutions would be necessary to support the transition? What might the separation of powers mean in a system long based on either dictatorial unanimity or ideological consensus? How would an atomized and passive public and an entrenched elite accustomed to substantial bureaucratic privileges respond to such reforms? Often unsure of his route, Gorbachev improvised along the way.

Such confusion was somewhat inevitable given the subject positioning of the progenitors of change. These were hardly outsiders with some extrinsic source of independently evolved and formulated ideas; they were, in American parlance, the consummate insiders. Their educational, professional, and even personal lives had centered around the system they now hoped to reform. This limitation in their operational experience was bound to restrict their vision. Knowing no other path, they were stifled in their understanding of where the country needed to go and how it might get there, and even in their sense of where it presently stood.

As Viktor Sergeyev and Nikolai Biryukov argue, the combination of Soviet historical revisionism and the censorship of scholarly and public discourse "achieved its aim: not only the man in the street, but the intellectual elite, too, fail to understand the society they live in."[27] Vladimir Kudriavtsev, among the most accomplished within Gorbachev's circle, thus admits that the latter never had "such expectations then of what the future would bring. . . . We profoundly misunderstood the underlying psychology and nature of the system that emerged through seventy years of Soviet rule. We did not realize what Russia had become."[28]

In the end, close proximity to and engagement with the system hindered

---

Canadian Studies. Interview in English, 10 August 1993. Hereafter Vlasihin, interview of 10 August 1993.

26. Andrannik Migranyan, member of presidential council. Interview in English, 4 February 1994. Hereafter Migranyan, interview of 4 February 1994.

27. Sergeyev and Biryukov, *Russia's Road to Democracy*, viii.

28. Vladimir Kudriavtsev, vice president, Russian Academy of Sciences, and academician of law, 17 August 1993. Hereafter Kudriavtsev, interview of 17 August 1993. In January 1994, however, Kudriavtsev (interview of 31 January 1994), attempting to defend the actions of President Yeltsin in September and October 1993, was unwilling to describe *these* highly unusual events as surprising. Rather, they were "to be expected."

their understanding of its true character. This flawed perspective underlay Gorbachev's expectation that the Communist Party could win free elections in the Soviet Union and his misreading of a free Eastern Europe's willingness to remain within a Soviet sphere of influence. Yet this naïveté as to how bad things had gotten was simply one of the "limits of the people who tried to do this."[29]

In their defense, however, the confusion of which Gorbachev's circle stands accused was nearly universal, as was their inexperience. While some, such as Andrannik Migranyan, were writing as early as 1989 on the nature of authoritarian transformation, even he must confess that "there simply was no realistic idea of how to change a totalitarian regime into a democratic one."[30] Never before had such a political sea change been attempted. Even the closest analogy, the constitutional transformation of Spain under Franco, was only marginally helpful as a guide, given the relative political and economic stability of transitional Spain as compared with the Soviet Union.

Viewed in this light, Gorbachev's most telling failure may not have been a lack of knowledge, but a lack of interest in making real and lasting changes beyond the economic arena. As Gorbachev was concerned primarily with opposition to his economic reforms, he focused on breaking away from the old decision-making process and not on creating a new one.[31] Thus did he obliviously speak of returning power to the soviets. Yet this was an impossible goal; the emasculated soviets were in no position to play any serious role. This suggests that Gorbachev either had little grasp of history and its lessons or, more likely, felt little commitment to substantive political restructuring in the first place. For him, democracy and constitutionalism were not ends in themselves but simply means to the ends of economic reform.[32]

While we can never know whether the latter is definitely true, the erratic character of Gorbachev's reforms lends this interpretation some credence. It appears that his institutional and structural reforms were not intended, or expected, at the outset. This would explain why discussion of them came relatively late in *perestroika*. This view is also supported by the talk of a draft Soviet constitution, which Kudriavtsev and others acknowledge existed but

29. Elena Lukasheva, scholar of human-rights law, Institute of State and Law, 11 August 1993. Hereafter Lukasheva, interview of 11 August 1993.

30. Migranyan, interview of 4 February 1994.

31. Biryukov, interview of 18 November 1993.

32. Robert Tucker, professor of politics, Princeton University. Comments at presentation of Nikolai Biryukov, Princeton University, 15 November 1993.

suggest was never seriously considered for adoption.[33] At the start, then, Gorbachev's goals were finite and limited. However, things soon moved beyond his control and "life forced him to change his view."[34]

It became apparent that openness alone would not clear the path of economic reform. *Glasnost*, "without a precise plan for legislative work," was an inadequate force for change.[35] The Party and conservative bureaucracy would not be broken by rhetoric alone. The relatively blunt and disperse character of Gorbachev's alternative power base—the still weak Soviet public—made opposition to his reforms quite easy. Recognizing as much, Gorbachev turned to the restructuring of the Soviet constitutional order as the path forward.

As we move on to consider Gorbachev's structural reforms, it should be noted that as a crash course in the relatively foreign ideas of constitutionalism and the rule of law, this early period of rhetoric was significant in "raising the public's expectations for political change and economic results."[36] It opened the floodgates of change that would eventually remake the political scene and radically alter the direction of Russia's constitutional future.[37] While Soviet scholars and politicians had long spoken of two kinds of democracy—western and Soviet—Gorbachev's early years in power caused the conventional wisdom to acknowledge that "there are civilized, democratic states and though we are not one now, we must become one." This shift from Soviet constitutional expressions to universalist ones, at the core of Gorbachev's rhetoric, would soon come to be accepted by all but the smallest minority in Russia.[38] Even the vaguest of commitments to the rule of law by Gorbachev and his entourage released forces that would soon overwhelm the Soviet Union and its leaders.

33. Kudriavtsev, interview of 31 January 1994.

34. Migranyan, interview of 4 February 1994.

35. V. L. Entin, "Law and Glasnost," in Butler, *Perestroika and the Rule of Law,* 108.

36. Robert Sharlet, "The Fate of Individual Rights in the Age of Perestroika," in Barry, *Toward the "Rule of Law" in Russia?* 204.

37. Yegor Kovaldin, adviser to the president, Gorbachev Foundation, and expert witness to the 1993 Constitutional Conference, 21 July 1993. Hereafter Kovaldin, interview of 21 July 1993.

38. Fyodor Burlatski, president, Academy of Natural Sciences of Russia, and former adviser to President Gorbachev, 1 February 1994. Hereafter Burlatski, interview of 1 February 1994.

CONSTITUTIONAL RESTRUCTURING

Developments thus moved beyond the abstract "literary version" of constitutionalism originally intended by Gorbachev's circle.[39] From simple rhetoric, there followed a variety of changes and transformations that radically altered the state of Soviet politics. "Mere words began to change the face and nature of the constitution very much." For the reformers, "it was time to come up with Plan B."[40] As Gorbachev realized the need for concrete change, he initially focused on the internal affairs of the government and the Party. He imposed massive cuts in the bureaucracy, reducing the number of ministries by 30 percent and cutting the staff of the central ministries by 23 percent. In two years, one million bureaucrats lost their jobs.

But the Soviet apparat, built by Stalin into the power nexus of the Soviet government, was well prepared to fight back.[41] "Jealous of their jobs, their privileges, and their power over the economy, the politically oriented *apparatchiki* did everything they could to make the new laws on economic reform unworkable."[42] As they grew increasingly secure in their positions during the eighteen years of Brezhnev's stagnation, the *nomenklatura* had perfected the art of resistance.

In tandem with these moves against the entrenched bureaucracy, Gorbachev moved to restructure the internal operations of the Communist Party in January 1987. By insisting on a greater plurality of opinion in Party debates, Gorbachev hoped to allow those amenable to his reforms to overcome the resistance of the conservative forces that opposed them. His Party reforms thus included the introduction of secret balloting and a greater role for ordinary Party members, whose traditional role in policy discussions Gorbachev described as grossly inadequate. Yet these changes also met fierce resistance from senior Party functionaries who correctly feared that the distribution of power would be at their expense.

At an impasse, Gorbachev realized the need for a radical reformation

39. Kudriavtsev, interview of 31 January 1994.

40. Nikolai Topornin, professor of constitutional law, Moscow State Institute of International Relations. Presentation in English (as part of a seminar on Russian constitutional issues), 27 July 1993. Hereafter Topornin, presentation of 27–28 July 1993.

41. Through the 1920s Stalin used the post of general secretary, a marginal one when he was designedly selected for it, to build an alternative power base in the burgeoning Party secretariat. It is testament to his success that the Communist Party's general secretary remained the highest official in the Soviet Union until Gorbachev created an executive presidency in 1990.

42. Cameron Ross, "Party-State Relations," in Huskey, *Executive Power and Soviet Politics,* 61.

beyond that which he had previously envisioned. This acceleration of reform became explicit at the Nineteenth All-Union Conference of the Communist Party in June 1988, when Gorbachev openly embraced the concept of a *pravovoe gosudarstvo* and declared it to be the defining characteristic of the new political order. He further called for the creation of a new legislative body, the Congress of People's Deputies, as well as a variety of other institutional changes.

As we turn to the substance of the constitutional restructuring promulgated by Gorbachev in late 1988, it is important to note the immense contribution of Andrei Sakharov, the dissident Soviet physicist and recipient of the Nobel Peace Prize, to the shift in Gorbachev's constitutional reforms from words to deeds. Sakharov, more than anyone, took up the banner of constitutionalism half-heartedly raised by Gorbachev and made it a functional tool of revolution. On 16 December 1986, Gorbachev's historic telephone call to Sakharov released him from internal exile in Gorky and allowed him to return to Moscow.[43] From then until his death in 1989, and even after, he "epitomized . . . legal reform in the popular consciousness."[44]

Sakharov's most prominent battle was his campaign to amend article 6 of the 1977 constitution, which enshrined the Communist Party's monopoly on power and declared it to be the "leading and directing force of Soviet society and the nucleus of its political system."[45] This struggle was as important to the legal consciousness of the public as it was irrelevant to the actual political situation. Though article 6 was finally amended, after several delays that badly damaged public esteem for the Congress,[46] only the failed coup of August 1991 would finally end the Party's political influence. A change of

43. Peter Juviler, "Human Rights After Perestroika: Progress and Perils," *Harriman Institute Forum* 4 (June 1991): 5–6.

44. Louise I. Shelley, "Legal Consciousness and the *Pravovoe Gosudarstvo*," in Barry, *Toward the "Rule of Law" in Russia?* 64.

45. The 1977 constitution is available in translation in *Current Digest of the Soviet Press* 29 (9 November 1977): 1–13. Reprinted in Robert Sharlet, *The New Soviet Constitution of 1977* (Brunswick, Ohio: King's Court, 1978).

46. The Congress's reputation was damaged not only by the delay in its amendment of article 6 (avoided until the Third Congress in March 1990), but by the manner of its eventual consideration of the issue. Having ignored the democratic opposition's motion for the amendment of article 6 at the Second Congress, in December 1989, the Congress now heeded the call of the Party itself, which had finally concluded that a " 'voluntary' abdication" was preferable to a "violent overthrow." By awaiting the Party's cue, however, the Congress painted itself as simply a mouthpiece of the Party's will. See Sergeyev and Biryukov, *Russia's Road to Democracy,* 168–71.

wording in a document drafted sixty years after the Party's rise to power cannot be overemphasized. Yet Sakharov fought this battle and earned an initially resistant Gorbachev's enmity, not for this limited structural victory, but for the psychological one Gorbachev himself feared from this change in the constitution.[47]

In Sakharov's insistence that article 6 be amended, beginning at the earliest sessions of the newly established Congress, the Soviet people saw for the first time that the will of the Party and state could be effectively resisted—and rejected. Such a prospect, unimaginable only a few years before, encouraged a new view of the relations of state and citizen, one increasingly favorable to the latter. Sakharov's interest in and anxious concern with the constitution created, for the first time, a sense of the constitution as a living document whose revision could effect real change. Previously, the public "did not believe this piece of paper can [sic] change anything." Sakharov thus "introduced the idea of constitutionalism, about which there was previously no great discussion." Absent his influence, suggests Vyacheslav Nikonov, himself a constitutional scholar, none of those interviewed herein would have even known what was meant when I spoke of "constitutionalism."[48]

Sakharov's draft for a new constitution—the Constitution of the Union of Soviet Republics of Europe and Asia—with its emphasis on human rights and responsive, limited government, further encouraged this new way of thinking.[49] Possibly the most widely read Soviet or Russian draft constitution, including the one now in force, it instilled in public consciousness a sense of constitutionalism's relevance to their own lives. With it, interest in the law, if not yet respect for or understanding of it, spread. People began to speak of the law (*pravo*) and the passage of new laws (*zakoni*) as a means out of the state of crisis.

Sakharov thus played an immeasurable role in creating a receptive climate for a new constitutional order and in pressing Gorbachev to put forth his proposed constitutional amendments and begin his restructuring of the Soviet state in 1988. Most prominent among this first wave of amendments to the 1977 constitution (adopted by an extraordinary session of the pre-reform Soviet "parliament" in December 1988) was the creation[50] of a

47. Vyacheslav Nikonov, legal expert, International Reform Foundation. Interview in English, 23 July 1993. Hereafter Nikonov, interview of 23 July 1993.

48. Nikonov, interview of 23 July 1993.

49. Translation available in *FBIS, JPRS Report—Soviet Union: Political Affairs* (19 January 1990), 1–5.

50. The Congress was established under article 108 of the constitution.

new two-tier legislature, consisting of the Congress of People's Deputies and a working Supreme Soviet[51] composed of 542 members elected from the Congress's ranks.[52]

A similar institutional arrangement had existed under the 1918 constitution of Communist Russia, as well as in the first Soviet Constitution, adopted in 1924. It was, however, dispensed with in Stalin's 1936 constitution and disappeared until its revival in 1988. Selection of this parliamentary structure was in keeping with Gorbachev's portrayal of his reforms as a return to the principles and goals of the revolution. "The revolution," he declared in a television address, "continues."[53]

Coupled with this set of amendments was a new election law that liberalized election procedures and the means of candidate selection. However, it also set out an unusual arrangement for the election of the 2,250 members of the Congress. Under its terms, 750 seats would be filled by "social organizations," meaning, for all intents and purposes, the Communist Party and its ancillaries—the Young Communists (*Komsomol*) and various labor-union organizations. In this way the Party was assured that it would not lose control of the Congress and the political process.

Furthermore, the Congress would elect the permanently sitting Supreme Soviet, not the general public, further divorcing the parliament from public control. Critics such as Avgust Mishin, the preeminent Soviet constitutional scholar, point to these limitations on the democratic process to impugn the broader intentions of Gorbachev's reforms: "It has now become evident that the authors of the constitutional reform of 1988 had other goals than creating a strong and representative parliament that was capable of working effectively in a system of separation of powers. Their aim was to create legal-consultative bodies that could give legal character to the dictates of the Communist Party."[54]

---

51. This working parliament was a true novelty. It can be quite favorably compared with the institution of the same name that existed under the unamended 1977 constitution, a rubber-stamp body that was in session only several days each year. The latter, of course, officially adopted the 1988 package of amendments.

52. Amendments available at *Vedomosti SSR*, no. 49, item 727 (1988); also published in *Pravda*, 3 December 1988 ("On Amendments and Additions to the USSR Constitution [Fundamental Law]") and 4 December 1988 ("On Elections of USSR People's Deputies"). The various amendments are available in translation in *Review of Socialist Law* 15, no. 1 (1989): 75–118.

53. Cited in Sergeyev and Biryukov, *Russia's Road to Democracy*, 93; see 93–96.

54. Avgust Mishin, "Constitutional Reform in the USSR," in Barry, *Toward the "Rule of Law" in Russia?* 364. For further discussion of the limitations of the 1989 election, see Sergeyev and Biryukov, *Russia's Road to Democracy*, 101–9.

Notwithstanding such legitimate criticisms, the elections represented the beginnings of a Soviet "civil society." Sergeyev and Biryukov best characterize the ambivalences of the 26 March 1989 election as such: "Now Gorbachev and his colleagues were planning to hold—for the first time in Soviet history—a genuine election, instead of staging a phoney one as usual, but at the same time they deemed it necessary to 'insure' themselves against all conceivable risks."[55] With the convening of the First Congress on 25 May 1989, however, a new stage in Soviet constitutional history had begun.

Soviet watchers well remember the public broadcasts of the first sessions of the Congress, which were viewed avidly on television screens across the country. "The country was in an unprecedented state of suspense, glued to television sets."[56] So high was the level of public interest that daytime transmissions had to be discontinued, as too many workers were skipping work to watch the broadcasts, producing a 20 percent drop in productivity during the First Congress.[57] The Soviet people now had their first glimpse into the workings of their government structures.

Yet the greatest significance of the Congress was its shift of the venue of governance and reform from the Party to itself. The importance of this change became apparent at the very first session of the Congress, as deputies declined to do as instructed and obediently join preestablished political groupings, instead setting up blocs of their own design. Prominent among these independent clusters of deputies, in a foreshadowing of what lay ahead, were the reformist New Moscow Deputies, led by Boris Yeltsin.[58]

Judicial reforms were another essential, though less publicized, element of the 1988 constitutional restructuring. Centered around the Law on the Status of Judges,[59] these were designed to enhance the independence and authority of the judiciary, long the weakest branch of the Soviet constitutional order. Among the changes introduced were the lengthening of judicial terms from five to ten years and a change in the means of judges' selection.

---

55. Sergeyev and Biryukov, *Russia's Road to Democracy,* 100.

56. Sergeyev and Biryukov, *Russia's Road to Democracy,* 113.

57. Sergeyev and Biryukov, *Russia's Road to Democracy,* 113. See W. E. Butler, "Perestroika and the Rule of Law," in Butler, *Perestroika and the Rule of Law,* 12.

58. Frances Foster-Simons, "The Soviet Legislature: Gorbachev's 'School of Democracy,'" in Barry, *Toward the "Rule of Law" in Russia?* 127.

59. *Vedomosti SSR,* no. 9, item 223 (1989). Available in translation, with analysis, in Jane Henderson, "Law on the Status of Judges in the USSR," *Review of Socialist Law,* no. 3 (1990): 305–38. This was followed by the Law on Court Structure of 13 November 1989.

In place of elections, judges would now be appointed by the soviet[60] one administrative level above their own jurisdiction. This, it was hoped, would ensure their freedom from undue local pressure.

Most significant among the judicial changes, however, was the establishment of the Committee for Constitutional Supervision[61] by amendment of article 125 of the constitution.[62] With the passage of its enabling law on 23 December 1989,[63] the committee was brought into being and its twenty-five members elected by the Congress to ten-year terms. Sergei Alekseev, a well-known constitutional scholar, became its chairman. Constitutionally independent of the other branches of government, the committee was charged with the task of constitutional review. While not authorized to itself declare laws or acts unconstitutional, it could charge the Supreme Soviet or Congress to do so (though without sanction for non-compliance). On the other hand, laws that the committee found violated citizens' rights were automatically suspended, without the necessity for further legislative action. Under article 121 of the 1977 constitution,[64] the presidium of the pre-reform Supreme Soviet had nominal powers of constitutional review, but these were never, in fact, exercised. Thus the very creation of the Committee for Constitutional Supervision was quite meaningful.

This significance was borne out by the committee's various determinations, often highly publicized and involving controversial decisions and practices of the executive and legislative branches. These helped to heighten public understanding of limited government and the checks and balances central to constitutionalism. "The impact of this clash between the guardian of the new *pravovoe gosudarstvo* and [the institutions] that represented the old unitary system was the first victory for the idea of a *pravovoe gosudarstvo* over the Soviet concept for the organization of the state."[65]

---

60. Local or regional councils.

61. Often termed the Committee for Constitutional Oversight (*nadzor*).

62. Subsequently renumbered as article 124 by the amendment of 14 March 1990. Notably, the strongest opposition to the committee's creation came from the Baltic representatives and from several leading democrats, who feared it would require constitutional reform to be consonant with the obsolete and undemocratic 1977 constitution, making the committee a body of reaction, not of reform. This gave rise to a peculiar situation in which the conservative *nomenklatura* proclaimed the rhetoric of the rule of law and human rights, while their liberal counterparts sat silent. See Sergeyev and Biryukov, *Russia's Road to Democracy*, 157–59.

63. Law of 23 December 1989, article 21, paragraph 3, *Vedomosti SSR*, no. 29, item 572 (1989). Traditional Soviet practice, carried forward into the present day, requires that enabling legislation be passed to bring certain constitutional provisions into force.

64. Article 121, section 4.

65. Ger P. Van den Berg, "Executive Power and the Concept of *Pravovoe Gosudarstvo*," in Barry, *Toward the "Rule of Law" in Russia?* 145.

An early decision of the committee declared that internal passports (*propiski*), an intimate part of the life of every Soviet citizen and one dating back to the earliest years of the Soviet state, violated international human-rights norms. Another proscribed the practice of not publishing certain government acts, especially those impacting upon human rights. Most well known, however, was the committee's 13 September 1990 nullification of Gorbachev's politically motivated decree (20 April 1990) banning public demonstrations in the center of Moscow.[66] The importance of the committee's bold decision in this case cannot be overestimated. It laid the foundation for a judiciary equal to its fellow branches in the minds of the people and in the principles and practices of the government itself.[67]

Concern with autonomous judicial action of this sort, as well as the increasing independence of the Congress, brought Gorbachev to reconsider his earlier opposition to the creation of an executive presidency. "Originally frustrated with the Communist Party as a vehicle of reform, Gorbachev abandoned the parliament as well in favor of the presidency, an instrument of rule that he believed would be at once more responsive and powerful."[68]

In late 1989, amidst growing economic and ethnic chaos, Gorbachev found himself without an effective institutional base from which to govern. "Practical political problems" thus drove Gorbachev to amend the constitution once more and create yet another new institution.[69] With the aid of Kudriavtsev and others, he drafted his Law on the Presidency, which the Supreme Soviet approved in February 1990 and the extraordinary Third Congress amended to the constitution several weeks later.[70]

With the strains of economic disintegration setting in and setting off a public outcry, however, Gorbachev was unwilling to face the will of the people. He was thus elected to the powerful post of president, not by popular vote, but by vote of the Congress. His close victory even in the Congress, with 1,329 of 2,245 possible votes, probably justified his fears. Yet this approach was manifestly inconsistent with the principles of constitutional democracy. Moreover, under the Law on the Presidency (section II), the president was to be elected by direct suffrage; however, the law (section III)

66. See *Izvestiia*, 15 September 1990.

67. See V. P. Kazimirchuk, "On Constitutional Supervision in the USSR," in Butler, *Perestroika and the Rule of Law*, 148–56.

68. Eugene Huskey, "Executive-Legislative Relations," in Huskey, *Executive Power and Soviet Politics*, 98.

69. Mishin, "Constitutional Reform," 365.

70. The Congress simultaneously amended article 6 to limit the Party's role and to allow for the creation of alternative political parties.

made an exception for the first occupant of the presidency (and, conveniently, the author of the law), who was instead to be chosen by the Congress.[71]

Aside from its patent appearance of illegitimacy, this election procedure would also prove politically disadvantageous. Later the popularly elected Yeltsin would badger Gorbachev about his fear of the electorate, describing himself as the only legitimately elected official in the country. Absent a popular mandate, Gorbachev would eventually find himself, as Sakharov predicted, without a core of centrist supporters to sustain his views and initiatives.[72] "Election of the president by the Congress, legitimate enough from the standpoint of the national political tradition and quite acceptable under different—more stable and less dramatic—circumstances, could hardly be effective as a means of overcoming the crisis of power" existing in the Soviet Union by 1990.[73]

In the new president's initial interactions with the Congress, the public began to appreciate the workings of an independent executive and legislative branch. Their early conflicts over economic reform and other issues heightened public understanding of the give-and-take of the new constitutional order. Balanced by the growing authority of the Committee for Constitutional Supervision, the president and Congress gave Russian constitutionalism some structure. "A kind of muted Soviet separation-of-powers doctrine began to take shape, including demonopolization of the Party and the emergence of new executive and judicial institutions to complete the triad of powers."[74] This crash course in constitutional politics was essential both to its participants and to the public at large. Few had forgotten that "Stalin became a dictator through constitutional bodies—through the Congress and through the government."[75] Consequently, a restoration of faith in such institutions was a critical first step.

In its attempts to build coalitions and work with the executive branch, the Congress manifested the beginnings of parliamentary democracy at work, passing sixty-nine bills into law in its first eighteen months, a good start for a group of beginners.[76] It must be credited, if not for great advances, then at

---

71. Like the American presidency, that of the USSR was tailored to its first occupant.
72. Juviler, "Human Rights After Perestroika," 7.
73. Sergeyev and Biryukov, *Russia's Road to Democracy*, 174.
74. Sharlet, *Soviet Constitutional Crisis*, 94.
75. Boris Topornin, director, Institute of State and Law, and academician of law, 21 July 1993. Hereafter Topornin, interview of 21 July 1993.
76. Huskey, "Executive-Legislative Relations," 92.

least for some basic ones in its passage of a broad range of legislation on public freedoms. This included the Law on the Press and Other Mass Media (June 1990), the Law on Freedom of Conscience and Religious Organizations (October 1990), and the Law on Public Associations (October 1990).[77] Most important, however, was its Declaration of Individual Rights and Freedoms, passed on 5 September 1991[78] as its last act.

Of course, these acts were incomplete in many ways and required complex enacting legislation to actually come into force. They left gaping holes in their protections as part of elaborate compromises designed to ensure their passage.[79] Yet these laws, quite prominent in the public eye, helped to enhance public awareness of individual rights and freedoms and thus played a substantial role in the development of constitutionalism. In the course of parliamentary debates surrounding their passage, the public became aware of particular pieces of legislation and their relevance to their own lives. "The very discussion of individual liberty gave people a sense of real freedom for the first time. The change in their consciousness of their rights and their autonomy from the state thus took root."[80] Freedom became a norm that could no longer be denied them.

The Congress, however, ran into difficulties due to its unusual and generally ineffective structure. Rather than imitating western parliamentary models based on bicameralism and a clear-cut separation of powers, Gorbachev borrowed his two-tier parliament from the revolutionary institutions of the 1924 constitution. The rationale behind this unfortunate decision remains unclear.[81] The late Avgust Mishin, among the strongest of Gorbachev's critics in the Soviet legal community, saw the Congress's built-in defects (including its unwieldy size) as further evidence of Gorbachev's lack of sincere commitment to true democracy and public participation. The Con-

77. Respectively published on: 12 June 1990 in *Vedomosti SSR,* no. 26, item 492 (1990); 1 October 1990, *Vedomosti SSR,* no. 41, item 813 (1990); and 9 October 1990, *Vedomosti SSR,* no. 42, item 839 (1990).

78. *Izvestiia,* 7 September 1991.

79. See Peter Juviler's discussion of this legislation: "Human Rights After Perestroika," 2–3; "The Soviet Declaration of Individual Rights: The Last Act of the Old Union," *Parker School Bulletin of Soviet and East European Law* 2, no. 8 (1991): 3–4, and unpublished excerpts from Juviler's *Human Rights and Democracy in Post-Soviet Systems: The Ordeal of Freedom.*

80. Valeri Yegorov, scientific secretary, Russian Political Science Association, 2 February 1994. Hereafter Yegorov, interview of 2 February 1994.

81. Nikolai Biryukov, professor of philosophy, Moscow State Institute of International Relations. Presentation at Princeton University, 15 November 1993; Sergeyev and Biryukov, *Russia's Road to Democracy,* 111.

gress, Mishin insisted, was "merely a facade Gorbachev could show off to the West to help him justify demands for increased foreign aid."[82]

It is equally likely that Gorbachev was simply not as concerned with the Congress's effectiveness as a working parliamentary body as he ought to have been. Even if not quite a "facade," Gorbachev hardly meant for the Congress to become an independent and uncooperative opponent. Structural flaws were compounded by the continuing influence of the Communist Party, which opposed Gorbachev's reforms and still saw the appropriate measure of the constitutional order and its players as their *partinost*, or "partyness."

Faced with continued Party opposition to his reforms, Gorbachev's advisers called on him to split the 20 million–member Party into a conservative Communist bloc and a social-democratic bloc under his own leadership.[83] This, they predicted, would encourage the development of distinctive multi-party institutions and ideologies, as well as a more stringent political discipline. More effective policies would result, and public participation in the political process would increase. "Society was ready for this, even if the Party was not."[84] Yet Gorbachev feared this path, worrying that a move beyond "controlled democracy"[85] might lead to the Party's collapse. The Party's subsequent failure, notwithstanding Gorbachev's heroic efforts to save it, suggests that a decision to divide it might well have increased its chances for survival.[86]

The potential impact of the Party's division on the development of constitutionalism was rooted in the persistence of the elites as the key to constitutionalism in the late 1980s. Fyodor Burlatski, an adviser to both Nikita Khrushchev and Mikhail Gorbachev, as well as editor of *Literaturnaya Gazeta,* one of Russia's largest newspapers, is as much a member of the elite as anyone. Consequently, it was no surprise to hear him insist that: "The problem of democracy in Russia is a problem of the political elites, not the masses." Elite behavior, from bureaucratic accountability to legislative professionalism, would make or break constitutionalism in Russia.[87]

---

82. Mishin, interview of 14 August 1993. See also Sergeyev and Biryukov, *Russia's Road to Democracy,* 165.

83. It is interesting to note that while most of Gorbachev's former advisers with whom I spoke were unwilling to generally criticize his decisions, all of them made a particular point of commenting on Gorbachev's "mistake" of not dividing the Communist Party.

84. Kudriavtsev, interview of 31 January 1994.

85. Sergeyev and Biryukov, *Russia's Road to Democracy,* 110.

86. It is important to note that the Communist Party of the mid-1990s is an entirely distinct Party from that of the Gorbachev years—under new leadership, with a new political ideology and a revised history, it now even advocates the development of the free market.

87. Fyodor Burlatski, president, Academy of Natural Sciences of Russia, and former adviser to President Gorbachev, 14 August 1993. Hereafter Burlatski, interview of 14 August 1993.

Notwithstanding his bias, Burlatski *was* right. For much of the time we are concerned with herein, and at least until 1990, this was probably true. During Russia's first revolution in 1917 and second in the 1980s, the public was not yet ready to grapple with questions of constitutionalism. Oppressed under the tsars and repressed under their Bolshevik successors, Russians had little room for concern with vague notions of individual liberty, democratic accountability, and limited government. These were beyond their range of vision.

Dissidents and academics, the so-called intelligentsia, did stand outside the narrow circle of political elites, did have a grasp of these issues, and could theoretically have carried them beyond the Kremlin walls; yet up until the early 1990s, they continued to lack a sufficiently political role to politically educate the masses in any significant way. Though the intelligentsia was far more influential under Gorbachev than it had ever been, an attempt to draw the general public into the debate around constitutionalism and into the process of its creation was still beyond their capacity.[88] While I will later argue that this understanding of the political elites as the gravitational center of legal and constitutional reform is no longer appropriate, it still held true under Gorbachev.

As a result, questions of constitutionalism actually were, in some sense, internal Party matters. The breakup of the Communist Party could thus have had quite an impact on the development of constitutional values in Russian society. This is apparent as we survey the political scene today. Across the entire political spectrum, nearly every major party in existence, regardless of its politics, spawned from the Communist Party or its membership.[89]

Yet Gorbachev remained unwilling to divide the Party. In his view, the Party ought to remain intact, as this was its best chance for renewal and success; a division of the Party, to the Bolshevik mind-set still strong within him, was contrary to the historical progression of Soviet politics.[90] Though Gorbachev had often admonished his listeners that reform "must begin with

88. It seems quite likely that Gorbachev's early decision to release Sakharov from exile was meant to solicit the latter's assistance in his efforts at reform. And while Sakharov may have proven far less cooperative than Gorbachev had hoped, he undoubtedly did serve as a bridge in the shift of political influence from the *political* elites to a broader class of elites, and from there to the general citizenry.

89. There is, of course, one exception, the most threatening and dangerous faction of all, Vladimir Zhirinovsky's neo-fascist Liberal Democratic Party (LDP). See Sergeyev and Biryukov, *Russia's Road to Democracy,* 69.

90. See Sergeyev and Biryukov, *Russia's Road to Democracy,* 69.

ourselves," when it came time to translate this message into action, it proved to be more words than deeds.[91]

In the end, regardless of the initially positive response afforded them, Gorbachev's changes failed in the most basic respect: they were ineffective. Although new institutions were put in place, the elites' underlying values, inadequately addressed by Gorbachev and his reforms, remained largely the same. As a result, necessary economic and political reforms were not carried out, the state of chaos was prolonged, and the government began to crumble.

The huge size of the Congress made it stodgy and unresponsive, ill-equipped to keep up with a nation in flux.[92] With the heated debate over the amendment of article 6 at the Second Congress in December 1989, the parliament had begun to implode; but Gorbachev, with his low prioritization of effective parliamentarianism relative to economic reform, failed to recognize or address this crisis. The Congress gradually turned to politics rather than the law as its raison d'être, and amidst political infighting, even the most basic lawmaking functions were forgotten. Gorbachev's expectation that new institutions would transform the system into a constitutional order operating as in the West had failed. Yet he came to recognize this too late. Caught up in "bigger" concerns, he fiddled as his own Rome burned.[93]

Increasingly Gorbachev moved to the right, where he hoped to find a new base of power and the tools to bring stability to the country. In Georgia in 1990, and elsewhere, he acted to rescind some of the reforms already in place. Aleksandr Yakovlev, a law professor active in the Soviet Congress and as Yeltsin's representative to the Russian Parliament, defends Gorbachev's moves as necessary to the progress of reform. "Zig-zagging like a ship," he describes Gorbachev, "first to the left, then to the right, but always forward."[94]

But Gorbachev's actions in Lithuania, which was clamoring for independence at the end of 1990, cast doubt on whether forward and backward might not better characterize his moves. On the night of 12 January 1991, a

91. Dimitri Olshanski, chairman, Department of Political Psychology, Institute for Political Analysis. Interview in English, 7 August 1993. Hereafter Olshanski, interview of 7 August 1993.

92. On the minimal number of deputies that were able to speak at the Congress's sessions due to its huge size, see Sergeyev and Biryukov, *Russia's Road to Democracy*, 163–64.

93. Andrei Avakyam, department chairman, faculty of law, Moscow State University, 9 August 1993.

94. Aleksandr Yakovlev, *The Bear that Wouldn't Dance: Failed Attempts to Reform the Constitution of the Soviet Union* (Manitoba, Canada: Legal Research Institute of the University of Manitoba, 1992), 268.

harsh economic blockade against Lithuania escalated into an attack by special military forces that left thirteen civilians dead in the capital of Vilnius. Whether this step was ordered by Gorbachev or not, his subsequent call for a temporary suspension of the Law on the Press (and its freedoms) in response to *Moscow News*'s "Bloody Sunday" coverage of this use of force makes clear his increasing disdain for the constraints imposed on him by the law—even a law of his own making.

Gorbachev amassed increasing power to rule by executive decree. First granted by the Supreme Soviet on 24 September 1990 for eighteen months, these powers were grudgingly expanded and made permanent by the Congress in December of that year. Gorbachev began to rule as a monarch, with decrees "increasingly arbitrary and controversial."[95] Use of such extra-legal instruments of power, as it became the norm, signaled Gorbachev's unwillingness to live up to his own constitutional rhetoric and within his own constitutional limits. The Soviet Union, he declared, "is not ready for the procedures of a law-based state."[96]

The legislature responded in kind, with increasing opposition to the president. This, however, undermined the Congress's own internal relations, which finally collapsed into a struggle of "one against one" amongst its members.[97] In the end, "too much hope and popular expectation was pinned on the USSR Supreme Soviet"—hope that it could not possibly live up to.[98] By 1991 the law was more central than ever, but it had ceased to play a salutary role. Once again, it had become a bargaining chip in the political process and a tool in the application of power.

If not imbued with a deeper substance, *president* and *Congress* were mere words. They could not, as Gorbachev had hoped, break the Soviet Union away from the past and drag an entrenched bureaucracy and an inert mass into the future. While valuable instructors, their success was premised on supportive attitudes and a climate of cooperation and institutional faith. "New forms of political life cannot exist without the appropriate political culture: for it is the soil without which the transplanted exotic flower will fade."[99] Without a strong civil society or a party system that could provide

95. Sharlet, *Soviet Constitutional Crisis,* 95.

96. David Remnick, "'We Are Already in a State of Chaos'; Gorbachev, Beset by Deputies' Protests, Appeals to People for Peace," *Washington Post,* 19 December 1990, A1.

97. Zorkin, interview of 2 February 1994.

98. Vladimir Entin, "Lawmaking Under Gorbachev Judged by the Standards of a Law-Based Society," in Barry, *Toward the "Rule of Law" in Russia?* 360.

99. Sergeyev and Biryukov, *Russia's Road to Democracy,* ix.

such a grounding, the new constitutional process "created corporations fighting each other and not trying to cooperate."[100] As the Congress collapsed into bickering between a massive conservative bloc, a swing "marsh" in the center, and a smaller liberal camp, which refused to work together *or* with the president, the public lost interest. They decided their new institutions would not generate solutions, but only more problems.

Gorbachev's critical failure was to inadequately emphasize the development of an ordered civil society in creating his new constitutional order.[101] He believed in limited democracy more than in limited government, and thus failed to achieve either. Though he established the requisite institutions for a new constitutional order, he failed to act effectively, and personally, to imbue them with a lasting constitutional spirit, thereby condemning them to failure. Gorbachev opened a Pandora's box by singing the praises of the law and the constitution, yet continuing to use them not as arbiters of the process but as tools within it.

This might have been expected. These early institutions failed to work because not only Gorbachev, but members of the Congress and the general public as well, did not fully want them to. They ran "against the suspicious attitude toward representative democracy embedded in the national political culture."[102] The basic view of government in Soviet society differed fundamentally from the view with which we have been analyzing their actions. The Russian concept of government has long been of a benign leadership that simply does the right thing. Rooted in the traditions of Eastern Orthodoxy, this follows from a sense of the simple peasant knowing best, but only as part of the mass, as part of a "mystic unit" represented and embodied by the government, whether it be the tsar or the parliament. This attitude implicitly discouraged attempts to limit government and viewed the right of revolt and even its tamer corollaries as dangerous and regressive.[103] Though largely destroyed amidst the public cynicism of recent years, this conception of government remained powerful enough during Gorbachev's reign to stifle efforts to create a pluralistic, limited government.

Yet Gorbachev's constitutional structures did have their influence. "The First Congress of People's Deputies had in itself been an event unique in Soviet history. For the first time in the past seventy years there had been a

100. Migranyan, interview of 4 February 1994.
101. Biryukov, interview of 18 November 1993.
102. Sergeyev and Biryukov, *Russia's Road to Democracy*, ix.
103. Biryukov, interview of 18 November 1993.

legal opposition active within the country's uppermost body of power."[104] Equally important, the Russian republic came to follow the same institutional path, creating its own Congress, Supreme Soviet, and presidency in 1990 and 1991. These brought to the forefront the figure who would become Gorbachev's nemesis and a major actor in the final months of the Soviet Union and in the continued development of constitutionalism into the mid-1990s. Russia, under Boris Yeltsin, inherited the institutions of Gorbachev's constitutional order, yet similarly failed to embrace the deeper transformation they required.

THE AUGUST COUP

Though *verkhovenstvo prava*, the supremacy of law, has been sorely lacking in Russian history, there has been some tradition of formal legalism or *verkhovenstvo zakonov*, the supremacy of laws. As noted at the outset, neither Russia nor the Soviet Union lacked an intricate order of "law in books." This legalism did not extend to all areas of jurisprudence but was quite elaborate nonetheless. One should recall, in this vein, the legal realists' victory over the legal nihilists in the 1930s and Stalin's adoption of the 1936 constitution, a highly structuralized and formal legal document, which laid the groundwork for a hyper-codification of Soviet law. Through 1985, this tendency toward a detailed constitutional and legal framework divorced from reality grew progressively stronger.

Intended primarily for public consumption, this mantle of strict *zakonost* or legalism was selectively invoked to lend legal legitimacy to the government's already existing religious or, under the Communists, ideological authority. Stalin thus made a public display of his 1930s show trials, elaborating exacting, though imaginary, charges and an entire prosecutorial leviathan to lend his patently coercive regime the appearance of respect for law. Thirty years later, it was with similar care that the persecution of political dissidents was carried out in keeping with the procedural norms of the criminal code.[105]

104. Sergeyev and Biryukov, *Russia's Road to Democracy*, 166.
105. Vlasihin, interview of 10 August 1993. The deeper *zakonost* of the later period was evident in that the 1965 trial of Andrei Siniavsky and Iulii Daniel was, at least, publicly and vigorously contested in court, even if not necessarily decided with full neutrality.

It is a testimony to this tradition, as well as to the heightened sense of constitutionalism that had emerged since 1985, that when a group of conservatives in Gorbachev's cabinet determined to remove him from office and turn back his reforms in August 1991, they cited the constitution in their defense, even holding a press conference to explain their position. Taking care to include the inept and inconsequential vice president Gennady Yanayev among their ranks, the self-styled State Committee for the State of Emergency (*GKChP*) cited an obscure subparagraph of the constitution on the vice president's succession to the presidency,[106] and Gorbachev's purported illness, as justification for the committee, chaired by Yanayev, to take power. Among the influential defense minister Dimitri Yazov, prime minister Valentin Pavlov, internal minister Boris Pugo, and KGB chairman Vladimir Kryuchkov,[107] the insubstantial Yanayev clearly had no place. He merely served to secure the committee a tenuous foothold of constitutional legitimacy.

Such concerns with legitimacy had mattered little thirty years earlier, when another Soviet reformer, Nikita Khrushchev, was swept from power by a palace coup. In 1964, press releases and public appearances did not figure prominently in Leonid Brezhnev, Aleksei Kosygin, and Nikolai Podgorny's plans. Yet now, concerns of legality and a felt need to prove its legitimacy were at the forefront of the committee's worries. To the demonstrators on the street, the coup leaders seemed to be oddly "fascinated by the idea of doing everything 'constitutionally.'"[108] Surprised by this, an aspiring humorist came up with "The Constitutional Game," a witty amusement that occupied many of those gathered around the White House as we awaited the arrival of the committee's tanks.[109] Photocopied by the dozens and distributed hand to hand, this hastily thought-up game required participants to flip a coin (a kopeck or two), move their game piece (usually another kopeck), and, depending on where they landed, assume the role of one or another of the committee members and imaginatively conjure up his explanation of the coup's legitimacy.

106. Article 127, section 7.

107. Other members of the committee were Oleg Baklanov, Vassily Starodubtsev, and Aleksandr Tizyakov, representatives of the Party, agrarian, and industrial elites.

108. Vladimir Dashkevich, "Plot and Counter-Plot," *Independent Newspaper from Russia* 2, nos. 12–13 (August 1991).

109. The seat of the Russian government during the Soviet years, an imposing white edifice on the bank of the Moskva River, was commonly referred to as the White House. It is now the seat of the Russian Council of Ministers (the Government) and the prime minister.

Gorbachev's rhetoric of a *pravovoe gosudarstvo* thus appears to have had some impact on elite consciousness. At the highest levels of power, the law had acquired a greater procedural, though still not substantive, meaning. Rather than simply involving the appearance of legality, Soviet legalism now extended to a tenuous compliance with the law as well. Of course, this must not be overdrawn, as the committee's compliance only reached the letter of the law and not its spirit. Even this, however, was a step forward, suggesting a "greater reliance on law and constitutional process as the new 'rules of the game.'"[110]

Yet this papier-mâché constitutionalism would not suffice as it once may have. Popular western impressions of a massive uprising against the coup are unfounded, but the public demonstrations in Moscow and other urban centers were relatively substantial. More important, acceptance of the committee's empty rationalization of their actions could not have been less. Even the passive majority, viewing events on their television screens at home, found the committee's facade of legality laughable. Repeated avowals of commitment to the constitution and detailed explanations of Gorbachev's illness could not assuage people's doubts. They were no longer content with the *ex post* justification of illegal practices with empty legalistic phrases; they now insisted on compliance with both the spirit and the letter of the law.

Even if limited in scope, the well-publicized defense of the White House, in which Yeltsin and the Russian leadership held forth during the coup, conveyed an important lesson in public control: for the first time in Russian history, power was seen to stem from and reside with the people.[111] The combined force of the army, the internal police, and the KGB appeared ineffectual when faced with open public opposition. As the tanks stood opposite the "Defenders of August," the use of force suddenly seemed illegitimate. In the public eye, the law had prevailed over the kind of raw power that had been the primary instrument of Russian civil authority for centuries. Even in its bluntest form, in the absence of institutionalized mechanisms of any sort, the law had proven itself a powerful defender of rights and liberties and a guarantor of the political order. This lesson in democratic authority thus helped to heighten public respect for a constitutional order of law.

In reality, the efficacy of law, and even citizen democracy, only partially

110. Sharlet, "Citizen and State," 118.
111. Anatoly I. Rakitov, chief, Analytic Centre of the Presidential Administration, 3 August 1993. Hereafter Rakitov, interview of 3 August 1993.

explain the collapse of the coup attempt. It failed because of many factors, including the military's unwillingness to fire on demonstrators in so public a forum, the committee's incompetent failure to effectively muzzle the press, and, quite significantly, the opposition of the middle elites, which effectively isolated the committee from the levers of power.[112] However, our concern herein is not with the politics of the coup but with its bearing on public consciousness. The impact of public opposition and the role of the law are therefore correctly noted among the coup's significant aspects.

Boris Yeltsin's prominent role in opposing the coup heightened its impact on public consciousness of the significance of the law. Yeltsin had long done everything in his power to render President Gorbachev politically impotent. He exhorted Russia to declare its independence, campaigned against Gorbachev's political candidates, and appropriated essential national resources on Russian territory. No one had done more to strip Gorbachev of authority and influence by means of political machinations and maneuverings.[113]

Nonetheless, upon learning of Gorbachev's overthrow, Yeltsin immediately took to the barricades in defense of the standing constitutional order and its legitimate representative. Gorbachev, he insisted, was the recognized executive authority of the Soviet Union and could not be removed at the whim of the military and, in a cunning accusation on Yeltsin's part, the Communist Party.

The association of the Party with the coup plotters—though not founded on any explicit evidence of direct involvement—stigmatized the Party with the taint of illegality. Though there is little indication that the Communist Party per se played any substantive role in the planning or execution of the coup, this stigma of illegitimacy would become the Party's mark of Cain and would later be used by Yeltsin to justify its gradual removal from its once lofty position of influence and authority.[114]

Thus was the final link of Party and state severed on 24 August 1991, when Gorbachev stepped down as general secretary. The association of the Party with the coup was so complete, explained Gorbachev, that continuation of his responsibilities as president was incompatible with service as leader of the Communist Party. Having survived years of restructuring and even the repeal of its constitutional domination of the political landscape,

112. David Lempert, "Changing Russian Political Culture in the 1990s: Parasites, Paradigms, and Perestroika," *Comparative Studies in Society and History* 35 (July 1993): 642.
113. Topornin, interview of 21 July 1993.
114. Boris Kurashvilli, professor, Institute of State and Law, 24 July 1993. Hereafter Kurashvilli, interview of 24 July 1993.

the Party lost the final remnants of its legitimacy for what may have been the one illegal act it did not commit. With Gorbachev's resignation as general secretary, followed by the Supreme Soviet's passage of its law "For the Purpose of Preventing Attempts to Carry Out a *Coup d'Etat*," which suspended the activities of the Communist Party in the Soviet Union, the end came into sight. "The final destruction of the old system" had begun.[115]

Returning, however, to Yeltsin's opposition to the coup: In the public consciousness, Yeltsin appeared to have risked his life and defended his avowed enemy, all in the name of the law. Of course, this understanding was simplistic, as Yeltsin's own power would have been undermined were the coup to have succeeded.[116] Yet by his actions and the motivations attached to them, the law became a banner under which he could rally public support. Constitutionalism moved to the center of public discourse. For the first time, Russians felt they understood dissidents' demand that the Soviet Union simply live up to its own constitutional norms.[117]

The rhetoric of the "defense of August," blasted from megaphones on the steps of the White House, was critical to this impact. It suggested a break with the past and implied a cooperation of the *Russian* parliament and president in just the ways that Soviet institutions had failed to collaborate. Speech after speech suggested that such cooperation would turn back the coup and then move the country forward. This vision created a renaissance of interest and hope in constitutional structures as potential vehicles of progressive change, now within Russia's own constitutional framework.[118]

FINAL GASPS OF THE UNION

Yet the aftermath of the coup had a dark side as well. Yeltsin, a former Party boss, instinctively reacted to victory in the tradition of extra-legality that

---

115. Belyaeva, "Russian Democracy," 8.

116. Mishin, interview of 14 August 1993.

117. This legalist strategy was, for many years, standard practice for dissidents facing trial. They would demand exacting prosecutorial compliance with their due-process rights, hoping thereby to show the emptiness of formal Soviet guarantees of rights and liberties. This practice seems to have first been applied in Siniavski and Daniel's 1965 trial for assisting in the publication of *samizdat* (underground) journals. See Valery Chalidze, *To Defend These Rights: Human Rights in the Soviet Union* (New York: Random House, 1974).

118. Topornin, interview of 21 July 1993.

was the norm for the Communist apparat. In addition to prominent decrees banning the Communist Party and confiscating its property, which the Russian Constitutional Court would later rule unconstitutional in part, Yeltsin ordered the arrest of many opponents and even detractors, violating due process and other rights by holding them without charge or even evidence of wrongdoing. He simultaneously suspended several major news-papers, including *Pravda,* the Communist Party's official organ. This deci-sion, though quickly rescinded, demonstrated the continued fragility of civil rights in Russia and the lack of sophistication in the legal consciousness of the senior elite.

In this climate of duress, a set of interim institutions was established at the all-Union level, including a State Council composed of the Union and republic presidents, a new, two-chamber Supreme Soviet, and an inter-republic Committee for the Economy. These were of dubious constitutionality, but legality was brushed aside in their creation, as Yeltsin's allies insisted "that observation of the letter of the law . . . yield to considerations of political expediency."[119] The haphazard creation of these bodies itself predestined their failure, a result that was only hastened by Yeltsin's forcible comman-deering of the major all-Union ministries, including the Finance and Internal Affairs ministries, which he placed under sole Russian control.

Among the many aconstitutional blows to Russian legal consciousness in the fall and winter of 1991, the most detrimental came in December, when public faith in the law and legal order was shaken to its core. On 8 December 1991, in what Gorbachev's circle still calls the "Byelorussian coup," the presidents of Russia, Ukraine, and Byelorussia (now Byelorus) met in Minsk (now Mensk) and announced the creation, by administrative fiat, of the so-called Commonwealth of Independent States. This confederate body initially included only the three Slavic republics but invited all the Soviet republics to join. Significantly, Yeltsin and his fellow leaders' announcement came in the midst of ongoing negotiations on Gorbachev's revised Union Treaty, a document intended to reshape the relations of the Soviet republics into a lasting federative structure. These negotiations were quite prominent in the media, as prevention of the original Union Treaty's ratification appears to have motivated the timing of the August coup.[120]

The pre-coup version of the treaty was drafted and negotiated on the basis

119. Sergeyev and Biryukov, *Russia's Road to Democracy,* 191.
120. The coup attempt began on 18 August 1991, two days before the scheduled signing of the Union Treaty by nine republics and the central government.

of the 17 March 1991 All-Union Referendum, in which a majority had voted for the retention of some form of union.[121] The referendum was admittedly "a purely central initiative, put forward without consultation with the republics."[122] The results were thus skewed by the wording of particular questions and by boycotts in several regions. Yet this had not prevented the three Slavic republics from participating in treaty negotiations up to this point—both before and after the August coup.

A new draft treaty, more favorable to the republics' interests than earlier drafts, was thus near completion in December 1991, and its ratification was expected at any moment. There had even been some humorous discussion in several newspapers about the selection of a new name for the Union. The new political structure, it was suggested, should be selected based on the first letter of its descriptor, in order to ensure the adoption of an appealing acronym. Thus did *Nezavisimaya Gazeta* express its opposition to a "confederative" structure, as this would require the use of letters that would make for a less fluid acronym than would a "federation."

Gorbachev appears to have sincerely seen the Union Treaty as the next step toward a new, more viable constitutional order, and not as an attempt to stall the Soviet endgame he had inadvertently set in motion. His closest political advisers in the Union Treaty negotiations, Yuri Baturin and Giorgi Shakhnazarov, believed the treaty would add the second leg to a two-part constitutional system already framed by the Declaration of Individual Rights and Freedoms, passed three months earlier, in September 1991. These two documents would form the outlines of a new constitutional order that would evolve further with the continuation of the reform process in both the political and economic arenas.[123]

Elena Lukasheva, a Soviet scholar of human rights, supports this view, suggesting that the Declaration of Individual Rights was "intended to be the constitutional keystone of a new federal or confederated USSR."[124] This

---

121. Armenia, Estonia, Georgia, Latvia, Lithuania, and Moldavia, the six republics that continued to oppose the treaty in August, had boycotted this earlier vote.

122. Staff of the Commission on Security and Cooperation in Europe, *Presidential Elections and Independence Referendums in the Baltic States, the Soviet Union and Successor States* (August 1992), 28.

123. Giorgi Shakhnazarov, head, Political Science Department, Gorbachev Foundation, 3 February 1994 (hereafter Shakhnazarov, interview of 3 February 1994); and Yuri Baturin, law and national security adviser to the Russian president, 11 August 1993 (hereafter Baturin, interview of 11 August 1993).

124. Juviler, "The Soviet Declaration of Individual Rights," 3 (citing personal communications with Dr. Lukasheva).

understanding was also acknowledged by the preeminent Sovietologist John Hazard.[125] Sitting in a meeting with Shakhnazarov when he learned of Yeltsin's new commonwealth, I can attest to his complete surprise and utter consternation. "What," he wondered aloud, "are they trying to do?"

What might have been the results of Gorbachev's rejected path of constitutional development? Though entirely speculative, it is reasonable to believe that this route to constitutionalism may have been far more effective. Such a gradual formulation and strengthening of the constitutional order, somewhat like the piecemeal development of constitutionalism in Great Britain, may have provided just the sort of educative function Russian society most needed at that stage.

The three leaders' decision to break off the treaty negotiations (in which they appeared to be participating in good faith) and to establish the new commonwealth was nominally justified by the results of the 1 December 1991 Ukrainian referendum. In this vote, 60 percent of the Ukrainian public voted for independence from the Union. This, it was argued, made Ukrainian acceptance of even the watered-down Union Treaty impossible. And without Ukraine, it was true, no union was viable. The preamble of the commonwealth's charter also asserted that recent months had seen a near complete collapse of central authority, making any further prolongation of the life of the Union meaningless.[126] Yet this argument fails to acknowledge the three republics' own role in rendering the central government impotent, and the potential of the Union Treaty to revive it. Nor does it explain the republics' participation in negotiations until the very last minute.

Regardless of what practical justifications might exist, this was clearly a circumvention of both Soviet and international law, intended primarily to remove Gorbachev from power. It ignored the terms of the standing constitution and was designed to destroy the old system, not to create a new one. It is significant that both those in Gorbachev's circle, such as Fyodor Burlatski, and those in Yeltsin's camp, such as Aleksandr Yakovlev, recognize this to be true. Thus does the former speak of the creation of the commonwealth as a "major setback" to the development of constitutionalism,[127] and the latter as a "break in legal continuity."[128]

125. John N. Hazard, "The Evolution of the Soviet Constitution," in Barry, *Toward the "Rule of Law" in Russia?* 106.

126. "Texts of Declarations by 3 Republic Leaders," *New York Times*, 9 December 1991, A8; and "Soviet Disarray: Accord on Commonwealth of Independent States," *New York Times*, 10 December 1991, A19.

127. Burlatski, interview of 1 February 1994.

128. Yakovlev, *The Bear That Wouldn't Dance*, 274.

Yeltsin cut off contact with Gorbachev and ignored or brushed aside the efforts of Soviet constitutional structures to address lingering political questions. These institutions, including the newly restructured parliamentary bodies, were left to languish and die. This occurred in subsequent weeks as quorums could not be achieved for sessions, and their respective chairpersons were forced to declare them closed. Finally, Gorbachev himself resigned on 25 December 1991, citing his inability to carry out his duties as president. As widely noted in the press, Gorbachev was quickly shuffled out of the Kremlin. Apparently, Yeltsin even ignored agreed-upon terms for his departure. Even to liberal politicians such as Vyacheslav Nikonov, no great friend of Gorbachev, this entire chain of events was "quite illegal."[129]

Yet the impact of this "coup" on legal consciousness is difficult to gauge. The elites probably accepted it as an appropriate and not unexpected use of political force, notwithstanding its lack of constitutional legitimacy. It is also unclear whether it significantly affected the legal consciousness of the general public, which no longer respected Soviet power structures as representatives of a constitutionally, and democratically, sanctioned political order. Delegitimized by circumstance and by their own failures, these institutions lacked the legal respect of the people; consequently, some argued, they could be attacked with impunity.[130] Regardless of the extent of its impact on legal consciousness, however, the Union's sudden dismemberment was undoubtedly perceived as a victory of power over law.

A more fluid transition, one to which Gorbachev had acceded (as he could have readily been made to do), would have greatly enhanced public perception of Russia's political processes. Far better use could have been made of the rhetoric of August, and its vision of moving ahead, to justify Yeltsin's decision to dispense with the Soviet Union. Hastily implemented as it was—and following so closely upon the attempted coup of the State Committee for the State of Emergency—this decision appeared to simply be another, more successful, effort to remove Gorbachev, only this time by the liberals and democrats, not by the conservatives and Communists. It was thus a "particularly self-destroying" decision by Yeltsin, who would have been wiser to have acted at the Union level rather than to have simply brushed it aside.[131]

129. Nikonov, interview of 23 July 1993.
130. Klamkin, interview of 4 February 1994.
131. Biryukov, interview of 18 November 1993.

Mikhail Gorbachev, history will likely determine, was "more effective as a teacher than as a politician."[132] In his seven years in office, he transformed the Soviet nation at both the instituitonal and the societal level. Though not always his intention and, occasionally, contrary to his will, these changes laid the foundation for both branches of constitutionalism, establishing new institutions and institutional principles, while simultaneously raising consciousness of individual rights and the axiom of limited government. "Despite his ultimate inability to manage the social forces he had unleashed, Gorbachev's legacy to Russia has been an emphasis on constitutionalism."[133] Thus was it appropriate that the last act of the Soviet Congress be its passage of the Declaration of Individual Rights and Freedoms in September 1991.[134] If nothing else, Gorbachev had surely changed the "rules of the game."[135]

Yet because Gorbachev proved unwilling to fully embrace the principles of constitutionalism he himself had heralded, he left a mixed legacy of one step forward and one step back. Unsure of where he wished to go, he left the nation similarly perplexed. At the end, asserts Peter Juviler, a scholar of Soviet law and human rights, Gorbachev "symbolized more than ever, within himself, the unresolved conflicts of transition from old Communist loyalties and values to new democratic commitments."[136] Now, resolution of these conflicts would be in the hands of an independent Russia.

132. Sharlet, *Soviet Constitutional Crisis,* 4.

133. Robert Sharlet, "The Russian Constitutional Court: The First Term," *Post-Soviet Affairs* 9 (January–March 1993): 1.

134. Passed on 5 September 1991. *Izvestiia,* 7 September 1991. See Juviler, "The Soviet Declaration of Individual Rights."

135. Sharlet, "Citizen and State," 118.

136. Juviler, "Human Rights After Perestroika," 1.

CHAPTER TWO

THE RUSSIAN FEDERATION

As we seamlessly move from the Soviet Union to independent Russia, some will argue that it is a mistake to conjoin them in our discussion. Rather, they feel a sharp line ought to be drawn between Soviet history and the post-Soviet present. This may or may not be true with regard to the broader debate on Russo-Soviet historical continuity, both in 1917 and 1991; it is not a concern with reference to the issues considered herein. The legal traditions of Russia and the Soviet Union are sufficiently intertwined,[1] and the Communist order sufficiently Russified in its psychology, that no sharp distinction is necessary with regard to legal consciousness.

As for constitutional structures, the central institutions of newly independent Russia (with exceptions such as the Russian Constitutional Court) directly paralleled those of the Soviet Union. This would be expected, given their establishment in 1990 and 1991, when Russia remained a Soviet republic.[2] We can thus reasonably approach constitutionalism's development as one fluid line. Though Aleksandr Solzhenitsyn, a staunch Russian patriot who condemns Soviet rule as a form of foreign occupation, would not be pleased with this formulation, application of Robert Tucker's continuity thesis seems most appropriate.

The legal nihilism and later formalism of the Soviet Union were rooted in the divinely sanctioned legal arrogance of the tsarist period. As the tsar was God's vicar, what law could possibly stand above him? "*Pravo: kuda dishlo, tuda vyishlo,*"[3] went a traditional peasant saying, proving that a weak

---

1. This is true with regard to the Soviet Union and post-communist Russia, even if less so as regards the Soviet Union and tsarist Russia.

2. See Hoffmann, 45–46 ("The Yeltsin period is a direct outgrowth of the Gorbachev period").

3. "The law: where it is led, there it will go."

constitutional order and limited respect for the law were not peculiar creations of the Soviet era but had a long history in Russia.

The Soviet period did add a particularly virulent cynicism to these tendencies. Whereas no constitution was in force until the final years of Imperial Russia, Soviet leaders made them centerpieces of public propaganda, purporting to them great significance though they lacked any at all. Marxist perceptions of the law as a bourgeois tool of influence and power also aggravated legal cynicism. However, as was noted early on, the theoretical notion that the law, like the state, would "wither away" was quickly dispensed with by the Bolsheviks. They "had to be more practical," so instead chose to twist the law into one of their favorite instruments of power, further undermining respect for it.[4]

Beyond the substantive continuities of Russia and the Soviet Union, it should be remembered that the only home most Russians have ever known is the USSR. Their upbringing, education, and professional life revolved around Soviet ideology and propaganda. Consequently, Soviet attitudes were still prevalent among both the elites and the masses in 1991. Public conceptions of capitalism and democracy did shift under Gorbachev, but at the deepest level these changes were not nearly so pronounced. Instinctively, the majority of Russians still have a difficult time accepting the wealth and opulence they now find alongside poverty and homelessness on their streets. The same can be said of attitudes toward democracy, with support for greater openness paradoxically coupled with calls for strong-arm solutions to Russia's ills.

This is also true of legal consciousness. While progress has been made, Russia still operates on many of the same constitutional and legal premises that have motivated it throughout this century. Thus did Yeltsin and independent Russia inherit from Gorbachev's Soviet Union both substantial changes and lingering challenges on the path to constitutionalism. Constitutionalism remained a work in progress.

EARLY CONSTITUTIONAL DEBATES

The development of constitutionalism in Russia, both before and after December 1991, revolved primarily around the drafting and adoption of a

---

4. Richard Thornburgh, "The Soviet Union and the Rule of Law," *Foreign Affairs* 69 (Summer 1995): 15.

new Russian constitution. To badly reword Tip O'Neill's famous aphorism,[5] all politics in Russia was constitutional. Unsurprisingly, one of the first acts of the Russian Congress, elected in 1990, was to establish a Constitutional Commission to revise Russia's 1978 constitution (a near-clone of the 1977 Union constitution). Through 1990 and 1991, a wide range of individual academics and politicians, as well as both liberal and conservative groups, authored draft constitutions. Constitutional themes and terms of reference held center stage in the media.

The evolution of reform policies was also framed in constitutional terms, as many of the political and economic reforms of the early 1990s involved amendments to the 1978 Russian Constitution.[6] This increased public interest in constitutional reform and in the role that the law might play in "real life." Unfortunately the great expectations thus born would later be disappointed, and legal consciousness undermined, when Yeltsin's relations with the Congress soured and legal reforms ceased to effect real progress.

Yeltsin began his national career as chairman of the Russian Congress of People's Deputies, a post to which he was elected after the establishment of the Congress in 1990.[7] With the Congress's creation of a Russian presidency and Yeltsin's popular election to this position in the spring of 1991, he nominated his deputy, Ruslan Khasbulatov, to succeed him as chairman. Thus did the political relations of the president and parliament begin as a cooperative venture, one enhanced by their common defense of the constitutional order and the White House in August 1991. Furthemore, though not a completely democratic parliament, the Russian Congress was representative of the wide spectrum of Russian politics.[8] Accordingly, the public had great expectations that their independent, cooperative, and increasingly legitimated constitutional structures would act constructively. As this failed to materialize, the work of Yeltsin and the Congress drew increasingly less

5. The former Speaker of the U.S. House of Representatives was fond of noting that "All politics is local."

6. Beginning in 1988 this had been true of Gorbachev's policies as well, but in a less explicit and consistent manner. See Robert Sharlet, "The Prospects for Federalism in Russian Constitutional Politics," *Publius: The Journal of Federalism* 24 (Spring 1994): 117.

7. On the creation and election of the Russian Congress and Supreme Soviet, see Michael Urban, *More Power to the Soviets: The Democratic Revolution in the USSR* (Hants., England: Edward Elgar, 1990); and Thomas F. Remington, "Parliamentary Government in the USSR," in Robert T. Huber and Donald R. Kelley, eds., *Perestroika-Era Politics* (Armonk, N.Y.: M. E. Sharpe, 1991).

8. Belyaeva, "Russian Democracy," 8.

public interest. The notion of showing sessions of Congress on television, as had once been the norm, grew farcical. By late 1992, "people didn't believe that decisions from above had any relevance" to their own lives. Having initially placed too much faith in their infant institutions, the people soon came to have none.[9]

Again, the basic failure was one of effectiveness. Though many laws were adopted, the most essential ones were ignored. Economic reform floundered while the political elite engaged in battles that were irrelevant to the needy citizen. Even Vladimir Lafitski, a critic of Yeltsin and staunch partisan of the Russian Supreme Soviet, notes that Yeltsin ought to have used his authority, including extraordinary powers granted by the Supreme Soviet in November 1991, more actively to move reforms forward.[10] Yet he failed to do so. Criticizing this failure, Erik Hoffmann points to the "substantive elements of democratic consolidation," including economic growth, as critical aspects of constitutionalism's development.[11] Absent such substantive progress, public faith in the constitutional order cannot not be sustained.

Amidst growing hostility between the president and parliament (beginning in late 1991, with the collapse of their common enemy, the Soviet Union[12]), the Russian Constitutional Court came into being. It attempted to moderate what was increasingly being defined by both players and spectators as a black-and-white battle of good and evil (with the assignation of the former and latter determined by one's political persuasion). The court, suggests its former chairman, who eventually would himself become a political partisan, tried to demonstrate that there was not one parliament, but many, and that the president was not good or bad, but both and neither at the same time.[13]

Meanwhile, the constitution that the court had to defend was gradually becoming an empty shell. By 1992, having been amended over four hundred

---

9. Olshanski, interview of 7 August 1993.

10. Vladimir Lafitski, chief research fellow, Institute of Comparative Law. Interview in English, 31 January 1994. Hereafter Lafitski, interview of 31 January 1994.

Erik Hoffmann argues, in fact, that the moment for decisive action by Yeltsin was in the weeks immediately following the August 1991 coup attempt. His prestige and authority at that moment could have justified any and all steps necessary to modernize and reform both government structures and the economy. Hoffmann, 30.

11. See Hoffmann, 21–23.

12. The vote of the Supreme Soviet to annul Yeltsin's decree declaring a state of emergency in Chechen-Ingushetia, a precursor to the more recent conflict over that region, was the first interbranch salvo.

13. Zorkin, interview of 2 February 1994.

times, it was filled with all the holes and contradictions of a document long ago superannuated institutionally, politically, and economically. Even the democratic faction, the most constitutionally oriented segment of the Russian elite, "openly demonstrated that it had not any particular respect for the old constitution."[14] The latter was increasingly ignored, and by late 1992 it was difficult to find an up-to-date copy of it, even among Russian officials.[15]

This added fuel to the fire of efforts to adopt a new constitution, efforts that had ebbed and flowed since 1990, when they were centered almost entirely on the work of the Constitutional Commission of the Supreme Soviet. As chairman of the parliament and later as president, Yeltsin nominally chaired this commission. Nonetheless, in the three years the commission met, Yeltsin attended only one or two of its sessions. Its vice chairman, Ruslan Khasbulatov, also rarely attended. For these men, long members of the Communist apparat, the constitution was simply not a serious concern. The commission's day-to-day operations were thus left to its executive secretary, Oleg Rumyantsev.

Led by the ambitious Rumyantsev, the commission drew a wide array of political and popular concerns into its discussions, hoping to initiate a broader public dialogue on the constitution.[16] As their debates progressed and draft documents were produced, the latter were entered into the public record and published in the commission's journal, *Konstitutsionnyi Vestnik*. Though discontinued in October 1993, with Yeltsin's suspension of the parliament, this remains the most comprehensive collection of material on the key constitutional questions facing Russia today. The *Vestnik* also revealed the commission's strong interest in American constitutionalism, with articles on Alexander Hamilton (*"Gamil'ton*, Federalist 9") and American separation of powers (*"Amerikanskaya model'"*)[17]

With these articles and other official documents and commentaries, the commission attempted to raise the awareness of particular constitutional issues among both the elites and the general public. Its members and staff saw this as an essential element of their work.[18] In this regard the commis-

14. Biryukov, interview of 18 November 1993.

15. My own efforts to locate a copy for my research in October 1992, either at the Russian embassy in Washington or in Moscow, were to no avail.

16. Nikonov, interview of 23 July 1993.

17. Respectively, in 10 (February–March 1992), 128–34; and 14 (December 1992), 107–67.

18. Vladimir Lafitski, adviser to the Constitutional Commission of the Supreme Soviet, 11 August 1993 (hereafter Lafitski, interview of 11 August 1993); and Ivan Fedaseyev, secretary, Constitutional Commission of the Supreme Soviet, 13 August 1993.

sion did have some impact as "a tool of instruction." But as even Vladimir Lafitski, an adviser to the commission, admits: "This cannot be exaggerated. Everything is in a context, and ours was a turbulent one. Given more time, more security, and maybe a different country"—he laughs—"maybe we could have made a *real* difference."[19]

The commission's constitutional drafts, produced in November 1990, October 1991, and February 1992, outlined a mixed parliamentary-presidential system, with, in the early drafts, only a slight superiority of the parliamentary branch. They inculcated the separation of powers and were deeply considered documents that revealed an acute awareness of constitutionalism. This is no surprise. Rumyantsev and his similarly youthful advisers and associates on the commission[20] were ardently committed to the importance of legal culture and constitutionalism. They were (and may still be) the most eloquent and committed adherents of the rule of law to be found in Russia.

Yet youthful hubris had its costs. They undoubtedly saw themselves as the Jeffersons and Madisons of Russia—scholar-politicians who would long be remembered as Russia's founding fathers. As the political cauldron grew hotter, they therefore joined the battle and moved to the right with the parliament rather than remaining the neutral academics and professionals they were. The commission politicized its draft by making its presidential post weaker. These revisions, made in an attempt to keep up with politics, rendered the hybrid constitutional structure of their draft convoluted and unworkable; if adopted, this draft would likely have produced constitutional gridlock.[21]

This corruption of their own work, argues political philosopher Nikolai Biryukov, was in keeping with an apparent "inferiority complex" of the Supreme Soviet as a whole. This led the parliament to "forfeit the strategic interests of the democratic movement" (of which, contrary to western media analysis, it was undoubtedly a part) for immediate power and influence. The Constitutional Commission, like its parent institution, came to operate with "irrationality and a lack of sagacity," allowing "tactical considerations to prevail over dispassionate consideration" in its work.[22] Rather than maintaining its focus on constitutionalism, the commission turned to the shifting sands of politics. And here, in the end, it was bound to lose ground.

19. Lafitski, interview of 31 January 1994.
20. Most were in their thirties.
21. Sharlet, "Citizen and State," 120.
22. Biryukov, interview of 18 November 1993.

By January 1993 Yeltsin had broken with the commission and assembled his own group of associates, who set to work on a draft more favorable to the president. This sudden interest in constitution drafting, which he had long ignored, came at the strategic moment when, like Gorbachev before him, Yeltsin found his "constitutional frame to be too tight." Only then did the constitution become a real issue for him.[23] Yeltsin's efforts, unsurprisingly, lacked the legal precision, deep thinking, and finesse that had characterized the process until this point.[24]

Yeltsin began to speechify incessantly about the constitution's critical role and the need for a new constitution. As a result, political opponents such as Andrei Galovin, founder of the right-of-center *Smena*-New Politics faction, accused him of using this discussion to distract attention from the failure of his economic reform program.[25] Yeltsin's sudden interest in and political maneuvering around the constitution thus turned a process that had remained largely apart from the vicious politics of the period into yet another chip in the game. Hereafter, "in the constitutional bazaar of Russian politics, the participants 'shopped' for arguments and justifications with which to legitimize attacks and counterattacks."[26] Yeltsin adviser Giorgi Satarov boldly argues that this stage was necessary and that "the constitution had to be joined in the political conflict" if it was ever to enter the public consciousness.[27] Even if necessary, however, the chaotic and acrimonious way the constitution came to be used as weapon and shield was clearly detrimental to the spirit of law. "Yeltsin stumbled and destroyed public respect for *any* constitution in the process."[28]

Draft constitutions began to appear daily in the press, not as prescriptions for a new constitutional order, but rather as attempts by their authors to secure political influence. Gradually the public lost faith in constitutional discourse. The constitution, no longer above the political conflict, became simply another instrument in it. This was particularly unnecessary, given the

---

23. Nikolai Troyitski, legal editor, *Megapolis-Express,* 20 July 1993. Hereafter Troyitski, interview of 20 July 1993.

24. Mishin, interview of 14 August 1993. Mishin was initially invited to work with the drafters but made himself persona non grata by repeatedly insisting on compromise with the commission.

25. Andrei Galovin, member of Russian Supreme Soviet, and chairman, *Smena,* New Politics, 20 July 1993. Hereafter Galovin, interview of 20 July 1993.

26. Sharlet, "The Prospects for Federalism," 117.

27. Satarov, interview of 4 February 1994.

28. E. A. Paen, chairman, Presidential Working Group on National Politics, 28 January 1994. Hereafter Paen, interview of 28 January 1994.

relative similarity of all the drafts. The various draft constitutions, by Anatoly Sobchak (mayor of St. Petersburg), by the commission, by the Presidential Working Group, and even by the Communists, were not nearly as divergent as the public debate painted them to be. While variant in defining the exact competencies of each branch, all the drafts incorporated the same institutions and were founded on the same constitutional principles.[29]

Thus even the leftist Draft Constitution of the Russian Soviet Federated Socialist Republics called for the "development of market relations," "various forms of ownership," and "a multi-party system."[30] A comparison of the commission's draft and the presidential one that emerged out of Yeltsin's June–July 1993 Constitutional Conference also reveals substantial similarities.[31] Naturally, the president's position vis-à-vis the parliament was superior in his constitution, and vice versa in the parliament's draft. In neither, however, was the balance of power entirely skewed to one side. On federal issues they were interchangeable. Finally, a less explicit enumeration of individual rights in Yeltsin's draft was balanced with a shortening of the list of potential caveats to such rights found in the commission's draft.[32] Notwithstanding limited differences, the drafts were all on the same wavelength. Their divisive caricature in the political debates of late 1992 and 1993 was therefore unnecessary.

This convolution of the debate opened the door for those who opposed reforms generally, as well as any new constitution that would make them possible. Right-wing politicians such as Sergei Baburin, leader of the red-brown National Salvation Front, a peculiar coalition of left and right, thus argued that the "need for a new constitution was not an actual problem" but was simply being used by Yeltsin "as an instrument in the political conflict."[33] The centrist Galovin similarly described the lack of a new constitution as a "thought-up problem and mirage of Yeltsin." This entire debate, Galovin insisted, ignored the existence of "a modern constitution of a democratic government [the 1978 constitution] that is more effective and more democratic than even the United States Constitution!"[34] Such empty

---

29. This would be increasingly less true of later presidential and parliamentary drafts.

30. Berman, "The Rule of Law and the Law-Based State," 56.

31. See Rita Moore, "The Path to the New Russian Constitution," *Demokratizatsiya* 3 (Winter 1995): 44–60.

32. Sharlet, "Citizen and State," 122–24.

33. Sergei Baburin, member of Russian Supreme Soviet, and president, National Salvation Front, 20 July 1993.

34. Galovin, interview of 20 July 1993.

rhetoric inevitably undermined public perception of the importance of a new constitution. Yet such arguments were the unavoidable result of the political machinations around the constitution that Yeltsin had stirred up.

Another unfortunate tendency of this period was the close association of drafts with specific individuals: there was the president's draft (drawn up by Alekseev and Shakhrai), the Communist Slobodkin draft, Rumyantsev's parliamentary draft, Sobchak's federal draft, and others. This degraded the public sense of a constitutional document as beyond the immediate vicissitudes of the political debate and its present players. Taken to its troubling conclusion, this personalization of the constitutional process implied that a constitution deserved only as much respect as its author. The American Constitution could not survive such a test, let alone any Russian analogue.

Equally important was the public's gradual loss of interest in the constitution-drafting process. A public-opinion poll in May 1993 thus found 68 percent of those surveyed to be unfamiliar with either the presidential or the parliamentary draft.[35] Public interest and engagement in the constitutional and political reform process peaked in the days and months after the August 1991 coup. Jaded by divisive debates and the lack of substantive economic progress since then, the public could no longer care less. Their activism, which had gradually built up under Gorbachev, had then steadily declined and now stood at a low ebb. Discussion of constitutional reform, at the heart of the public debate about political and economic reform in early 1992, had come to be considered idle chatter by 1993. Whereas the amendment of the constitution's provisions on land ownership had once been the focus of efforts toward land reform, now questions of vouchers and auctions were most prominent.

By mid-1993 it had become almost impossible for me to discuss constitutional issues, even with educated Russians who had been deeply interested in the constitution and its amendment only a year before. As one student put it, "the constitution was no longer seen as relevant to the progress of reform or

---

35. In a public-opinion poll surveying 1,081 people on 30 May 1993, the question was asked: "Are you familiar with the drafts of the new Russian constitution?"

Familiar only with the presidential draft:	11 percent
Familiar only with the Constitutional Commission's draft:	6 percent
Familiar with both drafts:	15 percent
Not familiar with either draft:	68 percent

(Survey by the Public Opinion Foundation, published in its journal, *Within Sight*, June 1993)

to one's personal life. We didn't care."[36] Some step was therefore necessary to break the "unending routine" that the constitutional debate had become.[37]

THE CONSTITUTIONAL CONFERENCE

In the spring of 1993, Yeltsin's conflict with the parliament came to a head when the Eighth Congress of People's Deputies, meeting in March, passed resolutions intended to sharply limit the president's authority over the economy and over the composition of the government. At the close of the Congress, in a nationally televised address on 20 March 1993, Yeltsin announced the introduction of "special rule" by the president. While this never materialized (for reasons I will consider when discussing the Russian Constitutional Court), the announcement resulted in the 25 April 1993 All-Russian Referendum, resistance to which had initially provoked Yeltsin's address. In this vote, the public was polled as to their support for the president and the parliament. Its results can be, and have been, challenged in many respects, including the phrasing of the questions, the doubtful value of a vote compelling citizens to choose between one branch of government and another,[38] and the tabulation of results by presidentially appointed counting commissions. However, legitimate or otherwise, the announced results of the referendum showed Yeltsin, and even more surprisingly his economic-reform program, to have stronger public support than the parliament.

Faced with waning public interest in his drive for a new constitution and wanting to capitalize on these results, Yeltsin used the referendum as grounds to call for a Constitutional Conference to be held starting 5 June 1993. Public-opinion polls showed greater support for this approach to the adoption of a new constitution than for any other.[39] Many scholars also

---

36. Mikhail Mossin, student, Moscow State Institute of International Relations, 2 February 1994.

37. Sergei Alekseev, *"Kliucheviye zvenya Konstitutsiya," Russian Monitor* 2 (1993): 29.

38. Considering the possibility of an analogous vote in the United States reveals its peculiarity.

39. In a series of public-opinion polls of roughly one thousand people through the month of May 1993, asking "Who should adopt the new constitution of Russia?" roughly half of those polled consistently responded, "a specially created constitutional conference." (Survey by the Public Opinion Foundation, published in its journal, *Within Sight*, June 1993)

promoted such a body as the most effective forum for the drafting, if not necessarily the adoption, of a new constitution.[40] Of course, whether public or scholarly support, or even concerns of effectiveness, were actually behind Yeltsin's decision is impossible to know. Indeed, it may be either side of the same coin to say that Yeltsin called the conference to stabilize the constitutional order or that he wished "to use it simply to solve his own problems by acquiring more power."[41] For him, these goals may have been synonymous. Regardless, their result was the same—the conference was convened in June 1993.

The Constitutional Conference brought together 762 representatives from a wide spectrum of professions, persuasions, and political associations to discuss Yeltsin's proposed constitution (and summaries of two thousand comments and proposals regarding the draft) in five working committees. In two of these, the Federal Organs of Power and Subjects of the Federation, the most controversial political issues were addressed. The other three, Political Parties, Entrepreneurs and State Enterprises, and Municipalities, concentrated on narrower, less-volatile issues. The participants were from various political factions, social organizations, and interest groups in the country. They included writers, filmmakers, academics, financiers, and others. All sixty-seven regions and twenty-one of the twenty-two republics (with the exception of the already troubled Chechnya) were also represented, making the gathering, in the words of one participant, a veritable "who's who of Russia."[42] Organizers Sergei Shakhrai and Aleksandr Yakovlev

---

40. See V. Bogdanor, "The Constitution and the Transition to Democracy," in Butler, *Perestroika and the Rule of Law,* 174. See also Jan Zielonka, "New Institutions in the Old East Bloc," *Journal of Democracy* 5 (April 1994): 102–3.

41. Kovaldin, interview of 21 July 1993. Also Ludmila Zavadskaya, professor of law, Institute of State and Law, and participant in the 1993 Constitutional Assembly, 5 August 1993. Hereafter Zavadskaya, interview of 5 August 1993.

42. Kovaldin, interview of 21 July 1993.

The first group, consisting of 162 people, represented federal organs, including members of the Congress of People's Deputies, and members of its Constitutional commission (95 people); representatives of the president and the government (50 people); factions of the Supreme Soviet (14); and the Academy of Science (3). The second group consisted of 176 representatives of members of the Federation, including leaders of the republics, leaders of executive and legislative bodies and of territories, provinces, the autonomous province, autonomous regions and the cities of Moscow and St. Petersburg; as well as 176 experts in law. The third group was composed of 26 people representing local self-government chosen by the Union of Russian Cities, the Union of Small Cities, the Russian Association for the Revival and Development of Historic Small and Medium-Sized Cities, and other organizations. The fourth group represented 36 political

described the conference as a "round table of political consensus,"[43] designed to be "broadly representative, quite open, discussing everything [sic]."[44] Yet the many flaws in the design of the conference undermine this partisan view of its nature.

To begin with, the conference would have had greater legitimacy if its participants had been elected rather than invited by Yeltsin.[45] Notwithstanding the representativeness of Yeltsin's choices, "only an elected assembly could be labeled truly independent."[46] Such a body could have been elected for the single task of adopting a constitution, further enhancing the autonomy of its participants. Shakhrai argues that a popular election would have produced a populist body lacking necessary expertise in constitutional issues.[47] But this fails to acknowledge the efficacy of citizen democracy[48] and can be contrasted with William Buckley's expressed desire to be led by the first hundred people in the Cambridge telephone book rather than by the faculty of Harvard University (an impractical suggestion for Russia, given Moscow's lack of a comprehensive phone directory). Moreover, Shakhrai's concern with a populist constituent assembly could have been readily addressed. Most simply, a contingent of experts could have been appointed to complement the elected delegates.

---

parties—16 considered "democratic," 11 considered anti-Yeltsin, and 4 centrist—public associations (64); trade unions (58); and religious denominations (17). Other participants came from a wide variety of social organizations including the Assembly of Democratic Forces of the Northern Caucasus, the Confederation of Peoples of Russia That Were Subjected to Repression, the International League of Numerically Small Peoples and Ethnic Groups, and the Senezhskoye Forum. Fourteen creative unions, three veterans' organizations, three human rights organizations, two ecological organizations, the All-Russia Society for the Disabled and others also sent representatives. The fifth group represented producers and entrepreneurs, including delegates from the Russian Union of Industrialists and Entrepreneurs, the International Stock Exchange and Commodity Exchange Union, the Hermes joint-stock company, the international Association of Enterprise Executives, the League of Entrepreneurs and Cooperative Members, the Russian Agro-Industrial Union, and the Chamber of Commerce and Industry [in Moore, 59 n. 12].

43. Sergei Shakhrai, deputy prime minister, 6 August 1993. Hereafter Shakhrai, interview of 6 August 1993.

44. Aleksandr M. Yakovlev, plenipotentiary representative of the president to the Federal Assembly. Interview in English at his home, 5 February 1994. Hereafter Yakovlev, interview of 5 February 1994.

45. Nikonov, interview of 23 July 1993.

46. International Reform Foundation, "We Need a Different Constitution, and It Must Be Adopted Without Haste," *Nezavisimaya Gazeta*, 7 December 1993.

47. Shakhrai, interview of 6 August 1993.

48. No surprise to critics of Shakhrai, described by some as the "little Stalin."

Rigid control over speaking times and limited opportunities to speak, as well as the predominance of Yeltsin supporters, were other problems. The audience thus shouted down Ruslan Khasbulatov as he attempted to read his opening statement; angered, Khasbulatov walked out with seventy representatives from local parliaments, calling the conference a "sham." Such abuse ought to have been prevented or at least punished. Communist Yuri Slobodkin's subsequent ejection for "disorderly conduct," after he attempted to introduce a new draft for discussion, added insult to injury.[49] Such errors of judgment lent credibility to the claims of Yeltsin's opponents that this was not a genuine constitutional assembly but a rubber-stamp forum designed to lend legitimacy to a document that lacked any at all.

These opposition parties had already compromised by attending the conference notwithstanding their initial threat to boycott it, thereby making actual debate and constructive progress a real possibility. Yeltsin's circle should therefore have made far more effort to compromise and thus keep them in attendance. The unwillingness of the organizers to do so may suggest that they aimed to minimize their opponents' role from the outset. As a result of these missteps, however, public perception of the conference may already have been undermined in its opening hours, even though five thousand amendments to the presidential draft would later be proposed and much compromise actually made with the parliament's draft. Instead of acting as they did, suggests Boris Kurashvilli, one of the authors of Slobodkin's leftist draft, the organizers should have averted such attacks on the conference by including other drafts from the beginning.[50]

Time constraints that Yeltsin's entourage placed on the conference as a whole also thwarted its effectiveness. The ten days allotted for working group discussions were far too few.[51] Rather, the participants should have been "made to sit for a while" and hammer out the basic issues one by one, thus lending the working groups' conclusions far greater validity and legitimacy.[52] In contrast, the formalistic Brezhnev constitution, after nearly fourteen years of internal discussion, was published in *Pravda* in June 1977 and opened to several months of public debate, which generated a variety of

49. See Dwight Semler, "Summer in Russia Brings No Real Political Progress; Federative Issues Dominate Constitutional Discussions," *East European Constitutional Review* 2 (Summer 1993): 20.

50. Kurashvilli, interview of 24 July 1993.

51. Elena Lukasheva, scholar of human-rights law, Institute of State and Law, 1 February 1994. Hereafter Lukasheva, interview of 1 February 1994.

52. Nikonov, interview of 3 February 1994.

changes and adjustments. Though few of these were especially substantive, this "mass political socialization campaign," in which 140 million individuals participated, was itself quite significant.[53]

For that matter, even Stalin's 1936 constitution, one completely devoid of substance, was put forth for discussion and debate throughout the summer and fall of 1936.[54] As Yeltsin legal adviser Yuri Baturin admits, "six months would have been more appropriate for this endeavor."[55] Undue haste gave the conference the appearance, and possibly the function, of "trying to solve present problems" rather than laying out lasting norms of public behavior and government practice.[56]

The much-criticized closed sessions of the conference were modeled on those of the Philadelphia Constitutional Convention.[57] It was hoped that this would encourage many participants, whose politics would never allow them to publicly consult and cooperate, to instead work together and reach consensus. Most attendees spoke positively of this decision and its beneficial effects.[58] In the closed, "business-like atmosphere of the Conference," even the uncooperative Vladimir Zhirinovsky could compromise and cooperate.[59] Ludmila Zavadskaya, another participant, repeatedly expressed her surprise to see Zhirinovsky raise his hand and wait his turn.[60]

This aspect of the discussions may also explain, in part, Zhirinovsky's decision to come out in favor of the constitution in the 12 December 1993 referendum, making him, outside the liberal camp, the only supporter of its ratification and perhaps the one who ensured its victory. Yakovlev might thus be correct to call the conference a "crash course in the parliamentary creation of law."[61] Here, diverse members of Russia's social and political

53. See Sharlet, *Soviet Constitutional Crisis,* 43.

54. Topornin, interview of 21 July 1993.

55. Baturin, interview of 11 August 1993.

56. Mikhail Piskotin, editor, *People's Deputy,* 6 August 1993. Hereafter Piskotin, interview of 6 August 1993.

57. Aleksandr M. Yakovlev, legal adviser to the president. Interview in English at his home, 14 August 1993. Hereafter Yakovlev, interview of 14 August 1993.

58. Zavadskaya, interview of 5 August 1993; Kovaldin, interview of 21 July 1993; and Aleksei Simonov, director, Glasnost Institute, and representative of the Confederation of Journalists' Unions to the 1993 Constitutional Conference, 30 July 1993. Hereafter Simonov, interview of 30 July 1993.

59. Serge Schmemann, Moscow bureau chief, *New York Times,* 17 July 1993. Hereafter Schmemann, interview of 17 July 1993.

60. Zavadskaya, interview of 5 August 1993.

61. Yakovlev, interview of 14 August 1993. See *Konstitutsionnoe Soveshchanie* 1 (August 1993).

elite came together to acquire firsthand experience with the process of consensus-building.

Yet this mystical process was shrouded from the public eye with far too little explication and clarification. Without adequate public explanation, the closed conference sessions seemed synonymous with "the murky and clouded political processes that had prevailed in Soviet politics for years."[62] Given the divisive political environment of the day, public understanding was especially critical. In its absence, opponents of the process could compellingly describe the discussions as a "monologue, not a dialogue," and argue that the conference "was not meant to create any sense of constitutionalism at all, but simply to force Yeltsin's will on the people."[63] Inevitably, partisans of the Supreme Soviet would draw parallels between the public endeavors of the parliament's Constitutional Commission and the closed proceedings of Yeltsin's conference, especially those of the Constitutional Arbitration Commission that worked the committees' proposals into a final conference draft.[64]

Yeltsin and his entourage failed to take the time to carefully educate the public and explain their approach. Yet their well-intentioned but paternalistic view that the government, like the Father Tsar, could build constitutionalism from the top and simply present it to the people, was no longer viable. The conference organizers failed to realize that "the process of drawing up a constitution is itself an important element in the creation of a democratic political culture." Only if the people were included in this process would it mean anything to them.[65]

It is evidence of how deeply ingrained this paternalistic attitude is among the Russian elite, however, that Aleksandr Yakovlev, as thoughtful a scholar as one could imagine, could reflect upon reform under Gorbachev and criticize it as "a process of *nomenklatura* liberals coming together at the *dacha* to write laws which they give to the people as a gift"—yet could himself conceive and carry out a tellingly similar process when his own opportunity arrived. While Yakovlev defensively distinguishes the conference he helped plan from Gorbachev's efforts, describing the former as "an inclusive gathering where the voice of the people, and not that of the leaders,

---

62. Robert Sharlet, professor, Union College. Telephone interview in English, 16 June 1993. Hereafter Sharlet, interview of 16 June 1993.

63. Vlasihin, interview of 10 August 1993.

64. Led by Vladimir Kudriavtsev, this commission ultimately decided which proposals would be incorporated into the draft and which would not.

65. Bogdanor, "The Constitution," 171. See also Faundez, 356.

was heard," this characterization seems tenuous at best.[66] This was, in reality, neither what the conference was about nor how it actually worked. Yakovlev and his cohorts, for all such rhetoric, still did not appreciate the fact that progress now depended on a dialogue with the people, not one above them.

Notwithstanding these criticisms, the Constitutional Conference did produce the draft that, with adjustments, would be voted into force as the Constitution of the Russian Federation five months later, in December 1993. Moreover, the conference's internal workings represented a great leap forward. Here, an institution broadly representative (in form, if not entirely in substance) of the political, economic, and social spectrum of Russian society had emerged and cooperatively functioned. Soon after the conference, Yakovlev correctly declared that the persistence of this style of political interaction was the key to the country's sociopolitical development.[67]

Had greater attention been paid to the conference's public face and to preventing the withdrawal of its conservative participants, the Constitutional Conference could have radically influenced not only its participants but the general public as well. The final 133-article draft of the conference did, in fact, draw extensively from the parliament's draft, principles, and even specific provisions that had been brought in by both the working groups and the final drafting commission.[68] The draft, in the end, was not dissimilar from that of the parliament, with the more than five hundred amendments that had been made in Yeltsin's original in order to create it. A true product of compromise and consensus, the draft's only serious failing was the exclusion of Yeltsin's opponents from the process of its creation. It passed with the support of 433 of 585 voting participants in late July. Its legitimization in the legal consciousness of the masses, however, had been incompletely carried out by the conference. This was now the critical task.

ADOPTION OF THE DRAFT AT ALL COSTS

As the Constitutional Conference had made no provision for the adoption of its constitution, the next step remained unclear. While some argued that the

---

66. Yakovlev, interview of 14 August 1993.

67. Aleksandr M. Yakovlev, speech at the Kremlin, 26 July 1993.

68. Including reductions in the power of the president, ranging from limits on his veto power over federal constitutional laws (articles 106 and 107) and on his power to dissolve the Duma, to a shortening of his term from five years to four, making it concurrent with that of the parliament.

conference itself could vote to adopt the draft, this would have been an empty victory given the conference's partisan composition. The Congress of Peoples' Deputies was unlikely to pass Yeltsin's draft or (it had become increasingly clear) any such document. The deputies' many institutional privileges, benefits hard to come by in Russia, made their agreement to any constitutional restructuring that would threaten their positions or shorten their terms (which should have run to 1995) unlikely at best. At the other extreme, Yeltsin immediately rejected the constitution's adoption by presidential decree as too patently illegitimate.[69]

After some hesitation, he elected to present the draft to each subject of the federation[70] for its consideration. If two-thirds of the subjects could be convinced to support the draft, Yeltsin's advisers believed this would lend it sufficient legitimacy to allow Yeltsin to adopt it on this authority alone. His inner circle promptly issued forth to the regions in an all-out drive to press for ratification.

Yet this was a futile endeavor. It should have been clear to Yeltsin at the close of the conference, when only five republics voted in favor of the draft, that nowhere near two-thirds of the relatively conservative regional governments, many still controlled by Soviet-period holdovers, would support his constitution.[71] Moreover, even the tepid support at the conference was bought with a broad range of concessions on the sovereign status of the various subjects and on the discrepancies in tax rates between the regions and republics. In return for ratification, the subjects now demanded further concessions that would have stripped even more power from the central government and set the stage for the Russia's dismemberment.

Yet without these concessions, there was little hope that the draft would "survive the trip."[72] In the political climate of late 1993, with a growing tax revolt in many of the republics and increasing support for the decentralizing concept of "federalism from below," widespread regional support for any national constitution was an impossibility.

Recognizing the failure of his direct campaign among the subjects, Yeltsin took a new approach to using them to adopt his constitution. In mid-

69. Shakhrai, interview of 6 August 1993.

70. Translated literally from the Russian, a "subject" is any of the component political subdivisions of Russia, including republics, regions, oblasts, and others.

71. Semler, "Summer in Russia," 21. Many of the regional parliaments were further biased against the draft on account of their conservative, pro-parliamentary politics. Sharlet, "The Prospects for Federalism," 121.

72. Semler, "Summer in Russia," 21.

September he managed, after much effort, to convene an "organizational meeting" of the Federation Council, the upper chamber of the legislature outlined in his still-unadopted draft constitution. If the members of the Federation Council, over which Yeltsin had some influence,[73] could be cajoled to vote for the draft's adoption, Yeltsin would use this as evidence of regional support and adopt the draft directly. By this peculiar means, he would bypass his opponents in both the Congress and the regional parliaments. However, the Federation Council balked at this imposition, refusing to declare itself a permanent body and thus foiling Yeltsin's plans once again.[74]

After this second defeat, Yeltsin took a strategic step that further undermined legal consciousness. Dating back to the Treaty of Union signed by Russia, Ukraine, Byelorussia, and Transcaucasia on 30 December 1922, federalism had always been a central element of the Russian constitutional order. In Russia's Declaration of Sovereignty of 12 June 1990,[75] in the adoption of the Federation Treaty in 1992, and in the increasingly prominent role of the subjects in the debates about the future constitutional order, federal questions were at the forefront. Beginning with the active courtship of the subjects by both sides during the April referendum,[76] federalism's importance had only increased in 1993. Yet now, realizing he could not win his constitutional battle in the regions, Yeltsin simply brushed them aside.

Having often spoken of the great significance of the subjects as he attempted to justify adoption of his constitution on the basis of their support alone, Yeltsin now ignored them.[77] For him, it was clear to even the most casual observer, federalism had not been a constitutional principle but a political tool. This tendency toward a federal realpolitik would become even more obvious with the changes Yeltsin made in the draft constitution during November 1993—dropping the Federation Treaty out of the text and giving its clauses on federalism a much more centrist tone. Finally, the December referendum on the constitution, discussed below, was the culmination of Yeltsin's disavowal of the subjects: the subjects, either as autonomous

---

73. Though its members sit as representatives of the subjects, the president had significant indirect influence over their selection (see article 95 of the constitution).

74. The regions gained much from the instability at the center and thus were little inclined to help put an end to it.

75. Russia's declaration was followed by similar ones by the other republics, except for the three Baltic republics, which had declared their independence earlier in 1990.

76. See Sharlet, "The Prospects for Federalism," 119–20.

77. Sharlet, "The Prospects for Federalism," 121.

entities or as composites of their citizens, were irrelevant to the referendum's result.[78] Overnight, what had been Russia's "biggest stumbling block" became a non-issue in Yeltsin's rhetoric and politics.[79]

Yeltsin's blatantly politicized attempt to circumvent the Congress's authority over ratification of a new constitution by turning to the republics had already cast doubt on the legitimacy of the constitutional process. His subsequent, and sudden, reversal on the role of the subjects made public cynicism about the constitution and the issues it addressed inevitable. Meanwhile, the parliament did its share to encourage this state of affairs. After a 16 July 1993 report by Rumyantsev on the Constitutional Commission's progress, delivered within days of the Constitutional Conference's conclusion, the Supreme Soviet passed a bill "On the Procedures for Adopting the Constitution of the Russian Federation." This legitimate but politically motivated declaration simply reaffirmed the two established procedures for adoption: first, by vote of the Congress, and second, by means of a referendum holding to the requirement of support by a majority of the electorate.[80] Devoid of any new substance, the bill's only purpose was to cast a stone at Yeltsin's efforts.

Soon after, the Supreme Soviet drew up a package of amendments to the 1978 constitution that would have rendered the president a figurehead. It also prepared a set of additions to the criminal code that would impose criminal penalties on ministers who failed to obey orders of the parliament. These were readied for presentation to the Tenth Congress of People's Deputies in November 1993, when they were likely to be adopted. During August, the Supreme Soviet also passed a new privatization law placing the latter under parliamentary control, as well as a budget plan that included subsidies and welfare spending that would undermine most of Yeltsin's reform efforts to date.

Faced with this onslaught, Yeltsin finally chose to hold a public referendum. Having turned to the subjects to circumvent the Congress, he now decided to turn to the people to circumvent the subjects. Yet he was not entirely confident of success on this path, with good reason. Given popular opinion at this stage and the masses' distaste for everyone and everything political, it may have been "better for the president not to leave anything to

---

78. This was a change from prior plebiscites, in which support by a majority of voters in a majority of subjects was required, in addition to a majority of the total popular vote.
79. Semler, "Summer in Russia," 20.
80. Semler, "Summer in Russia," 21.

the people," as their response was entirely unpredictable.[81] As long as an active parliament continued to oppose Yeltsin and the Constitutional Court sat as a forum of judgment that would hold him to the official requirements for a referendum, he was not guaranteed the public support he needed to adopt his draft. This concern led to the events of September and October 1993, foreshadowed by Yeltsin in August, when he spoke of an unspecified "September offensive" for which he was preparing.[82]

On 21 September 1993, in a television address, Yeltsin declared that Russia was "experiencing a profound crisis of its state structure," one that had to end.[83] Declaring the standing constitutional order to be defunct, he announced Decree no. 1400, "On the Step-by-Step Constitutional Reform of the Russian Federation." He disbanded the Supreme Soviet, suspended parts of the constitution, and enjoined the Constitutional Court from meeting until after new parliamentary elections. This decree was quickly followed by others that banned the publication of several conservative newspapers, including *Den* and *Sovetskaya Rossiya,* and imposed censorship restrictions on several centrist journals that had spoken out strongly against his initial decree.[84] Though these restrictions were quickly lifted under strong political pressure, the president, claiming to be stuck in a corner by the "provocations" of the parliament, insisted such measures were the only way out of the crisis.

The subsequent arming and isolation of several hundred supporters of Vice President Aleksandr Rutskoi and parliament Speaker Ruslan Khasbulatov in the White House is well known. Less publicized, but equally important from our perspective, was the decision of Valery Zorkin, chairman of the Constitutional Court, to call an emergency court session notwithstanding Yeltsin's decree. A minority faction of the court, led by Ernst Ametistov, publicly declared its refusal to participate. Directed by Zorkin, however, a quorum drafted and released a ruling rife with procedural errors, which declared Decree no. 1400 to be unconstitutional and called on the parliament to impeach the president. Meanwhile, the drama at the White House enthralled the public, which closely followed Orthodox Patriarch Aleksei II's attempts

81. Troyitski, interview of 20 July 1993.

82. I well remember sitting with several researchers at the Gorbachev Foundation, listening to Yeltsin's speech and curiously discussing what "preparations" he was engaged in, and for what sort of "offensive."

83. "Yeltsin's Address on National Television," official Kremlin international news broadcast (available on LEXIS: News, Sovnws), 21 September 1993.

84. *Nezavisimaya Gazeta* and *Segodnya.*

at compromise and the media's wild speculations as to the outcome of the crisis.

It was clear to all that the months (if not years) of gridlock and dual power in the Russian government had to end. The balance of power in Russia had long ago degraded into a paralysis of brinkmanship. And with the constitution "no longer showing the lines of power," there appeared to be no gradual, constitutional way out of this corner.[85] Recent Supreme Soviet decisions decreeing deputies' right to make indiscriminate use of military aircraft, claiming jurisdiction over the Ukrainian port of Sebastopol in violation of international law, and slowing down the process of privatization, among others, had undermined the parliament's legitimacy. There was no longer an adequate framework for minimal interaction, let alone cooperation, between the executive and legislative branches. This was not unlike the situation in the other former Soviet republics, with the exception of the Baltic states and Armenia.[86] Thus it may not have been either party's fault, but an inevitable impasse on the path away from the Soviet political order.

The bulk of the population seems to have recognized this dilemma and expected its resolution in a victory of presidential power. Given the volatile state of affairs they faced, the Russian people still acknowledged the place of raw political power in the country. Russian traditions of a strong executive, as well as public dissatisfaction with the stumbling Supreme Soviet, also underlay expectations that the president would prevail in the inevitable struggle. While it is unlikely that this exact scenario had been predicted before 21 September, the contours of its results were no surprise. The only surprise may have been Yeltsin's assurances of new parliamentary elections in December, followed by presidential elections in the spring.

Given all of this, Yeltsin's decree may have had only a limited impact on the public's sense of law and order—they "understood that the old constitution would not help resolve the crisis and that an exit had to be found."[87] The events of 3 and 4 October 1993, more destabilizing than months of political chaos, were quite another matter. A week after Yeltsin's pronouncement, negotiations to draw Yeltsin's opponents out of the White House had deadlocked. The occupants, it was revealed, had a large stockpile of heavy weapons on hand. Thus moved to end the standoff, Yeltsin sealed the building and cut off its electricity, water, and telephone connections. Em-

85. Klamkin, interview of 4 February 1994.
86. Paen, interview of 28 January 1994.
87. Burlatski, interview of 1 February 1994.

boldened by desperation, on 3 October Vice President Rutskoi directed a mob that had broken the troop lines surrounding the White House to storm the mayor's office and the Ostankino state television station. Heated street battles ensued at both locations and Yeltsin responded in kind, if not in proportion. Early on the morning of 4 October, special military forces launched a massive artillery attack against the White House and its remaining occupants. Within hours, as smoke billowed from the White House windows and over a hundred lay dead, the opposition surrendered.

This massive use of force to end Khasbulatov and Rutskoi's occupation of the White House came as a complete surprise to all observers. "I have known Yeltsin a long time," said Khasbulatov in the aftermath, "but I never expected this from him."[88] Only two years had passed since the putschists of August had failed as they could not bring themselves to fire on the masses gathered in defense of the same building. No argument of "need of state" could justify such a step then, and few saw any to justify it now.

Yet Yeltsin, having escaped the White House two years before and now seated in the Kremlin, acted in the old tradition of the tsar, the general secretary, and the president, and came out in force to crush the rebellion and silence his opponents.[89] The kind of attack—a bombardment that essentially burned the occupants out—intensified perceptions of impropriety. This was a "huge trauma to Russian legal consciousness," notes Fyodor Burlatski, even as he discounts the impact of Yeltsin's earlier decree. "Even if it was the key to the construction of a new constitutional order, it was not the right way out."[90] The public thought such official violence had been left behind with communism, yet it had now reappeared. With Yeltsin's attack on the White House, legality and constitutionalism appeared to the average Russian to be more subservient to power politics and brute force than ever—for Soviet brutality had never enjoyed such wide publicity. In the opinion of Vladimir Lafitski, a member of the staff of the now-defunct Constitutional Commission, Yeltsin's actions "ruined the legal mentality of the people." In their aftermath, "no one believed in law and the constitution anymore."[91]

It is especially interesting to consider the impact of Yeltsin's attack on the legal consciousness of the elites. In its aftermath, the elites' safety and security appeared as tenuous under democracy as it had been under Stalinism. The

88. Related by Mikhail Marchenko, vice rector, Moscow State University, and professor of law, 31 January 1994. Hereafter Marchenko, interview of 31 January 1994.
89. Burlatski, interview of 1 February 1994.
90. Burlatski, interview of 1 February 1994.
91. Lafitski, interview of 31 January 1994.

stability of the bureaucracy, the leitmotif of Brezhnev's years of stagnation, now seemed threatened. The ability to toe the party line had become the key to survival once more. On the other hand, Giorgi Satarov defends Yeltsin's actions and argues that this assessment is overdrawn. "Elites and masses alike saw these steps for what they were—simply a continuation of the political conflict . . . and its necessary conclusion."[92] The bolder Andrannik Migranyan even wonders whether a bit of fear will not "teach the elites some badly needed discipline."[93]

Yeltsin's escalation of the conflict, Satarov and Migranyan would argue, was necessary. The occupants of the White House and their supporters outside were armed and violent. Prior to Yeltsin's use of force, armed attacks had already been made on the mayor's office and the television station. This aggression, coupled with growing support for Khasbulatov and Rutskoi outside Moscow,[94] suggested a drift toward civil war that Yeltsin had to halt. "By the time the tanks opened fire, however, parliament, which had increasingly marginalized itself in the previous months and finally discredited itself by endorsing street violence, was a spent force in the long political struggle between the executive and legislative branches."[95] Yeltsin's portrayal of the parliament as a serious threat to the civil order, thus, is untenable. Yet even if we accept this argument, questions remain about Yeltsin's defense of his actions. Little was said or done in this regard. Apparently disinterested in maintaining public respect for law, Yeltsin only nominally attempted to justify his decision to seal off and attack the White House.

Yeltsin had tepidly acknowledged the unconstitutionality of Decree no. 1400 at the outset,[96] but he insisted on its legitimacy nonetheless, arguing that Russia's security was "more precious than formal obedience to contradictory norms created by the legislature."[97] Yeltsin made no additional

92. Satarov, interview of 4 February 1994.

93. Migranyan, interview of 4 February 1994.

94. Possibly as many as two-thirds of the subjects of the federation supported the occupants of the White House.

95. Robert Sharlet, "Russia's 'Ethnic' Republics and Constitutional Politics," *Eurasian Reports* 3 (Winter 1993): 39. In this vein, Sharlet has argued that the attack on the parliament might have been intended more as a message to the cantankerous regions battling Yeltsin over the division of powers, rather than as the only means available to end the separation-of-powers conflict in Moscow. Sharlet, "The Prospects for Federalism," 122; and Sharlet, "Russia's 'Ethnic' Republics," 39–40.

96. Not in his initial television address, but in subsequent statements by him and his advisers.

97. Quoted in Dwight Semler, "The End of the First Russian Republic," *East European Constitutional Review* 2, 3 (Fall 1993, Winter 1994): 109. As Yeltsin would write in his 1994

effort, however, to legitimate his *subsequent* decision to use military force to execute his decree. In his mind, the legitimacy of Decree no. 1400, which he felt he had established with his televised arguments of parliamentary illegitimacy, extended to its execution as well. "If he could ban the parliament," facetiously suggested Giorgi Shakhnazarov, a Gorbachev adviser, "he could bomb it as well. This was Yeltsin. This was his way."[98] Yet some further justification by Yeltsin was indispensable. That his decree was necessary did not make his tanks so.

The results of the April referendum, in which the public declared their support for the president and questioned the continued legitimacy of the Supreme Soviet, might have been one defense of this abrupt action. Though dissipated in its authority during the intervening five months, this vote remained a powerful rationale, one Yeltsin had emphasized in defense of the decree itself. Arguably, the referendum gave the president "carte blanche to reorder his relations with the parliament."[99] Too much time had already been lost since the people had spoken, he might have asserted, and the country could no longer wait on the Supreme Soviet. It was time to move forward, even at the cost of such force.

The old constitutional order, he might also have reasoned, had become defunct in the course of the radical changes in the country's political system since 1990.[100] And the new order could not be built with the tools of the old. Postwar German reconstruction, thus, was not carried out within the confines of the Nazi constitutional order.[101] Only by clearing the debris of its past could Russia step into the future.

Most broadly, Yeltsin could attempt to defend his actions on the basis of the urgent need for effective reform and the Supreme Soviet's continued resistance to this process. Yeltsin acted not at his own caprice, according to this argument, but at the will of people. As Yakovlev notes, "for the Russian people stability was worth more than the constitution."[102] Especially in light

---

memoirs: "But, oh! How I didn't want to break the law to extricate us from this tar baby." Quoted in Carl Linden, "The Dialectics of Russian Politics," *Problems of Post-Communism* 42 (January–February 1995): 10.

98. Shakhnazarov, interview of 3 February 1994.

99. Ernst Ametistov, member, Russian Constitutional Court, 4 February 1994. Hereafter Ametistov, interview of 4 February 1994.

100. He might have also made note of Khasbulatov's own lack of formal legitimacy, given his recall by Chechnya one year before. Vlasihin, interview of 10 August 1993.

101. Andrei Malgin, editor, *Stolitsa,* 3 August 1993.

102. Yakovlev, interview of 5 February 1994.

of Rutskoi's calls for his violent overthrow and the ensuing mob violence on 3 October, Yeltsin might suggest, he was not the enemy of constitutionalism, but its defender.

Any such defense might have sufficed. But his failure to forcefully present *any* argument for the legitimacy of the 4 October attack, as he had made the case for his original decree, gave the appearance that its legitimacy (or lack thereof) was ultimately irrelevant to him. By failing to defend his escalation of the conflict, he painted the entire process as criminal. This effect was only exaggerated by his suddenly defensive advisers' attempts to characterize the whole process as legal, a charade that harkened back to the empty legal rhetoric of Soviet newspeak. Thus was it disheartening to hear Ernst Ametistov, a legal scholar and member of the Constitutional Court, defend Yeltsin's actions by suggesting that he had "looked at certain articles of the constitution and not others, focusing his attention on the clauses delineating the people's power."[103] Such selective reading did not become a trained lawyer and judge, even if Yeltsin or his press spokesman might get away with it.

Regardless of which justification Yeltsin might have offered for his final moves, his failure to present any at all may have been his most serious error. By failing to speak of constitutionalism this once, Yeltsin engendered a climate in which "it became useless to speak of constitutionalism at all."[104] He appeared disinterested in legitimacy and legality and thereby tarnished not only himself, but all that followed from his actions as well.[105] Thus would the constitution, its division of powers, and even the new parliament come to be challenged as the illegitimate products of Yeltsin's criminal actions.

This sense of illegitimacy was heightened in the days after the bombardment of the White House, when an executive order expelled nearly 10,000 non-Russians from Moscow as part of an extra-constitutional drive to root out organized crime—one that was somewhat effective, though only fleetingly.[106] A curfew was imposed in Moscow, 6,000 individuals were arrested by the army, and anti-Yeltsin media outlets were placed under censorship,

103. Ametistov, interview of 4 February 1994.

104. Marchenko, interview of 31 January 1994.

105. See Sharlet, "The Prospects for Federalism," 121.

106. Louise I. Shelley, "Organized Crime in the Former Soviet Union," *Problems of Post-Communism* 42 (January–February 1995): 60; Stephen Handelman, *Comrade Criminal: Russia's New Mafiya* (New Haven, Conn.: Yale University Press, 1995), 289–90.

suspended, or, in several cases, banned altogether. Disloyal regional leaders and federal officials were sacked, and local and regional soviets were dissolved by presidential decree on 26 October.

Among these myriad anti-constitutional moves, the final blow to the constitutional picture Yeltsin had painted in defending his actions came with his sudden change of heart on the scheduling of presidential elections. Having previously announced that presidential elections would follow six months after those of the parliament in December, thereby reassuring those who saw his dissolution of the parliament as a step toward autocracy,[107] Yeltsin now stepped back from this commitment, declaring his intention to complete his term but not to run again in 1996.[108] This move sharply reduced what little faith the public still had in assurances from their constitutional representatives. Yet little protest was made to it, as few remained on the political landscape in a position to do so. In the public consciousness, argues one Russian lawyer, "while everything had been in the future in 1985, everything was now in the past."[109]

The ends of September and October, however, might still have served to redeem their means. "Russian political conflict had always been decided by force. Now force could be used to go beyond conflict," to the creation of a new political order. In this way, Ametistov optimistically suggested, the cycle of violence and political chaos might be broken.[110] Steps to adopt the draft constitution could now be taken, making force the midwife of stability. With his institutional opposition undermined, Yeltsin moved to place his draft before the Russian people in a referendum to be held along with elections to the Federation Council and State Duma, the upper and lower chambers of the new parliament, on 12 December 1993.

Through October and November, a rump Constitutional Conference reconvened to revise the July draft in light of the new political situation. Unsurprisingly, these revisions expanded presidential powers from the July

107. This promise could not have been more explicit. See Archie Brown, "The October Crisis of 1993: Context and Implications," *Post-Soviet Affairs* 9 (July–September 1993): 191 ("The presidential election will be on June 12, 1994. This has been determined and this is how it will be!") See also Yeltsin's 23 September 1993 decree, giving 1994 as the date of presidential elections.

108. Another promise he would later back away from.

109. Barenboim, interview of 3 February 1994.

110. Ametistov, interview of 4 February 1994. While Ametistov's intentions were sincere, it is nevertheless disconcerting to note that Stalin might have described his own rule, and the purges of an untold number of his citizens, in words not entirely dissimilar from those of Ametistov.

draft, providing: under article 83(a), the power to appoint the prime minister; under article 83(c), the power to dismiss the government; and under article 90(1), broader authority to rule by executive decree. Certain powers were shifted away from the State Duma and others were weakened, leaving it, for example, with only consent power over the president's selection of prime minister (and not the right of appointment) under article 111(1). In its final form, the constitution was thus premised not on the separation of powers, but on presidential supremacy. Respect for the separation of powers having dwindled among Yeltsin's circle by November, this was no surprise.[111]

As for the regions, the new draft dropped the Federation Treaty, leveling out the status of the previously unequal subjects.[112] Unitarism took the place of federalism in both the tone and substance of the constitution.[113] The sections regarding individual rights, on the other hand, remained largely unchanged and relatively strong. The potential for secondary infringements of rights probably increased, however, given the president's heightened powers of decree and emergency rule.[114] Erik Hoffmann describes the final draft as more "viable" than that of July.[115] In the climate of presidential supremacy of late 1993, this may well have been true. With presidential rule inevitable, it was probably better to adopt limited constraints Yeltsin would live within, rather than to demand significant ones he would simply brush aside.

His new draft, then, was put before the public and adopted by a small margin on 12 December 1993. Simultaneously, the constitution's new, two-chamber parliament was elected. Yet how odd it seemed to select deputies to a State Duma that one could, on the very same ballot, choose not to create. Beyond such existential criticisms, however, the referendum's substantive results can also be challenged.

To begin with, there is the distinct possibility that the vote was fraudulently tabulated. Electoral participation may thus have been 46 percent, rather than the 55 percent originally announced—an important difference,

---

111. Robert Sharlet, "Russian Constitutional Crisis: Law and Politics Under Yel'tsin," *Post-Soviet Affairs* 9 (October–December 1993): 328.

112. The July version had anomalously included the Federation Treaty, but also included an equality provision.

113. In contrast, however, a revised article 102 granted the Federation Council, as representative of the subjects, new powers of appointment and confirmation, and a new "states' rights" phrase was added in article 73.

114. See Sharlet, "Russian Constitutional Crisis," 328.

115. Hoffmann, 37.

in light of the requirement that 50 percent of the electorate participate for the referendum to be valid. The Central Electoral Commission, for reasons that remain unclear, used a lower base figure than the 107 million voters that were previously determined to have been in the electorate. Moreover, in a 4 May 1994 *Izvestiia*[116] article by Aleksandr Sobyanin, appointed by the president to examine the constitution's adoption (and fired after publication of this article), it was revealed that 9 million ballots appeared to have been falsified, lowering participation to 49 million voters, well below the required minimum. Further evidence suggested that regional authorities may also have presented inaccurate vote counts.[117] Yeltsin's decision to make use of presidentially appointed counting commissions (which themselves released, at various times, three different tallies of registered voters) encouraged such doubts about the results.[118]

On the other hand, the still-low participation rates that were announced and the extremely poor showing of Yeltsin's supporters in the Duma elections would seem to cast doubt on whether widespread fraud occurred. If it had, would the results not have been more favorable to those in the Yeltsin camp? Even absent direct tampering, however, Michael Urban argues that the very design of the electoral process encouraged certain results. Such instrumental structuring of the campaign and the election process—by limiting debate; reshaping electoral districts; and phrasing the referendum question on the ballot in a biased tone—was reminiscent of Soviet elections and cast doubt on the referendum's results regardless of any proof of explicit fraud. This was, in Urban's words, "democracy by design."[119]

The draft constitution was published in a few major newspapers a month before the election. This may have once guaranteed its wide distribution, but it no longer could, given the precipitous decline in the readership of nearly every newspaper in the country. As a result, it is unlikely that more than a small percentage of the citizenry perused the lengthy document, with its two parts, nine chapters, and 137 articles. An active debate about the draft's provisions might have remedied this. Again, it is instructive to recall the

116. *Izvestiia*, 4 May 1994, 4.

117. "Constitution Watch—Russia," *East European Constitutional Review* 3 (Spring 1994): 19–20.

118. See Sharlet, "The Prospects for Federalism," 123 n. 31. See also Vera Tolz and Julia Wishnevsky, "Election Queries Make Russians Doubt Democratic Process," *RFE/RL Research Report* 3 (8 April 1994): 19–27.

119. See Michael Urban, "December 1993 As a Replication of Late-Soviet Electoral Practices," *Post-Soviet Affairs* 10 (April–June 1994): 128, 128 n. 2.

process that surrounded the adoption of the 1977 constitution. The constitutional discourse in 1977, noted *Pravda* on its opening day, was meant to encourage "the further invigoration of all social life in the country."[120] The newspaper therefore set aside several pages in each issue for the discussion of constitutional questions. This could have easily been done in 1993 and would have ensured a more constructive and substantive debate on the constitution's merits.

It can be argued that with the exception of a few substantive changes, including the strengthening of the right to criticize officials under article 49 and the accountability of deputies under article 107, the 1977 discussions were little more than empty propaganda. Yet this misses the point. The Soviet leadership saw, as Yeltsin should have, that public discussion could be used as a "technique for mobilizing the population and encouraging citizen participation in policy implementation."[121]

Yeltsin worried, however, that absent the controls and filters available to Brezhnev in 1977, such discussion might overwhelm his true goal—the sure and speedy adoption of his draft.[122] But surely some happy medium could have secured both the short- and long-term needs of constitutionalism, providing for genuine public debate yet not jeopardizing the draft's eventual adoption. Yet when serious discussion began to emerge, Yeltsin immediately threatened to deny free television and radio time to those parties that used it to criticize the constitution. "Don't touch the Constitution!" he declared on 26 November.[123] This was justified, it was argued by Vladimir Shumeiko, a senior Yeltsin associate charged with carrying out the referendum (who also proposed at one point that parties critical of the constitution be removed from the ballot), since those parties running in the elections had tacitly endorsed the constitution by their participation and could not take back with one hand what they had given with the other. The threat to deny his opponents' television time was withdrawn two days later by Yeltsin, in response to the fire storm of criticism it provoked, but it had already revealed Yeltsin's low esteem for public discourse and debate.

While the draft constitution "was not worse than that of Gorbachev's commission," as Vladimir Kudriavtsev, a member of the latter, suggested,[124]

120. *Pravda*, 5 June 1977, 2.
121. Sharlet, *Soviet Constitutional Crisis*, 33.
122. On the 1977 discussions see Sharlet, *Soviet Constitutional Crisis*, 32–53.
123. Urban, "December 1993," 135, 135 n. 17.
124. Kudriavtsev, interview of 31 January 1994.

it needed to be sold to the public. It had to be shown to have substance. Stalin's 1936 constitution, one of history's most democratically worded constitutions, had mocked its substantive content by its adoption at the height of the aconstitutional purges.[125] Yeltsin's had to prove itself to be different. Furthermore, the draft could attract public interest, then support, and then faith only through a painstaking process of debate and discussion. Justice Zorkin, a former professor quite knowledgeable in American constitutional history, remarks that when the American Constitution and Bill of Rights were drawn up, "people turned to and focused on these documents. Only thus did they become part of the legal, political, and social culture of America."[126] If Yeltsin's constitution was to have real meaning for Russians, no less was necessary. Only an active, contentious debate would encourage public consideration and analysis of the document and thereby draw forth genuine public support rather than acceptance of the draft as the only reasonable alternative. Yet, sadly, the latter became the most powerful argument for the constitution's ratification. Some order, the logic went, was better than none.

Yeltsin's failure to comply with the Law on Referenda of 1990 or to justify his decision not to (a legitimate one, given the law's impossibly stringent requirements) undermined the results of the referendum as well. After several referenda held under the 1990 law, the public clearly understood its requirement of passage by 50 percent of the total electorate and not simply a majority of participants. With the participation of 55 percent of the electorate (assuming this number to be correct), the 58 percent voting for ratification of the draft indicates that roughly 31 percent of the populace was in favor, far from sufficient under the law as the public knew it. As a result, the low percentages voting in favor of ratification were inevitably noted by Yeltsin's opponents in the aftermath of the referendum. Kudriavtsev argues that the public had accepted this lower requirement as legitimate or else they would have opposed it—but it is unclear how they might have done so. Questioned in this vein, he refused to elaborate, insisting that he was "simply of a different opinion."[127]

Furthermore, those who failed to vote can be argued to have been in opposition.[128] Low participation rates and absenteeism in developed democracies, while not considered admirable, are not necessarily a critical issue.

125. Yegorov, interview of 2 February 1994.
126. Zorkin, interview of 2 February 1994.
127. Kudriavtsev, interview of 31 January 1994.
128. In the April 1993 referendum, polls indicate that non-participation was just this—a

Russia is probably no exception. Yet on this occasion, absenteeism may well have been "the result of the fourth of October. After that, the people no longer believed in the government and wanted to have nothing to do with it."[129] This seems reasonable. The unwillingness of 45 percent of the Russian electorate to participate in a vote on the constitutional structures and future of the country goes beyond a lack of interest in the politics of the liberal Gaidar versus the reactionary Zhirinovsky. Such non-participation may reveal a fundamental distaste for Russia's constitutional order as a whole. In such high percentages, the failure to take part may have shown "the Russian *mudzhik* [common man] to be against the new options of life."[130]

In the short term, low public interest and lack of participation may not have been critical issues. In fact, they may have made adoption of the constitution possible. Given the lack of western constitutional traditions in Russia, Migranyan argues that it is "not important for the public at large to know how the constitution was created, but only for the political elite."[131]

Yet the weak level of political legitimacy provided by elite, rather than popular, constitutionalism is an inadequate foundation for a lasting constitutional order. If public participation and legal consciousness is not important today, it must somehow be made so. Elite legal consciousness may once have been adequate for the creation of constitutionalism, but the face of Russia has changed. Thus, as we turn to Part II and Russia's constitutional future, the place and perspective of the people will be an increasingly prominent theme.

In addition to adopting the constitution, Russian voters also elected the Duma and Federation Council on 12 December 1993. These results, it will be remembered, shocked the entire world community. By the end, anti-reform parties including the leftist Communists and Agrarians and the rightist Liberal Democratic Party held 182 seats to the reformers' 164 seats. Yegor Gaidar's liberal Russia's Choice party emerged with the largest bloc of seats (96), but it was followed by the LDP, the Communists, and the Agrarians, with 70, 65, and 47 seats, respectively, making the latter the dominant parties in the Duma. And while this was not the product of a mass

---

sign of opposition to the entire system. Richard Rose, "Russia As an Hour-Glass Society: A Constitution Without Citizens," *East European Constitutional Review* 4 (Summer 1995): 40.

129. Burlatski, interview of 1 February 1994.

130. Dimitri Olshanski, chairman, Department of Political Psychology, Institute of Political Analysis. Interview in English, 2 February 1994. Hereafter Olshanski, interview of 2 February 1994.

131. Migranyan, interview of 4 February 1994.

exodus away from the democrats, but simply of the centrist "swamp" voting against the "liberals,"[132] it was still billed as the end of economic liberalization and democratization in Russia. Neither of these predictions, of course, proved to be true, and the constitution's new political order has proved far more effective than had been expected. But this is already the history of the Second Russian Republic, born on 25 December 1993 with the entry into force of the new Constitution of the Russian Federation.

Before we turn to the new Russia, it will be helpful to specifically analyze the institution of the First Republic that probably impacted upon the development of legal consciousness, and its undermining, more than any other—the Constitutional Court. The very fact of this institution's existence, it is fair to say, is powerful evidence of the radically altered landscape that constitutionalism faces in Russia today. Its history, however, is evidence of how challenging a landscape it remains.

THE CONSTITUTIONAL COURT
OF THE RUSSIAN FEDERATION

The Constitutional Court, the first incarnation of which appeared in October 1991, has arguably been the "strongest example and manifestation of respect for law" to emerge in Russia since Gorbachev resurrected the role of law in Soviet society.[133] This should come as no surprise, given that the court was Russia's first truly post-Communist institution.[134]

It is evidence of the mixed legacy of the court's subsequent deeds, however, that Robert Sharlet must ask, in assessing its tenure from 1991 to 1993: "Did the young Court mitigate or intensify the severity of the separation of powers conflict?"[135]

The court was formally established on 15 December 1990, when the Second Russian Congress adopted its Law on Amendments and Additions to the Constitution of the RSFSR, which established the court by amendment

132. Inga Mikhailovskaia and Evgenii Kuzminskii, "Making Sense of the Russian Elections," *East European Constitutional Review* 3 (Spring 1994): 62–63.
133. Yegorov, interview of 2 February 1994.
134. Sharlet, "Russian Constitutional Crisis," 331. See also Sharlet, "The Russian Constitutional Court," 1–39.
135. Sharlet, "Russian Constitutional Crisis," 323.

of article 119 of the 1978 constitution.[136] This clause was given effect by the Law on the Constitutional Court (12 July 1991), which in turn led to the parliament's election of thirteen of the fifteen required justices at the Fifth Extraordinary Congress of People's Deputies on 29 and 30 October 1991.[137] While the selection process was unduly politicized and was criticized for producing only one justice with any prior judicial experience,[138] it nonetheless signaled the birth of a new legal order in Russia.[139]

Notwithstanding its inauspicious start, this first Constitutional Court of Russia would go on to play a central role in the constitutional and political developments of 1992 and 1993, until its suspension by Yeltsin's September 1993 decree. This role was unprecedented in Russian or Soviet history. During its two years in operation, the court received approximately thirty thousand petitions from citizens, government agencies, and nongovernmental bodies. While usually outside the court's jurisdiction and lacking merit, each of these applications was responded to by the court and its staff. It heard twenty-seven cases—nineteen reviewing laws and administrative acts upon governmental request, eight responding to citizen complaints. While minimal by western standards, this remains an achievement for a novice court whose cumulative membership had almost no judicial experience. Finally, notwithstanding well-warranted criticisms of the court for the conservative political bias that emerged during its second year, it should be noted, in all fairness, that an equal number of court decisions (ten) struck down parliamentary acts as struck down presidential acts, suggesting a difference between the court's heated rhetoric and its actual work.

The court burst onto the political landscape with its unexpected decision, handed down during its very first month in operation, to overturn President Yeltsin's decree merging the police and internal security forces into a single ministry under his command.[140] The creation of new ministries, it ruled, was the sole prerogative of the parliament. President Yeltsin's usurpation of this power violated the separation of powers. The court thus gave the principle of the separation of powers, only recently codified in the 1978

---

136. Article 119, paragraph 23; *Vedomosti RSFSR* no. 29, item 395 (1990).

137. The two vacancies, for reasons that remain unclear, were never filled. Later both liberals and conservatives would oppose efforts to fill them, for fear the new appointees might tip the court's political balance against them. The failure to fill the seats at the outset, however, remains a mystery.

138. Six were appointed out of academia and six from the parliament, while the last was a longtime prosecutor.

139. Sharlet, "Russian Constitutional Crisis," 323.

140. Decided on 14 January 1992.

constitution by a series of amendments, a real bite that no one had expected of it.

Most important about the decision, however, was the even more surprising willingness of Yeltsin, after some coaxing by Chairman Zorkin, to abide by it.[141] For until then, the possibility of a judicial body directly overturning an executive decision was little known in practice, even if extant on paper. Thus the case truly altered both elite and mass consciousness of the law and of the bounds it places on political authority. Suddenly the law was no longer a toothless tiger. Like the Committee for Constitutional Supervision's decision to overturn Gorbachev's decree banning demonstrations, this decision placed the law above power in the public eye.

The most important case heard by the first court was the Communist Party case, which occupied most of its first year of operation. The latter brought the court into the national spotlight but also catalyzed its descent into politics of the most partisan kind. It represented the beginnings of a constitutional jurisprudence in Russia, but the end of the Constitutional Court itself. "In terms of the development of a law-based state, this case may [have been] a watershed."[142] In the course of the court's drawn-out consideration of the case,[143] moreover, procedures and principles that still shape the court's operations emerged on an ad hoc basis. This imperfect rule-making process itself influenced the present court's decision to adopt its procedural regulations at the outset, unlike the first court, which never formally adopted its rules of procedure.

The case revolved around the constitutional and legal status of the Communist Party and whether, in light of this, Yeltsin could permissibly disband the Party and seize its property and assets. More specifically, the case concerned the constitutionality of Yeltsin's Decrees no. 79, 90, and 169, respectively of 23 and 24 August and 6 November 1991. With these decrees, Yeltsin first suspended the Communist Party and took its properties into temporary receivership, then banned the Party permanently and nationalized all its property holdings.[144]

A group of Communist Party deputies first set the case in motion with a 7 February 1992 petition to the court arguing the decrees to be beyond

141. Sharlet, "The Russian Constitutional Court," 6.

142. Carla Thorson, "The Fate of the Communist Party in Russia," *RFE/RL Research Report* 1 (18 September 1992): 1.

143. 26 May 1992 to 30 November 1992.

144. Notably, the Party was thereby rendered indigent, forcing the government to provide for its defense.

Yeltsin's constitutional authority. Faced with a compelling case against the decrees, Yeltsin's anticommunist allies chose a strong offense as their defense, deciding to complicate the case and put the Party on the defensive by cross-petitioning the court with their own case. In early May, just before the court was scheduled to begin hearings on the Party's petition, they filed a petition requesting that the court address the legality of the Party and determine its status under the constitution. The court proceeded to join the two petitions, diluting the Party's strong position on the decrees and leading to suggestions that Zorkin had himself encouraged the submission of cross-petition to weaken the Party's case.[145]

With the merger of the two petitions, the case came to encompass three distinct questions, each of a mixed legal and political character. The first was the largely factual question of whether the Communist Party had been involved in the attempted August 1991 coup against Gorbachev, the event that was the original impetus for Yeltsin's decrees. The second, and far broader, question was what kind of organization the Communist Party actually was. Resolution of this issue involved the submission of thousands of pages of documents and lengthy testimony as to whether the Party was reforming itself by August 1991 or was unreformable; whether the Party was the state, controlled the state, or was a separate entity therefrom, and whether its property was, in fact, state property.

Finally, the hearings addressed the constitutionality of Yeltsin's decrees themselves.[146] Only this last issue, the original one, was a truly legal question. The Party thus argued that the decrees violated both the division of authority within the executive branch (specific procedures existed for the Ministry of Justice to ban political associations) and the separation of powers between the executive on the one hand, and the legislature and the judiciary on the other. With little grounds for a response, Yeltsin was forced to rely on some rather weak reasoning: Because the Party was not registered properly under the law on associations and, regardless, because the latter law was not yet in force in its entirety, Yeltsin's team argued that the applicable law on the rights of political associations was a 1932 Stalinist decree that, unsurprisingly, permitted the executive to ban political organizations.

The long and contentious trial drew wide public and media attention, with

145. Zorkin appears to have had a series of *ex parte* meetings with deputies in Rumyantsev's circle and clearly supported their pro-reform, anticommunist views.

146. It should be noted that the court's final opinion was based on two different versions of the constitution, as the 1978 constitution was heavily amended between Yeltsin's August and November decrees.

all eyes anxiously scrutinizing the work of the fledgling court on this hot issue. A prominent example of the media spectacle that the case became was former president Gorbachev's refusal to respond to a summons to appear as a witness, Yeltsin's resulting decision to deny him a visa to travel abroad, and Gorbachev's consequent self-anointment as the first post-Soviet "refusenik."[147] The case was also perceived, by many, as a determining factor in whether Russia would move forward or remain caught up in its past.

This charged political atmosphere made neutral, effective decision-making by the court a near impossibility.

> For the Constitutional Court, the CPSU case presented opportunities, but also posed dangers. The proceedings afforded the Court a highly visible occasion to establish itself among elite and public alike as the indispensable "third branch" of government in the emerging separation of powers doctrine in Russia. . . . At the same time . . . [it] represented a classic "political question" that the Court was supposed to avoid.[148]

To the surprise of all, the court announced its decision only weeks after it closed its six months of hearings. The Solomonic decision set out in its 30 November 1992 opinion was clearly designed to serve the need for political stability, more than the requirements of the law. Disappointing to both parties, it did not stand on particularly firm legal ground either.[149] The court upheld the constitutionality of Yeltsin's decrees, but only as against the Party's national bodies, which could be logically implicated in the coup and which had most visibly merged into the state. The Party's national institutions thus should be distinguished from its local and regional cells, which Yeltsin could not constitutionally ban. The court similarly limited the confiscation of property, authorizing local Party groups to bring petitions

147. Sharlet, "The Russian Constitutional Court," 28.

148. Sharlet, "The Russian Constitutional Court," 22–23.

149. Published in *Izvestiia*, 16 December 1992. See Sharlet, "The Russian Constitutional Court," 29–30: "What are the implications of the verdict for all involved? In brief, the decision could be classified as good politics (it averted defeat for Yeltsin at a critical moment), dubious law (political expediency was the driving force, though dressed in legal garb), and inconclusive history (the verdict on the CPSU's involvement in the coup would have to await the forthcoming coup trial)."

The coup trial (of the senior cabinet members who attempted to overthrow Gorbachev) also failed to provide much of a historical retrospective, however, with all the defendants amnestied in February 1994 and the one defendant who insisted on a trial summarily acquitted.

in the regular courts to regain their property. Meanwhile, the court declared the questions that had occupied most of its time—on the true character of the Party—to be moot, as the national Party had already collapsed by the time of the decision.

While the court should not alone be blamed for this dubious legal judgment, in light of the pressures it faced from all sides, its decision to hear the case in the first place was mistaken.[150] As the hearings progressed, it became impossible to distinguish the legal proceedings from the political games of its central players. In the public eye, the court seemed to be caught in a tug-of-war between Yeltsin and the Party, rather than to be neutrally mediating their differences. This perception was encouraged by the parties themselves, who "spared no effort to 'try' their cases in the press."[151] They cast the trial in a political light and accused the court of proceeding along political rather than legal lines. And while this accusation was untrue, it served to undermine the court's credibility at its very inception.

Despite the inevitable mistakes and misjudgments by the inexperienced first court, our overall assessment of its two-year tenure should not be entirely negative. In many respects, it handled itself with "thoroughness, profession-alism, and without political bias."[152] In its work, the public observed for the first time a relatively open legal process in which till-then inviolable state powers were forced to answer for their actions, under the terms of the law, to a superior body of review. The court demonstrated the law's ability to check the power of even the greatest political forces in the country. Generally favorable coverage in the mass media portrayed the court as a neutral and authoritative arbiter of Russian politics. At least at the outset, by "carrying itself well," the court effectively advanced the role of the law on the political landscape and acquired "great authority in the eyes of the people."[153]

In fulfilling this wider political function, however, the court "interpreted its role too broadly and altered its prescribed position in the constitutional system."[154] It went beyond mere judicial review to act as a latter-day

150. In keeping with the Law on the Constitutional Court, the court could have rejected the case under its "political questions" rule (article 1, section 3). *Zakon o Konstitutsionnom Sude RSFSR* (law in the RSFSR Constitutional Court), *Vedomosti RSFSR*, no. 30, item 1017 (1991).

151. Sharlet, "The Russian Constitutional Court," 21.

152. Belyaeva, "Russian Democracy," 15.

153. Ernst Ametistov, member, Russian Constitutional Court, 16 August 1993. Hereafter Ametistov, interview of 16 August 1993.

154. Nikonov, interview of 3 February 1994.

"council of elders" empowered to mediate the turbulent battles of modern Russian politics, focusing on the separation of powers, and not individual rights, as its raison d'être.[155] Thus did seven of the court's first nine decisions declare executive or legislative acts unconstitutional. This scope of activity can be contrasted with that of the United States Supreme Court, which generally eschewed such bold jurisprudence for its first hundred years. A similarly gradual expansion of the Russian court's purview would have better allowed it to secure each step and thereby ensure its long-term viability and influence.[156]

A more careful jurisprudence would also have avoided the many procedural errors with which the court's decisions were rife. The renowned decision of 14 January 1992 annulling Yeltsin's merger, thus, was not even within the court's jurisdiction. Justice Nikolas Vitrouk, the interim chairperson in 1994, acknowledges that the court's political involvement during its first two years "resulted in systematic violations of procedural norms sacrificed for the sake of hasty and selective response to specific legal acts or even to simple political actions."[157]

Had the court limited itself to neutrally (and at times, deferentially) adjudicating the constitutionality of newly emerging government practices, it would have fulfilled its judicial responsibilities without having to shirk a mildly political role in Russia's chaotic transformation. This approach would have helped fine-tune Russia's constitutional structures and invaluably strengthen the legal consciousness of the nation. By not joining in the political melee, the court's authority and influence would have been better maintained; thereby, it could have satisfied the people's "great hope that the court might be a force above the fight."[158] Had it thus become a rallying point of constitutionalism in the political order, it is no exaggeration to say that it might well have changed the course of Russian history.

The court ought to have laid the foundations of a new constitutional order

155. There were, of course, exceptional cases that did focus on civil rights and even several prominent rights cases, including the decision to overturn Yeltsin's ban on the National Salvation Front (an anti-reform political party) as a violation of the freedom of association. These, however, were the exception.

156. U.S. Supreme Court chief justice John Marshall's carefully crafted opinion in *Marbury v. Madison* (1803) evidences the need for careful judicial politics, even in a legally oriented culture such as that of the United States. It is also evidence that judicial development came no easier to the United States than to Russia.

157. Nikolas Vitrouk, comments at Mentor Group Conference on Russian Constitutional Affairs, 14–18 November 1994. Conference report, 44. Hereafter Vitrouk, comments.

158. Ametistov, interview of 4 February 1994.

by focusing on its most basic elements. It was at this level that a substantive difference could be made. While possibly adding to its fame and glory, the court's rulings on the "big questions"—such as Yeltsin's 19 December 1991 merger decree and Tatarstan's referendum on independence[159]—were probably far more fleeting in their impact[160] than would have been decisions in cases addressing the nuts-and-bolts underpinnings of constitutionalism. Dull as they may have seemed, such decisions on individual rights and on the due process requirements for the administrative bureaucracy were critically necessary. With such decisions, the legacy of the first Constitutional Court (1991–93) would have been the basic principles of Russia's constitutional order, rather than memories of its bias and gross interference in political affairs beyond its authority.

Significantly, every member of the court and its staff with whom I spoke (including the ambitious former chairman, Valery Zorkin) had come to recognize this mistake by the end of 1993. Each noted, without prompting, the huge number of letters the court used to receive daily from every corner of the country and described these as the greatest indication of the court's contribution.[161] These letters—from farmers, industrial laborers, and other common people—requested that the court help Ivan Sergeevich repossess his confiscated cow or Elena Mikhailovna sell her plot of land. Such letters, though often of little legal merit, represented an emerging public sense of judicial rights and their potential defense in the courts. Early on, the public came to see the Constitutional Court as a forum where their rights might be defended. Ironically, then, the high profile afforded the court may not have been as significant for the cases it did decide as for those it did not.

The Constitutional Court thus played a constructive role in raising the legal consciousness of the Russian masses. Throughout Russian history the people, consequent to the character of the political regime, had had little comprehension of their rights as subjects of the law. The law's protection of them from their neighbor, let alone from the government, was seldom felt and consequently not much considered. For the first time, the court had

159. Decided on 13 March 1992.

160. Their decision ruling the Tatarstan referendum unconstitutional was, in fact, entirely ignored, with the only effort at enforcement consisting of an abortive attempt to cut off federal funds to the republic. Sharlet, "The Russian Constitutional Court," 7 n. 25.

161. This can be favorably compared with public attitudes toward Gorbachev's Committee for Constitutional Supervision, "whose advice was seldom sought. Eighteen of its twenty-three decisions arose on the [committee's] own initiative." Sharlet, "The Russian Constitutional Court," 8 n. 29.

begun to instill this sense of legal security and judicial remedy. Though not dissimilar from traditional Russian conceptions of a paternalistic government protector, that a court should assume this role and not the Father Tsar or a benevolent Party boss was quite significant. While the latter two might show mercy, the courts dispensed justice.

Yet the court did not capitalize on this unique opportunity. Looking to the top and not the grass roots, it focused on meta-institutional relations and ignored the development of constitutionalism at the bottom. It failed to follow through on its potential impact in this arena, leaving a need that still remains to be filled. Instead, the court "entered into the political game, and [its] role came to be discredited."[162]

In selecting its cases, the court concentrated on constraining the executive and legislative branches and mediating between them. In this ambitious task "the court inevitably compromised itself. . . . This was not what we knew," observes Justice Ametistov. "We knew law, not politics."[163] This approach reached its acme in December 1992 at the Seventh Congress of People's Deputies, when Zorkin intervened to negotiate a compromise between Yeltsin and Khasbulatov, who appeared to be on the verge of a catastrophic break. The compromise, "On the Stabilization of the Constitutional Order of the Russian Federation," was signed on 14 December 1992 and attempted to clearly delineate the respective authority of the executive and legislative branches over the government's composition and direction, the major point of contention.[164] Arguably, the court thus played a "critical role at the point of highest conflict between the Congress and President," one by which "the authority and stature of the Constitutional Court was raised even higher."[165]

Yet this role was far beyond the scope of the duties of the chairman or his court, even were one to interpret their authority quite broadly. Zorkin argues that given the perilous situation in the country and the threat of a permanent rift between the branches of government, this extra-legal intervention was necessary and actually helped strengthen the legal consciousness of the public. It showed that the "law" (apparently, as personified by

162. Lukasheva, interview of 11 August 1993.
163. Ametistov, interview of 4 February 1994.
164. Notably, a decision to leave the court's two remaining vacancies unfilled was also included in the compromise agreement, presumably at the request of a court fearful of further division in its own ranks. Sharlet, "The Russian Constitutional Court," 11 n. 34.
165. Belyaeva, "Russian Democracy," 15–16.

Zorkin) could be a successful mediator of power and that the rule of law meant order and stability.[166] Unfortunately, this logic runs dry.

Even if Zorkin's involvement, in the words of his former Moscow State University colleague Mikhail Marchenko, did "save the country" at a moment when "all were afraid of civil war,"[167] its negative consequences would arise later, when the well-intentioned compromise fell apart. By stepping in, the court made itself a player in a game from which it could not easily withdraw. Zorkin soon appeared alongside Vice President Aleksandr Rutskoi and parliamentary Speaker Ruslan Khasbulatov in the magazine *Stolitsa*'s portrayal of Russia's "three dark horsemen." The court sacrificed its primary duty to act within the law for a secondary interest in ensuring political stability. And having compromised itself once, it found itself unable to return from whence it came. Furthermore, political engagement divided the court itself. In contrast to its nine unanimous decisions in 1992, those of 1993 regularly included sharp and vigorous dissents.

On 20 March 1993, Yeltsin went on national television and dispensed with Zorkin's December compromise,[168] announcing a decree granting himself emergency powers, a decision that was prima facie unconstitutional. However, the court's 23 March 1993 opinion on the matter, though correct in principle, was quickly branded as illegitimately biased toward the parliament. The line between truth and opinion in the court's judgments was no longer clear to the public. It was now marked as a political partisan. Not surprisingly, its opinion was also procedurally flawed.

In its desire to quickly speak out, the court released its decision with inadequate consideration of the issues at hand, violating explicit constraints on the time required to reach a decision. Even before this, however, Zorkin had made premature public statements on the matter, appearing on television to denounce Yeltsin's decree as a coup d'état. Such public pronouncements were clearly impermissible under the court's charter and obligated Zorkin to recuse himself from the court's subsequent consideration of the case.[169] Furthermore, there was nothing for the court to even consider other

166. Zorkin. For other defenses of Zorkin's extrajudicial activities, see Sharlet, "The Russian Constitutional Court," 31 n. 85.

167. Marchenko, interview of 31 January 1994.

168. At the provocation, he claimed, of the parliament.

169. From the start of his term, Zorkin manifested little hesitancy about extrajudicially declaring his views, often in the most strident of terms. An example was his strongly worded response to Tatarstan's independence drive, including his suggestion that it would lead to "a situation a hundred times worse than Yugoslavia" (Sharlet, "The Russian Constitutional Court," 16). This is not entirely surprising, in light of the similar conduct of Sergei Alekseev,

than Yeltsin's televised comments. Yeltsin never produced the decree he announced and later backed away from several points made in his television address. Zorkin argues that this proves the value of the court's rapid response, suggesting it tempered the president's actions.[170] Yet such speculation cannot justify the kind of haphazard decision making the court should have avoided. Zorkin's public comments denouncing Yeltsin's television address and the court's hasty announcement of an unfounded technical ruling were far from standard procedure and provoked easy accusations of bias. Thus the court discarded any position on the legal high ground it still retained.[171]

In the course of his tenure, Zorkin ought to have made far better use of his eloquence and breadth of knowledge to convey the principles of constitutionalism to the general public. His articulate comments on constitutionalism and the rule of law in the early months of his tenure, scattered through the western press, had made him the hope of many observers of Russian law, including myself. Here was a man who might finally inspire the Russian people with faith in the law. Yet choosing to play high-stakes politics over low, he ignored Russian legal consciousness and became, according to Sharlet, the court's "most serious problem."[172]

This was likely the result of hubris, both personal and institutional. Zorkin wanted to make the institution he headed, the weakest arm in the constitutional order of Russia, a viable body that could check and balance the others. But he chose to approach this noble goal in an entirely wrongheaded manner. "While Zorkin's intentions were constructive, his self-image as champion of civil peace and savior of the Constitution involved him in the role of public mediator between the power branches, a role for which he had little political experience and only modest aptitude."[173]

Hoping to make changes overnight, Zorkin played a political game instead of the legal one he was better trained for.[174] He tried to finagle his

---

chairman of the Committee for Constitutional Supervision. Zorkin, however, took such conduct to new heights. See Sharlet, "The Russian Constitutional Court," 13–14.

170. Zorkin, interview of 2 February 1994.

171. Of 1,228 individuals polled on 27 March 1993 with reference to the court's decision, 43 percent considered the decision to have been incorrect, while 24 percent judged it correct and 33 percent were undecided. (Survey by the Public Opinion Foundation, published in its journal, *Within Sight*, April 1993.)

172. Sharlet, "Russian Constitutional Crisis," 323.

173. Sharlet, "Russian Constitutional Crisis," 324.

174. Notably, as an adviser to Rumyantsev's Constitutional Commission, he advocated establishment of a presidential republic, a surprising view in light of his later rhetoric.

way into a position of power and influence, rather than working for change by the more gradual means of public education and experience, his most effective tools. He wanted progress immediately and thus sacrificed it altogether. Justice Vitrouk, looking back on Zorkin's tenure as chairman, correctly observes: "I believe that the principal shortcoming in the Court's work during this period was its gradual transformation from a temple of justice into an instrument of political struggle as it drifted away from law and into the political fray."[175]

By the time of Yeltsin's September and October decrees dissolving the parliament and suspending the court, the public saw the court as simply the legal arm of the conservative parliament. The court's abortive attempts to annul the decree and impeach the president were ignored,[176] and shortly thereafter Zorkin was removed as chairman. Not until early 1995 would the court return to life, in a new form we will turn to in Chapter 4.[177] It is testimony, however, to the court's resilience and influence that it has been revived, with even Zorkin still a member.

Visiting Justice Zorkin at the offices of the court in February 1994, I was struck by the peculiar manner in which my arrival was registered. Rather than listing me in the general entrance logbook, as is common in all official buildings in Moscow, my name was placed on a separate sheet as a visitor to Zorkin. The supervisor at the door forcefully told his subordinate to make quite clear who I represented and where I came from. Just "university" would not do. It was necessary to note "Princeton."

I watched the same exceptional procedure take place with several other visitors arriving to see Zorkin as I departed from his office, clearly struck by the still-outspoken, but more subdued man with whom I had spoken.[178] "Constitutionalism does have a future in Russia," he told me. "I may not live to see it, but you surely will."[179] Later that night I was surprised to watch news coverage of a court press conference with all standing members in

175. Vitrouk, comments, 44.

176. Zorkin's efforts were not only legal, but political as well. He thus attempted to broker a settlement in late September by inviting regional leaders to Moscow to meet at the offices of the Constitutional Court and pressure Yeltsin to accept Zorkin's plan for joint elections.

177. On 13 February 1995 a full complement of nineteen justices elected Justice Vladimir Tumanov as their new chairman, and the court began its operations once more, almost a year and a half after its suspension in September 1993.

178. In fact, Zorkin later showed his cards, helping found an opposition political party—a clearly impermissible act for a Constitutional Court justice.

179. Zorkin, interview of 2 February 1994.

attendance, except one. Zorkin, who had been discussing the rule of law with me at three o'clock, as the court met the press, had not been invited. Justice Vitrouk, the interim chairperson, castigated the formerly political character of the court and announced its future intention to avoid interference in political questions. Yet with such politics in its own chambers, the future of the court itself remained an open question.

Thus do we find a mixed record of efforts during the last ten years to create a Russian constitutional order at once effective and legitimate. Having observed repeated stumbles in the attempt to create constitutional structures and an enlightened legal consciousness in the Soviet Union and the First Russian Republic, we may now turn to the new patterns of behavior and thinking whose introduction is critical to the success of this endeavor in the second incarnation of independent Russia. It may be true, as Oleg Rumyantsev suggests, having been beaten up and hospitalized on 4 October 1993,[180] that everything has been lost and Russia must start again from the beginning.[181] It is all the more important, then, that developments in the new Russia be deeply considered.

---

180. As well as almost evicted from his Moscow apartment, a fate avoided by his being elected to the Duma. Such are the incentives of political office in modern Russia.
181. Related by Lafitski, interview of 31 January 1994.

PART II

AN EMERGING PARADIGM

With time and serious effort, Russia will finally rise to its place among the community of nations and live up to the universal human standards it now can only aspire to.

—Aleksandr M. Yakovlev,
Adviser to the president of Russia,
interview of 5 February 1994

Having outlined the successes and failures of Russia's attempts at constitutionalism up to the adoption of the new constitution and the election of its new institutions in 1993, we now have a landscape on which we may elaborate a more adequate approach to the emergence of constitutionalism in the Second Russian Republic. I will consider the history of the constitution's transitional period (1994–95) as well as the prospects for Russian constitutionalism following the first parliamentary elections (December 1995) and presidential elections (June 1996) to be carried out under the new constitutional order. As this constitutional order, born in December 1993, establishes and secures itself during these early years, systematic and thoughtful action is more critical than ever. "Disintegrating authoritarian or totalitarian regimes are not necessarily emerging democracies, and disintegrating centrally planned economies are not necessarily emerging markets."[1]

Continued progress toward constitutionalism will consequently require carefully considered decisions and a conscious effort to ensure that the missteps of recent years are avoided. This necessitates, in the first order, the specification of a new set of principles to guide the development process. On these foundational principles, outlined in Chapter 3, I will then attempt to detail the particular practices and policies needed to ensure the successful emergence of constitutionalism in Russia, considering both the existence or absence of these policies during the first two years of the new Russia and their prospective adoption during the years ahead. It is in this task of application, considered in Chapter 4, that the battle for constitutionalism will be won or lost.

At the primary level of principle, there are two broad areas of necessary adjustment in Russia's approach to the creation of constitutionalism. To begin with, the strengthening of legal consciousness must take priority over the perfecting of constitutional structures. With the gradual stabilization and

---

1. Hoffmann, 26.

legitimization of the December 1993 constitution, a concentration on legal consciousness has become a practical possibility. Equally important is a shift away from Russia's revolutionary consciousness, premised on overnight change promulgated from the top. This approach has long characterized development in Russia and is the source of much of the chaos and instability that exists today. It must be adjusted if a stable constitutional order is to emerge and maintain itself.

Writing of the stubborn persistence of elements of Soviet political culture in the USSR in 1991, Robert Sharlet decried the ill effects of "such political traditions as the concentration of power at the top, rule from above, heavy reliance on police power, manifestations of elite legal nihilism (or circumvention of the law by officials), and . . . still largely unaccountable bureaucratic control over public life."[2] Sadly, Sharlet could also have been describing present-day Russia, in which each of these "traditions" still survives. The legal and political culture of Russia has thus remained stagnant, though its structures have been made anew. It is to this deeper level, then, that an organic *perestroika* must now extend.

2. Sharlet, *Soviet Constitutional Crisis*, 98.

CHAPTER THREE

PRINCIPLES

SOZNANIYE (CONSCIOUSNESS) VERSUS STRUCTURE

> For reasons entirely organic
> We have not been endowed at all
> With that quality wholly satanic—
> Common-sense in matters of law.
>
> Russian natures broad and wide
> Seeking truths eternal,
> Cannot be constrained inside
> Lawyers' rules infernal.
> —B. N. Almazov[1]

The weakness of legal consciousness in Russia and, as a Russian would describe it, its "narrow legal culture" remain the greatest obstacles to the emergence of constitutionalism and the stabilization of the political order. With a decade of constitutional reform having laid out a basic constitutional framework, this issue must finally take center stage. The effort to create a legal culture in a society largely without one is sure to be taxing, but as Aleksandr Yakovlev exclaims: "I don't believe we're so damn stupid that we can't learn!"[2]

An awareness of the need for the further development of legal consciousness has not been lacking. Vladimir Kudriavtsev and Elena Lukasheva, in what was a historic article for the Party journal *Kommunist*, argued in 1988

---

1. These satirical verses were directed at Konstantin Aksakov, a nineteenth-century Slavophile (a tradition of anti-western Russian patriotism). Nicolai Petro, "Informal Politics and the Rule of Law," in Barry, *Toward the "Rule of Law" in Russia?* 227–28.

2. Yakovlev, interview of 5 February 1994.

for the subordination of the state to society, invoking natural law principles they traced back to Plato, Aristotle, Cicero, Montesquieu, Locke, and Kant. They also expounded upon the interdependence of Soviet legal institutions and the legal consciousness of the people.[3]

In 1993 Viktor Sergeyev and Nikolai Biryukov brought legal consciousness to the forefront of scholarly debate with their wide-ranging and lengthy consideration of Russian political and legal culture, *Russia's Road to Democracy: Parliament, Communism and Traditional Culture.* The authors compellingly argued that the reform of Russian political culture was essential to the success of democratic reforms. *Perestroika,* they suggested, "managed to destroy the cohesion between the blocks of the [political] structure, turning it into a pile of broken brick but leaving the properties of the material untouched."[4]

Yet serious concern with legal consciousness, notwithstanding such eloquent presentation, has remained largely in the province of scholarship and academic theory. Among those we might describe, for lack of a better term, as the power elites,[5] the development of legal consciousness has been commonly ignored. Few in the leadership appreciated that an effective constitutional order must rest upon societal ideals and values that support it. Consequently they neglected social and political values in their implacable drive to create new constitutional structures, simply breaking Soviet structures into bricks rather than undertaking a deeper but more difficult "polymerization" of Russian political and legal culture.[6]

Russia's narrow legal culture might be less relevant if Russian social consciousness were undergirded by some other ordering principle, such as religion. Yet Bolshevik rule undermined the values of the Russian people. The resulting frailty of Russia's legal, political, and social consciousness generally was demonstrated by a Russian law professor's attempt to compile a list of his culture's values and ideals. Presenting this question to a group of fellow academics at the prestigious Institute of U.S. and Canadian Studies, he managed to glean only two—a concept of the Greatness of Mother Russia and some sense of an ability to withstand suffering.[7]

Russians' weak legal consciousness has long roots in their history, as law has never been admired in Russia, its role in society considered negligible, if

3. Berman, "The Rule of Law and the Law-Based State," 48.
4. Sergeyev and Biryukov, *Russia's Road to Democracy,* 14.
5. The Russian analogy to FOBs, or Friends of Bill, in the United States.
6. Sergeyev and Biryukov, *Russia's Road to Democracy,* 14.
7. Vlasihin, interview of 10 August 1993.

not detrimental. Leo Tolstoy, among the law's more expressive and eloquent detractors, regularly spoke of his hatred for jury trials as well as for legal title to property, which he believed belonged only to God. His preferred literary villains, of course, were lawyers and judges.[8] With Tsar Aleksandr II's judicial reforms in 1864, however, the law began to develop a life of its own, establishing roots among the urban elites, if not yet among the masses. This law commonly involved *zakon* (*lex*, laws) and not *pravo* (*jus*, law), but even this represented significant progress. Many have thus pointed to the final decades of Imperial Russia as a viable foundation for a renewed legal consciousness.

For with the 1917 Bolshevik Revolution, there emerged, in the words of Aleksandr Solzhenitsyn, "an entirely different world, a new planet."[9] Though prone to hyperbole, Solzhenitsyn's words do capture the changes in the legal order, as the revolution destroyed much of the progress made under the last three tsars.[10] The early years after the revolution witnessed the preeminence of legal nihilism, an eliminative approach that, in agreement with Marxist theory, aspired to the "withering away" of the law and defined the rule of law as the "rule of the ruling class." But by the 1930s this perspective had given way to "a new legal order in which politics was in command."[11]

8. It may say something for Tolstoy's view of law and property that a vicious legal battle is now raging over the rightful heirs to his home and property at *Yasnaya Polnya*.

9. Aleksandr Solzhenitsyn, quoted in David Remnick, "The Exile Returns," *New Yorker*, 14 February 1994, 81.

10. In reality, the Bolshevik legal culture that emerged was a product of both continuity and change. Even the revolution's most radical moves thus had antecedents both in Russian history and in mass psychology. As Roy Medvedev suggests,

> I am convinced the truth lies between these extremes. History cannot be interrupted even by a most radical revolution and, although by nature a social revolution signifies a decisive rupture from the former structures and the order of the old society, the character of the revolution and its consequences are related to the character and features of that old society. In revolution there is negation of the past, but there is also continuity, which is why it would be erroneous to take into consideration only one side of this interrelation of the past and the present and ignore the other.

Roy Medvedev, "On Stalin and Stalinism: Historical Essays," *Znamya* 4 (1989): 20. Similarly, Sergeyev and Biryukov posit that "the revolution of 1917 brought about a thorough transformation of the Russian political culture, but what emerged as the result of that transformation was linked by numerous bonds to what had existed before the revolution." Sergeyev and Biryukov, *Russia's Road to Democracy*, 51.

11. Eugene Huskey, "The Administration of Justice: Courts, Procuracy, and Ministry of Justice," in Eugene Huskey, ed., *Executive Power and Soviet Politics: The Rise and Decline of the Soviet State* (Armonk, N.Y.: M. E. Sharpe, 1992), 222. Hereafter Huskey, "The Administration of Justice."

Hereafter, the law would be constructively used by the Communist leadership, rather than ignored. Even more so than its monarchist precursor, this era "was the antithesis of the rule of law and a period that established a strong and unfortunate legacy for the contemporary period."[12] This instrumentalist view of the law, which survived into Gorbachev's tenure as general secretary, thus did more damage to Russian legal consciousness than did legal nihilism, by undermining respect for the law rather than simply brushing it aside.

Law became power. It lost its implications of justice, taking on a "special totalitarian form" that did not indicate right and wrong, but simply *mozhna* and *nyelza*—what was allowed and what was forbidden.[13] The law was not absent from society; it was more omnipresent than ever. But in form and not in substance. The law became simply "an obstacle to be outmaneuvered for survival's sake."[14] Gradually, however, in areas outside the state's political interest, including family law and certain areas of criminal law, the law began to acquire substantive meaning. These categories expanded and multiplied with Khrushchev's de-Stalinization and with the political stabilization and "codification" of the legal order[15] that followed his ouster in 1964. In 1977 this process of legalization culminated in the adoption of the highly legalistic Brezhnev constitution. Thus had the law come into its own by the 1980s.

When he came to power in 1985, Gorbachev inherited this mixed legacy. Yet, for the most part, he ignored the critical issue of legal consciousness. Strengthening the latter was not among the primary concerns of his reforms. His later violations of human rights, and legal norms he himself had established, suggest this disinterest extended to his own legal consciousness as well. Radical changes in attitudes toward the law were simply not a priority. "As in his initial efforts to reform the economy and political institutions, Gorbachev sought to achieve legal reform within the context of the existing structure of Soviet society. He sought not to dismantle, but merely to improve, the socialist system."[16] Gorbachev's legal reforms consisted of structural changes he hoped would encourage his economic reforms, not social and psychological ones that would transform Soviet society.

Consequently, he began with simple rhetoric, emphasizing not *pravovoe*

12. Shelley, "Legal Consciousness and the *Pravovoe Gosudarstvo*," 66.
13. Piskotin, interview of 6 August 1993.
14. Sajo and Losonci, "Rule by Law," 326.
15. Robert Sharlet's descriptor for Brezhnev's legalism.
16. Shelley, "Legal Consciousness," 68.

soznaniye (legal consciousness) or *gospodstvo prava* (the supremacy of law) but *pravovoe gosudarstvo* (the law-based state) and *gospodstvo zakonov* (the supremacy of laws). Soon finding such rhetoric inadequate to his goals, Gorbachev began a reform of Soviet constitutional structures; "constitution" became a "codeword of Soviet politics."[17] Reform, however, focused on the separation of powers and other structural principles of the legal state, not on its cultural underpinnings. Both Gorbachev and Yeltsin after him seemed to hope that constitutionalism could be built at the institutional rather than the individual level. They expected newly created institutions to become the focus of the people's "faith," until then directed largely at Communist ideology and the state that stood on its shaky foundations.[18] These institutions would serve as a lodestone for new political forces and lay the groundwork for further change. A strengthened legal consciousness might be a collateral effect of these reforms, but it was not their primary focus.

Given the dearth of existing institutions that might embody the higher principles of constitutionalism, this structuralist orientation was appropriate in many respects. A cursory assessment might also suggest that it was the easiest approach since "it did not involve abstract engagements with the Russian psyche."[19] Finally, it was rooted in Gorbachev's, Yeltsin's, and their advisers' assessment of western constitutionalism. Russian reformers correctly saw structural issues such as the separation of powers as the critical elements of constitutionalism in the West today.

Yet they did not recognize these as necessary but insufficient ingredients in their circumstance: while institutions alone may be adequate to the maintenance of constitutionalism, they will not suffice for its creation. The constraints of limited government cannot simply be imposed by law; they must run deeper. Great Britain, with its complete parliamentary sovereignty, is the extreme case, in which institutional limitations are nonexistent and legal consciousness alone constrains parliamentary action. The reverse scenario, however, is untenable. Structural innovations cannot serve as a proxy for legal culture in limiting government. Without the psychological foundations of limited government, Russia gained nothing by the artificial implantation of its institutions.[20] Lacking the former, Russia has been little served by the latter.

17. Sharlet, *Soviet Constitutional Crisis*, 105.
18. Belyaeva, "Russian Democracy," 6.
19. Baturin, interview of 11 August 1993.
20. Rakitov, interview of 3 August 1993.

This dilemma was heightened by circumstances in Russia during the last decade. While new institutions might influence legal culture in a climate of stability, "in conflict situations, underlying values prevail." Faced with a crisis, the Russian *mudzhik* was bound to show his colors, dispensing with unfamiliar arrangements and instinctively rejecting the law as he always had.[21] Cosmetic changes could not survive the increasing chaos of recent years. Structural reform thus proved to be dependent on the more challenging task of transformation at the psychological level, where the Russian public "still do not know what the law is and why they need it."[22]

Neither Vladimir Kudriavtsev nor Aleksandr Yakovlev, respectively advisers to Presidents Gorbachev and Yeltsin, was ignorant of legal culture or considered it irrelevant to Russia's development. They simply imagined that an institutionalized constitutionalism might give birth to an individualized constitutionalism. They hoped, apparently in vain, that they could avoid the more abstract question of legal consciousness at this early stage in the transition to democratic republicanism. Powerful and effective institutions would hopefully act as tutors in the principles of law and drag Russian elites to constitutionalism, with the public on their coattails. As David Lempert analogously explains, however, "while the one-party system and the lack of private property were one cause of political inequality, changing only these two features of the system does very little to change the deep structure of political power."[23] Russian reformers imagined that structural reforms would give rise to a new legal culture, not appreciating the extent of the damage wrought by Soviet rule on the already tenuous relationship of the Russian people with the law. At the end of seventy years of Communism, little fertile ground remained in Russian legal culture for the rooting of new constitutional institutions. The soil itself had to be retilled. Thus did the Bolsheviks face a less daunting task of transformation in 1917 than did the constitutionalists in 1987. Destruction came much easier than would construction.

The reformers' structuralist vision also failed to predict the complexity of maintaining new institutions and the extent to which their effectiveness would depend upon a supportive legal culture. Yet it is testimony to the attraction of this hopeful view of institutions' beneficial effects that there was little explicit disagreement with it during this period, even among

21. Biryukov, interview of 18 November 1993.

22. Schmemann, interview of 17 July 1993.

23. David Lempert, "The Proposed Constitution of Ukraine: Continuity Under the Banner of Change," *Demokratizatsiya* 2 (Spring 1994): 280.

analysts in the West. Full endorsement was not given to every element of this approach, but its underlying premise was never directly challenged.

The tendency to ignore the development of legal consciousness during the Gorbachev period took on a more virulent form under Yeltsin. Now the drive for structural change was so consuming as to foster complete disinterest in any negative impact it might have on legal consciousness. In his effort to reform the economy overnight and to quickly implant new institutions and a new constitution, Yeltsin proved willing to trample legality underfoot. Wishing to dispense with the Soviet Union and later the Russian Supreme Soviet—obstacles, in his mind, to constructive reforms and progress— Yeltsin ignored his constitutional constraints. Respect for law, rather than serving to reduce chaos, was seen by Yeltsin as a constraint on his efforts. Furthermore, Yeltsin's efforts centered nearly entirely on the necessary, but far from sufficient, goal of economic restructuring. Economic progress, he imagined, would legitimate his authority better than a "procedural" concern with constitutional niceties and the due process of law. With the best of intentions, Yeltsin determined that the adoption of his constitution took precedence over the expired legality that stood in its way and acted on this belief. Yet in doing so, he shattered the very legitimacy on which the success of his draft most depended. Such disregard for the law, sadly, characterized much of the Yeltsin presidency.

Legal consciousness, notwithstanding its benign, and even callous, neglect during the last decade, has begun to emerge. Though appearing only in fits and starts, it was manifest when striking Soviet miners demanded, in addition to higher wages, an independent judiciary, and when May Day protestors boldly ignored Gorbachev's ban on public gatherings in 1990, demonstrating that "millions of Soviet citizens [had] unlearned fear and experienced a sense of numbers and empowerment."[24]

These advances in legal consciousness must be built upon. Central to this effort is the constitution itself. As its institutions persist and continue to develop, and thereby extend their legitimacy, their potential impact on public consciousness will grow. Both the procedure and substance of their work must center on the stabilization of the law and the enhancement of its role in society. Effectiveness must finally go hand in hand with legitimacy— reforms must move forward and progress become apparent to even the most

24. Juviler, "Human Rights After Perestroika," 7.

cynical of observers. This will lend the constitution substantive value in the public eye. "Underlying psychology has remained quite negligent to the constitution," because it has had little opportunity to reflect itself in people's daily lives.[25] If it is ever to be respected or even read, it must come to do so. Yet as an elderly man driving me across Moscow in February 1994 wondered, "How can I possibly take time to read the constitution when I have to work day and night just to get by?"

A heightened legal consciousness thus also depends on social stability, which begins with economic stability. The economy's collapse has produced an environment of criminality and chaos that degrades both public behavior and underlying moral inhibitions. Once provided by religious culture and later maintained by ideology and fear, such personal limitations lack motivating force absent Orthodoxy and Communism. As constraints in the world around them collapse, individuals feel increasingly fewer limits on their personal conduct.[26] Such a climate of licentiousness is anathema to the development of legal consciousness and must be adjusted. This will likely require that aspects of a negative legal consciousness be reinstated to moderate certain conduct through fear rather than respect. With fewer internalized inhibitions, more extensive external ones may be temporarily necessary.

Political stability is also critical to the strengthening of legal consciousness. Only if a stable political order persists for a substantial period of time will the thinking of those within it begin to shift. Essential to such stability is a move toward cooperation and coexistence and away from "hierarchy, domination, and subordination," long the norms of political relations in Russia.[27] This is critical to the sustainability and effectiveness of any constitutional order. The elites must begin to think in the long and not the short term. Short-sighted thinking, analogous to that of flies living only for a day,[28] makes compromise and respect for the principles of order and gradualism difficult to maintain.[29] Only when Russia's leaders abandon their tunnel vision for a broader view will legal legitimacy take precedence over blunt force and compromise replace confrontation.

Most important, the Russian people still "do not see themselves as

25. Nikonov, interview of 3 February 1994.
26. Olshanski, interview of 7 August 1993.
27. Migranyan, interview of 4 February 1994.
28. An old Russian saying.
29. Lafitski, interview of 31 January 1994.

subjects of the law."[30] This will result from practical experience with the law, which alone can "make constitutionalism an underlying value."[31] Legal consciousness will emerge with the widespread introduction of baseline institutional structures that are both close to and intimately connected with the people. These institutions, including courts of the first instance, elected local representatives, and even the municipal police, can "provide a real understanding of and training in a new way of life,"[32] by gradually drawing the public into their operations at the most basic level of government. It is here that legal consciousness will first appear.

It is true that "legal culture changes slowest of all" and that it may require substantial time and patience for this process to run its course.[33] Yet the transformation of legal culture is no less critical for its difficulty. Only when people feel the law's impact and have intimate contact with it will they take their most important steps on the path toward a constitutional order at once effective and lasting.

EVOLUTION FROM BELOW

The recent history of constitutionalism in Russia has been consistent with long-standing Russian traditions of revolution from above. With few exceptions, the constitutional developments of the last decade have been promulgated and advanced from the top, with little engagement of or contribution from the public at large. Constitutional reform has also been characterized by a frenetic pace that has often done more harm than good.

Russians commonly see the world in black and white, with little gray in between.[34] They ascribe, in varying degrees, to a "cosmic dualism, a doctrine which holds that whatever happens in the universe is an episode in and a result of the unceasing struggle between two opposing principles, Good and Evil."[35] Culturally, this has been manifest in an extremism premised on a sense of unending struggle. In 1985 this impulse provoked a battle with the entrenched bureaucracy, succeeded by one with the Soviet

---

30. Klamkin, interview of 4 February 1994.
31. Biryukov, interview of 18 November 1993.
32. Biryukov, interview of 18 November 1993.
33. Satarov, interview of 4 February 1994.
34. Burlatski, interview of 1 February 1994.
35. Sergeyev and Biryukov, *Russia's Road to Democracy,* 10.

government, and finally with Communist ideology itself. Yet having slain these dragons, the struggle rages on against anything and everything.[36] "The political culture that has formed in the Soviet Union is prone to this type of dualism: the world was once seen as a battlefield of Socialism and Imperialism; it came to be viewed as an arena of struggle between Democracy and 'Partocracy,' the State and the Mafia, and so on."[37]

Russia has thus ignored Oleg Rumyantsev's concern that "reformation needs continuity during transition, and it needs a shift from revolution to evolution of Russian constitutionalism to foster a true and intelligible constitutional order."[38] During this critical juncture in Russian history, when careful thought is most necessary, this destructive force in the Russian psyche has inclined the nation toward fighting instead of thinking.[39] Consequently, rather than reforming Russia's sociopolitical order, recent developments have simply shifted power amongst the elites, and "the public still remains at the bottom."[40]

Instead of all the changes in the names of Moscow's streets and metro stations after the Soviet Union's collapse, muses Aleksei Simonov, a film producer and participant in Yeltsin's Constitutional Conference, it would have been better to have changed the one metro station name that remained the same—*Revolution* Square—and, having purged the country of this alone, gone on to gradually change all the others and the country as well.[41] To the contrary, recent years have been characterized by an anxious hurry to move forward. And, in fact, things have moved forward. Recall how few years have passed since Russia's constitutional transformation began with the Russian Republic's Declaration of Sovereignty in 1990. Compared with parallel developments in the United States' and Great Britain's history, this pace of change has been breathtaking. Yet speed, on occasion, may leave much to be desired.

This revolutionary psychology, and the anxious hurry it provokes, are incompatible with both the ordered evolution and careful line drawing implicit in the law and the type of constitutionalist thinking necessary for democratic development. Its "lively spirit," suggests Nikolai Berdyaev, has

36. Mishin, interview of 14 August 1993.
37. Sergeyev and Biryukov, *Russia's Road to Democracy*, 10.
38. Oleg Rumyantsev, comments at Mentor Group Conference on Russian Constitutional Affairs, 14–18 November 1994. Conference report, 13. Hereafter Rumyantsev, comments.
39. Lafitski, interview of 31 January 1994.
40. Lempert, "The Proposed Constitution of Ukraine," 279.
41. Simonov, interview of 30 July 1993.

thus kept Russia from its rightful place among the great nations of the world.[42] The problem is not revolution per se, for as American history demonstrates, revolution may even encourage constitutionalism. Rather, it is the lack of a defining and limiting focus for Russia's revolutionary consciousness, which allows it to extend indefinitely and expand endlessly, that is the problem. Russia is an undying revolution.

It is essential that Russia forgo this path of revolution and give up the "habit of abandoning existing institutions and norms in times of decisive social transformation," citing "revolutionary necessity."[43] The long precedents for this tendency, under the threat of Lenin's "enemies of the Revolution," Stalin's "people's enemies," Gorbachev's "enemies of *perestroika*," and Yeltsin's "dark forces of the past," make this shift toward conservation particularly challenging, but especially necessary as well. No longer can a congenital stance of confrontation serve Russia's interests.

A penchant for reform from above follows from this revolutionary way of thinking. Whether under tsarist, Bolshevik, or democratic rule, the Russian paradigm has consistently been one of radical change initiated and directed from the top. At the pinnacle stood a Peter the Great, a Stalin, or a Gorbachev—the paternalistic leader who knows best and boldly promulgates innovations of his own determination and design, often with little or no foundation in society at large. So prevalent is this practice that it is difficult to point to even one critical development or event in Russian history with deep social roots or impetus. As Nadezhda Mandelstam put it in her famous epigram: "In Russia everything always happens at the top."

Given the illiterate peasant mass that was long the heart of Russia, an inclination toward a powerful authority charged with directing change is not surprising. Such an approach was probably the most effective route of development. Yet it came with excesses for which the masses paid the toll, most obviously under Peter the Great and Stalin. Stalin's "reforms" thus returned public mentality to a state of passive serfdom from which it is still struggling to break free.[44] Because of this legacy, the masses remain disengaged from a reform process that is not theirs but their leaders'. American

42. Nikolai Berdyaev, *The Fate of Russia* (Moscow: Soviet Writers Publishing House, 1990), 90.

43. Belyaeva, "Russian Democracy," 7.

44. Peter Juviler, "Russia Turned Upside Down," in Peter Juviler, Bertram Gross, Vladimir Kartashkin, and Elena Lukasheva, eds., *Human Rights for the 21st Century: Foundations for Responsible Hope* (Armonk, N.Y.: M. E. Sharpe, 1993), 35.

anthropologist David Lempert, visiting a prestigious St. Petersburg law school, thus found students opposed to the introduction of participatory seminars and unwilling to involve themselves in efforts to improve the curriculum.[45] Such democratic impulses were foreign to them.

Lempert analogizes Russian passivity to that of Pacific islanders during World War II, who anxiously awaited the arrival of their "birds" from the sky—American cargo planes that would bring them food and other goods. "Rather than look to themselves and to create reform from bottom up, Russians [continue] to use the approach of looking up, not just for billions of dollars of Western aid and business investment, but to someone 'above' to save them."[46] This tendency, a product of Russia's long history of development from the top, stands in direct opposition to the needs of constitutionalism. True constitutionalism, founded as it is on a grass-roots legal consciousness, must have powerful roots at the bottom. Without public engagement in the legal and political process, it will never come about. Thankfully, however, Lempert's analogy is limited. Unlike their aboriginal counterparts, Russians remain a highly educated population, warranting higher expectations of their ability to adapt to alternative cultural, social, and political norms.

The constitutional reforms of recent years have been well in keeping with "the time-honored tradition of reform from the throne."[47] This trickle-down approach, it was hoped, would allow the rapid introduction of systemic changes to which the masses would be forced to assimilate their attitudes, psychology, and behavior. The general efficacy of this practice remains unclear. Perhaps revolution from above, as practiced in the economic sphere in recent years, may have been the most desirable approach for Russia. It was clearly not the appropriate route to constitutionalism. Given the complex shape of constitutionalism and the many elements that comprise and can potentially influence it, it cannot be imposed in any effective way. Only in a "managed free market" can it take root.[48]

Lempert's model of "social contract democracy," anchored in the work of Jean-Jacques Rousseau, is the most appropriate approach for Russia today. In this construct, constitutionalism will emerge as individuals form new

45. Lempert, "Changing Russian Political Culture," 639.
46. Lempert, "Changing Russian Political Culture," 643.
47. Sharlet, "The Fate of Individual Rights," 201.
48. At least a political free market, though some have argued an economic one as well, is necessary for the creation of constitutionalism.

social and political ties at the grass roots.[49] Rather than formal government institutions, the system will consist of the people themselves. Coming together in myriad non-official fora, from knitting groups to church choirs, from trade and civic associations to bowling leagues, citizen groups will create the sinews of a nongovernmental civil order. Associational groups and voluntary organizations will multiply and remake the face of Russian society. Gradually, a form of "direct democracy" will become the norm and "all large institutions [will] necessarily be subject to some kind of close control by the citizenry in order to achieve the goals of democracy."[50]

Among this democracy's tools will be juries, class action suits, private attorneys general (wielding statutory causes of action), and citizen review panels; essential to its effectiveness will be equal access to education, to counsel, and to the media.[51] Yet in Russia these practices can serve as more than instruments in the execution of democracy. They can also be the mechanisms of its creation, educating citizens in their rights and responsibilities. Finally, they can serve as a critical tool in the encouragement of public trust in the political order, a virtue both necessary and lacking in present-day Russia.[52]

Russian legal and political culture will thereby shift from weak to strong democracy. Rather than the public being limited to the occasional and sparse political engagement of referenda and elections, they will become an active part of the constitutional process,[53] thereby changing both the political order and the society itself. In this way the people will come to see themselves as part of the system, and the government as a close associate rather than as a distant enemy.[54]

Though the constitutional developments of recent years have been largely in keeping with the contrary traditions of Russia's history, with change emanating from the top, progress has been made toward constitutionalism from below. As *perestroika* took on a life of its own in the late 1980s, public

49. See Lempert, "Changing Russian Political Culture." See also Serge Schmemann, "Why Russians Can't Get Excited About a Constitution," *New York Times*, 14 November 1993, 5.

50. Lempert, "Changing Russian Political Culture," 634.

51. Lempert, "Changing Russian Political Culture," 634. One may recall, in this vein, the provisions for citizen suits in the USSR Environmental Protection Act of 1991.

52. See Richard Rose, "Postcommunism and the Problem of Trust," *Journal of Democracy* 5 (July 1994): 29.

53. See Lempert, "The Proposed Constitution of Ukraine," 294–95 n. 33. See also Benjamin Barber, *Strong Democracy: Participatory Politics for A New Age* (Berkeley and Los Angeles: University of California Press, 1987).

54. See Rose, "Postcommunism and the Problem of Trust."

discussion of laws pending before the Soviet Congresses increased,[55] initiating a process of public engagement with political structures. Suddenly the passivity of the Russian masses began to fade: "Without waiting for promised laws, individuals and groups had begun to appropriate to themselves implied de facto rights of a freer press, a wider range of permissible speech, and the virtually unprecedented acts of forming independent groups and taking causes to the streets."[56]

The public briefly rose up to grab what power it could. Due to mounting frustration and lack of success, however, it soon reverted to its traditional lethargy. From 1989 forward, participation and interest in political life has thus steadily declined.[57]

Russia's citizenry must again engage itself in the political processes not of the government alone, but of a broader civil society. In this vein, the introduction of mechanisms of public engagement is critical. Such mechanisms are a priority and must take precedence in the reforms now under way. Together with an expansion of nongovernmental societal interactions, public engagement in the workings of government is the key to a true citizen democracy and lasting constitutionalism.

MASSES AND ELITES

Consideration of the relationship of the Russian masses and elites, and its bearing on the development of constitutionalism, will help clarify the substantive significance of the previous section. For the evolution of constitutionalism from below is impossible in the absence of agents of change at the bottom and responsive actors at the top. This relationship is thus one of the most critical issues Russia faces today.[58] Robert Sharlet supports this view and describes the latter-day manifestation of Robert Tucker's "dual Russia" to be the dichotomy of the masses and the elites.[59] Consequently,

55. Articles 113 and 114 of the 1977 constitution, which respectively allowed for legislative initiatives by mass organizations and encouraged general public discussion of draft legislation, may imply an even earlier tradition of public participation, however weak it may have been.
56. Sharlet, *Soviet Constitutional Crisis,* 88.
57. Brown, "The October Crisis of 1993," 188.
58. See Hoffmann, 26–30.
59. Sharlet, "Citizen and State," 109.

the changes in this relationship since 1985 are particularly relevant to the emergence of constitutionalism in the years ahead.

The constitutional developments of this period have essentially been a story of the elite. They have controlled the scope and direction of legal and political developments, dragging the masses along when they could, or, when this proved impossible, simply leaving them behind. The elites did not concern themselves with mass psychology or public interest, as their autonomy allowed them to ignore these with impunity. As a result, issues of constitutionalism and the development of legal consciousness centered on the elites. As the agents of change in Russian politics, they determined how constitutionalism would develop. Thus do the events and politics explored in Part I primarily involve constitutionalism among the elite.

As of yet, the people had not become players in the constitutional or the political process. They remained pawns in it and, for the most part, could be discounted as an issue. In fact, some would discount the masses not only as autonomous players in the process but even as victims or passive subjects of change. Given the masses' negligible legal consciousness and their traditional passivity, this argument runs, the political and constitutional developments of this period were simply beyond their scope of awareness. The politicization of the Constitutional Court, it would thus be argued, did not affect the people's legal consciousness, as they lacked a baseline understanding of the court that would give this shift normative meaning.

Even if this is true, and mass legal consciousness per se has changed only slightly, a more basic transformation in mass psychology clearly has taken place. During the last decade, the activism and political engagement of the Russian public has undergone a seismic shift. While this activism has flourished and flagged, it has dramatically increased in the aggregate. The mass public demonstrations of the late 1980s, opposition to the attempted coup in August 1991, and the events of September and October 1993 evidence a public engagement with the political process not found in Russian political culture in the past. At the end of the first decade of Russia's reformation, this underlying current of activism has become a central theme in the constitutional and political development of Russia. Increasingly, the story of constitutionalism has become that of the masses.

The dynamic process of restructuring and reform, with all its twists and turns, has gradually slipped out of the hands of the elites. Gorbachev surrendered control of the reform process to the elites in the late 1980s. Control has now moved beyond the elites as well and been dispersed to the economic process, to local politics, and to the people themselves.

Although the elites have lost their autonomy in the development process, however, they have not abandoned their role. The masses remain constrained by a legacy of historical passivity and by an apathy born of the last decade's recurring frustrations. They require activation by the catalyst of the elites; the masses are now the force behind change, but its initial impetus must still come from the elites. A public long disengaged from the political process does not know how to translate its desire for change into reality. The elites must therefore set the ball in motion.

While not entirely dissimilar from the past, in which a vanguard of elites led the way, this modern-day relationship differs at its core. Viktor Sergeyev and Nikolai Biryukov speak of a new paradigm of state-society relations in which mutual dependencies and reciprocal relations are the operative norms. "The age of 'separate and unequal' classes of mass and elite has at last come to an end in Russia."[60] The sociopolitical system, rather than being the sole province of the elites, is now bipolar. No longer can elites act alone. Nor can the public, though more empowered than ever. For neither the masses nor the elites are an independent variable in the development of constitutionalism any longer; they are interdependent variables equally critical to the process. Like that of a tag team, their success depends on their capacity to work together, each accepting constitutionalism and playing its part to keep the process moving forward.

As this symbiotic relationship develops, its polarity will diminish. The elites and masses will be drawn closer and become increasingly difficult to differentiate. This has already begun. To a growing extent, elite views now parallel those of the masses. This narrowing of Russian class culture began in the legal realm with general secretary Yuri Andropov's discipline campaign in 1982. Unlike previous attempts at reform, this effort targeted the masses and elites in a similar fashion. With it, the *nomenklatura* began to forfeit one of their previously distinguishing traits—a privileged status before the law. The increasing multipolarity of Russian society, as the sharp dichotomy of masses and elites fades, will only further undermine detrimental divisions that have long shut many out of Russia's political processes.[61]

---

60. Biryukov, interview of 18 November 1993. See Sergeyev and Biryukov, *Russia's Road to Democracy.*

61. A distinct question is whether one can still speak of a Russian elite or whether it is now too sharply divided within itself to be categorized as such. Such division, to begin with, may not exist at an underlying level. Divisive politics do not always evidence fundamental political schism. Moreover, even an irreparable division of the elites will not doom the constitutional process. The deadlock of a divided elite may produce just the opposite result. By forcing the

Of course, the transformation of elite-mass relations will not be simple. Both groups bear heavy historical legacies that still influence their behavior. For the public, it is their passivity. Yet as the events we have discussed demonstrate, this has already begun to change and will continue to do so. As of the elites, it remains unclear whether they can bring themselves to function within the norms of a constitutionalism that they have so long stood above. Can they learn to rule both *under* and *by* law—and no longer *through* it? The elites may not be captives of their history either. Consider South Africa, a different nation with its own crises of transition: as recently demonstrated by F. W. DeKlerk and Nelson Mandela and the opposing elites they represent, a fundamental change in elite attitudes is possible.

The masses and the elites have reached a crossroads on the path of Russia's constitutional development. In order to move forward, they must become partners under the law. This solidarity has begun to appear, with better legislative representation, increasingly effective local government institutions, and gradual public engagement in politics at all levels. Whether these conditions will persist remains to be seen.

A New Paradigm

As a new Russia appears, a new political and social paradigm must emerge at its base. If Russia is not to descend into the ideological morass that has characterized much of its history, a paradigm appropriate to its constructive and orderly development is critical.[62] The evolutionary model of constitutionalism outlined above can provide the foundation for such an approach. Within the construct of constitutionalism's development and the participatory and ordering principles it inculcates, broader elements of Russian reform can be integrated. The progress of reforms will then hinge on the emergence of constitutionalism, just as the development of constitutionalism will depend on the success of reforms. As constitutionalism goes, so will go the country.

---

elites to turn to the people, division may create an environment amenable to public participation. See Hoffmann, 27, 35–36; and Philip Roeder, "Varieties of Post-Soviet Authoritarian Regimes," *Post-Soviet Affairs* 10 (January–March 1994): 98.

62. Vladimir Pastykov, "'Noviye russkiye': payavleniye ideologii (II)," *Polis* 3 (1993): 18.

A greater focus on legal consciousness and a more gradualist, grass-roots understanding of the development of constitutionalism are at the heart of this new paradigm. Constitutionalism must rise from below. It requires strong roots that will secure it, rather than simply an overgrown head, like the twenty-foot bust of Lenin in Siberia[63] that is bound to fall over eventually. As recent years have shown, if strong psychological underpinnings are lacking, the finest constitutional order will prove to be a house of cards, or at best a glass one. What is crucial, then, is "not the structures of government but the paramountcy of law."[64] Lacking the spirit of law, structures alone will not uphold constitutionalism.[65] Thus was the 1936 Stalin constitution, though based upon French and German constitutional models, quite easily twisted to Soviet totalitarian demands.

The stability of the concrete structures of constitutionalism requires an indigenous legal consciousness. It is reassuring to note that in contrast to traditional western assessments, modern Russia does have a heritage that can nurture a reborn legal culture. The awareness of the need for constitutionalism in the late imperial period and the substantive political reforms of the Provisional Government in 1917 provide historical precedents to which Russia may turn in its efforts to reestablish legal consciousness.[66] Of course, as Yakovlev reminds us, "it is impossible to enlighten people until they are perfect and then start building democracy."[67] Structures and consciousness must thus develop hand in hand. "Constitutionalism is not the culmination of the process of state-building. Constitutionalism must be seen as a process that includes establishing stable institutions within the democratic perspective of securing self-government."[68]

This result will not come quickly but will emerge out of an evolutionary process in which every step is careful and considered. Such a gradual emergence of constitutionalism is only natural, as the legal state is not the final step, but the first, on the path of Russian political development. As Bogdan Kistiakovski, Russian theorist of the *pravovoe gosudarstvo*, ex-

63. In Ulan Ude, Buryatia (a relatively small Siberian city), this bizarre "Lenin head," as the locals call it, must rank among the most unusual of paeans to the Bolshevik revolutionary.

64. Hoffmann, 25.

65. The recent practice of the president's State-Legal Administration (GPU) of employing psychologists on its staff may evidence an increasing awareness of this fact. Eugene Huskey, "The State-Legal Administration and the Politics of Redundancy," *Post-Soviet Affairs* 11 (April–June 1995): 120.

66. Juviler, "Russia Turned Upside Down," 31–32.

67. Yakovlev, interview of 5 February 1994.

68. Faundez, 359.

plained nearly a hundred years ago, "the law-based state is a school and a laboratory, where institutions of the future social edification are worked out."[69]

Increasing interaction of the masses with the institutions of government must emerge and blossom into a back-and-forth parlay between the public and the elite that allows each to positively influence the other. Such public engagement, coupled with a proliferation of associational groups and citizen-to-citizen interactions, will allow Russia to discard its model of revolutionary development directed from above and replace it with one of evolution from below. Paradoxically, the elite must take the first steps in this direction. The weak condition of Russian civil society makes a spontaneous emergence of constitutionalism from below an unlikely scenario. Elites therefore remain central to the process but must use their position to widen the political base and not to constrain it.

The "new Soviet man" was long seen as the key to Soviet development. The development of constitutionalism now demands a new Russian citizen. A common joke of the Gorbachev period is relevant. It described a meeting of two friends in the street: "In Sweden," one remarks, "they have a brilliant democracy. Do you think it will be possible for us to have this kind of democracy?"

"No," the friend replies.

"But why not?" asks the first.

"Because we don't have enough Swedes."

Lacking as it does in Swedes, Russia must now make do with Russians. Guided by the principles of effective constitutionalism, however, Russians may yet prove adequate to the task. This will become clear as constitutional principles are put into practice in the years ahead. "Constitutionalism is no longer a theory, but a practical need. If we can apply it to our lives, we will survive. And if we cannot, we will not."[70] It is the application of constitutionalism to Russia's present-day realities to which we must now turn.

---

69. Bogdan Kistiakovski, "*Gosudarstvo pravovoe i sotsialisticheskoe,*" *Voprosy filosofi i psikhologi,* no. 5 (1906): 506.

70. Nikonov, interview of 3 February 1994.

CHAPTER FOUR

PRACTICE

As we turn to the application of constitutionalism in particular issue areas since 1994 and in the years ahead, a brief comment on the relevant actors is necessary. The state remains at the center of policy making and will inevitably figure prominently in every aspect of constitutionalism's emergence, but it will rarely be the only player or even, on occasion, the key player. The mass media, academics, and the general public also have critical roles to play, and their influence, though less apparent than that of government bodies, may have an even greater indirect impact. Even where the discussion is focused on government activities, one should thus keep in mind the potential for an involved citizen, investigative journalist, or entrepreneur to significantly affect the process. Andrei Sakharov's impact on the development of constitutionalism is ample evidence of this. As the Russian Federation moves toward a new constitutional order, only the interaction of the public and private, the political and personal, will allow any policy prescription to promote the emergence of constitutionalism.

POLITICS

Compromise and Cooperation

Effective governance, the ultimate predicate of long-term constitutional stability, is intimately linked with the practices of compromise and cooperation. Yet these phenomena have largely been absent from Russian history, particularly in government relations. This scarcity is due in part to the theology of Orthodox Christianity and its more than one thousand years on Russian soil.[1] Orthodoxy has traditionally viewed compromise through a

---

1. Orthodox Christianity was established as the state religion in A.D. 988.

moral and religious construct antithetical to modern political dialogue.[2] In the opinion of the church, to compromise was to "sell out the truth," to concede to falsehood and thus to evil—a deed no faithful believer could accept.[3] In this view, expressed here in its strongest form, there is right and there is wrong. Having sought and found what is right, moral duty requires one to deny (without exception or flexibility) what is wrong. In the realm of politics, this conception helps explain the absence of any sense of a loyal opposition in Russian or Soviet mentality. Such a notion, in the Russian view, is an oxymoron.

Under Brezhnev, the insistence on consensus on all major decisions was a product of this same *Orthodox* mind-set.[4] Such consensus was achieved largely by a characterization of dissent as opposition to the entire mass of society, not simply to the ruling political order or its present-day elites. A vote *contra* was thus not an attempt to further society's development, but an effort to undermine its unity. As such, dissent inherently made one a traitor and an "Enemy of the People," with no further inquiry necessary.[5]

"Russians find it difficult 'to agree to disagree,' to compromise on large and small matters, and to tolerate different political, social, ethnic, and religious viewpoints."[6] Yet such compromise is the essence of constitutionalism in an evolutionary political and legal climate. Unsurprisingly, Russians frown upon the law's willingness to be "content with procedural, and not absolute, truth."[7] Instead, the traditional Russian mind-set aspires to *sovershenstvo zakona,* the perfection of law.[8] Yet such an aspiration, if it ever was realistic, will most assuredly not be realized in late twentieth-century Russia.

Russian philosophers such as Nikolai Berdyaev and legal scholars such as P. I. Novgorodtsev and Bogdan Kistiakovski reserved some of their strongest cultural criticism for this debilitating unwillingness to compromise, which each described as a great impediment to Russia's development and progress. Poor psychology even for a stable polity, this absolutist approach is even less

2. Biryukov, interview of 18 November 1993.
3. Caryl Emerson, professor of Slavic languages and literature, Princeton University. Presentation in English at Princeton University, 3 March 1994.
4. While it would seem unusual to speak of the "Orthodox" mindset of the Soviet leadership, this view of truth was so ingrained in the Russian psyche that it became more of a cultural value than a religious one.
5. Sergeyev and Biryukov, *Russia's Road to Democracy,* 76; see 147–50.
6. Hoffmann, 33.
7. Huskey, "From Legal Nihilism," 38.
8. Lempert, "The Proposed Constitution of Ukraine," 271.

appropriate for a nation in the midst of so massive a political and social transformation. If headway is to be made against any of the economic, political, or social ills facing Russia, a healthy respect for compromise is essential.[9] In a climate of flux, an obsession with "objective truth," which remains the aspiration of Russian politics today, will surely prove fatal.[10] Rather than drawing Russia closer to any sort of truth, this quest will only drag the country deeper into a morass of sociopolitical dislocation and eventual civil war. Sergeyev and Biryukov further link this search for correct answers to the failure to establish an effective representative democracy under Gorbachev and Yeltsin.

Soviet and Russian parliamentary bodies thus did not turn to the people on account of any public right to be heard or to participate in the democratic process, nor were their voices included in order to reach a closer approximation of truth. Rather, suggest Sergeyev and Biryukov, the people were turned to as the repository of an absolute truth, one that might be tapped by the parliamentary process. This unusual notion, they argue, produced exactly the opposite result from that which it implies—by dealing with the people as a "mystic unit" endowed with true knowledge, the parliament could avoid dealing with any given individual's concerns, or even the views of those blocs of voters whose voices would normally be heard and acknowledged in a representative system.[11]

Other results of this persistent opposition to compromise and cooperation include President Yeltsin's recurring failure to help establish a political party to represent the democratic faction, his lack of support for an independent mass media, and his disinterest in free and open public debate. Together, these are indicative of Yeltsin's strong commitment to absolute or objective truth as distinct from merely a "democratically legitimated" one.[12] The view of truth as singular, thus, has had an appreciable impact on Russian politics and the development of a new constitutional order since 1985.

While a willingness to compromise is necessary throughout Russian society, it must first take root in the political arena, and specifically in the Duma, the chamber that is the primary representative body in Russia today.[13] Its

9. See Albert Schmidt, "Soviet Legal Development, 1917–1990," in Barry, *Toward the "Rule of Law" in Russia?* 339–42.

10. Sergeyev and Biryukov, *Russia's Road to Democracy*, 27.

11. Sergeyev and Biryukov, *Russia's Road to Democracy*, 24–28.

12. Hoffmann, 31.

13. More so than the Federation Council, the Duma is perceived as the representative of the

disperse "ten-party system,"[14] which parallels the fractitious contours of the Russian political landscape, must prove itself capable of compromise. Among elites who "already have formulated their own interests" and are disinclined to yield in the least, the Duma must forge consensus and avoid a polarization that will ensure its own demise.[15] Should the Duma collapse into a divisive bickering reminiscent of the Supreme Soviet that the Russian public grew to loathe, its legitimacy and influence will quickly wane. It must instead find ways to cooperate and reach common ground even when there appears to be little.

Dating back to the first of their kind in Russia–the tsarist *Zemskie Sobori*[16]—representative institutions have had little appeal for the Russian people.[17] In the wake of the failures of Soviet legislative bodies and the Russian Supreme Soviet, public "disenchantment with the workings of parliamentary democracy" has only grown.[18] During the last decade, "people decided they did not like such bodies as they spent lots of money and talked too much."[19]

Faced with this presumption of guilt, the Duma and its members must take great pains to prove themselves capable of talking more, yet doing more as well.[20] If not, their legislative legacy may well parallel that of the farcical Soviet Congress of People's Deputies, which came together in a dilapidated

---

masses and not the elites. This is rooted in the selection process for council members, one somewhat divorced from the general public. The Duma, furthermore, is the primary lawmaking body, while the Federation Council acts as a check on its work.

14. In reality, there are even more than ten parties.

15. Migranyan, interview of 4 February 1994.

16. Some have suggested the existence of representative institutions as early as the ancient *Kievan Rus*, but the more recent *sobori* are most commonly acknowledged as their earliest heritage in Russia.

17. Thus did an elderly taxi driver in Moscow, whose view of the 1993 constitution I had asked (4 February 1994), extensively discuss his opinion of the president and government but fail to even mention the Duma, though he was driving me there. See also Sergeyev and Biryukov, *Russia's Road to Democracy*, 47–49.

18. Butler, "Perestroika and the Rule of Law," 12.

19. Burlatski, interview of 1 February 1994.

20. In a public-opinion poll of 1,203 individuals on 15 May 1993, the question was posed: "How do you rank the work of your representative in the Parliament [Russian Supreme Soviet] in serving your interests?"

I do not know or do not remember who my representative is:	43 percent
I do not know how my representative works:	31 percent
I rank it well:	11 percent
I rank it poorly:	15 percent

(Survey by the Public Opinion Foundation, published in its journal, *Within Sight*, May 1993)

state farm outside Moscow on 17 March 1992 (three months after Gorbachev's resignation) to revive the Soviet Union. Yet several of the buses carrying deputies from Moscow to Voronovo were lost on the way. Thus, only 150 die-hard Communists finally gathered in the barn in Voronovo late that evening, to find no electricity available. Undaunted, they still managed to adopt eighteen resolutions in the forty-four minutes they met. By candle-light, no less![21]

This is not meant to suggest a media-friendly Duma caught up in the will and whim of a fickle public. The Duma does well to focus on so-called procedural questions, notwithstanding public acrimony about deputies wasting time "talking about nothing." As any trained attorney can testify, such procedural questions are often nearly everything. The Duma must, however, prove itself as an institution of governance in the public eye if it is to succeed. As the parliament faces a pattern of the promulgation of laws by presidential and administrative acts,[22] United States Supreme Court Justice Robert Jackson's admonition to the U.S. Congress in the historic case of *Youngstown Sheet and Tube Co. v. Sawyer* (1952) may be relevant to the Russian Duma: "We may say that power to legislate for emergencies belongs in the hands of Congress, but only Congress itself can prevent power from slipping through its fingers."[23]

Doubts about the potential for compromise in the divisive political climate of today can be provisionally set aside. Occurrences such as Vladimir Zhirinovsky's participation in Yeltsin's 1993 Constitutional Conference have blunted their force. Zhirinovsky's willingness to compromise and cooperate during these discussions, as well as his behavior toward all those present in the practical manner of a true parliamentarian, is better evidence of the potential for political cooperation than even the most rigid jury could demand. Such conduct justifies cautious hope for the success of the Duma as a whole. Its members are no longer "valued . . . for their ability to struggle against or for communism, but for their professionalism and a constructive approach."[24] The persistence of the relatively stable, cooperative atmo-sphere of the transitional first Duma, which sat for an abbreviated two-year term, until the election of the first properly constituted Duma in December 1995, thus seems increasingly possible.

21. Sergeyev and Biryukov, *Russia's Road to Democracy*, 209–10.

22. Huskey, "The State-Legal Administration," 127.

23. *Youngstown Sheet and Tube Co. v. Sawyer*, 343 U.S. 579, 654 (1952) (Jackson, J., concurring).

24. Giorgi Satarov, "What Fate Lies in Store for the Parliament?" *Rossiiskiye Vesti*, 11 January 1994.

The potential impact of deputies' willingness to cooperate on constitutionalism's development, as demonstrated in their adoption of bills ranging from the new Civil Code to new bankruptcy and securities laws by large and diverse majorities, is immeasurable. "For the creation of constitutionalism," notes Dimitri Olshanski, a Russian political psychologist and failed candidate to the Duma, "it is enough in principle that there is a good example of constitutional behavior at the top."[25] If the 1995 Duma can persevere on this path, it will help to erase the unfortunate legacies that have long stood in the way of compromise.

As mentioned, the parliament has already made great strides in this direction. The first speaker of the Duma, Ivan Rybkin, who was elected on the Communist-oriented Agrarian party ticket, opened a broad window for compromise in the name of stabilization and further reform. His meeting with Yeltsin in March 1994, soon after his election, "to discuss coexistence and cooperation" between the executive and legislative branches, a goal they agreed to focus on and support, was a first step in this direction and an example for future executive-legislative relations.[26]

The assignment of committee chairpersons in the first Duma symbolizes the new mentality necessary for continued progress. Realizing that an attempt to appoint chairpersons and their deputies individually would take months, members agreed to a compromise point system under which various factions would assign allotted points to one position or another. Three points were necessary for deputy speakers, one point for each committee chairperson, and a half point for each deputy committee chairperson. This may not have been the most democratic approach and did not always result in the best candidate getting the job. Yet it represents, in essence, the attitude of practical compromise the Duma must maintain if it is to serve as the "school of democracy" its predecessors failed to become.[27]

Consensus in the Duma, however, cannot be simply oppositional—unity born of a common confrontation with the executive. Rather, compromise within the Duma must coexist with a willingness to cooperate with those beyond it. It must be inter- as well as intra-institutional. As Hoffmann observes, "the relevance of national government bodies may depend on their

25. Olshanski, interview of 7 August 1993.

26. Steven Erlanger, "Russian Battle: Stage Is Reset," *New York Times*, 2 March 1994, A10. Hereafter Erlanger, "Russian Battle: Stage Is Reset."

27. *Izvestiia*, 30 May 1989, 1.

ability to cooperate with one another and with their regional and local counterparts."[28] Unless the various branches work harmoniously, reform will be impossible and the constitutional order will never mature.

To begin with, the patterns of Soviet political mentality and behavior that have survived the collapse of Communist rule must finally be uprooted. Until the birth of the Second Russian Republic, "the change in political mentality was not as fundamental as it appeared, and the rupture, however radical, with the communist ideals did not mean rupture with the communist political culture."[29] Yet if democracy and constitutional change are to prove lasting, a break with the latter is essential.

Russia's constitutional bodies must learn to interact according to the terms of the constitution. Having long been simply an instrument in the political struggle, it must now become the functional basis of the political infrastructure.[30] The Duma and Federation Council must avoid confrontation with the president on the basic terms of the constitution until the system has been given time to stabilize itself. Such confrontation would undermine the legitimacy of the constitution, the president, and the parliament itself,[31] rendering the entire constitutional order ineffective.[32] Moreover, it could provoke a repeat of Yeltsin's acts of September and October 1993, with all their dire consequences. Even if the constitution does not provide the best terms for how the branches of government should interact, it is an adequate beginning.

The separation of powers is now "practically implanted in Russia, even if not in its classical form."[33] The constitution's delineation of powers is therefore best upheld. Ambitious politicians should no longer twist the principle of checks and balances to justify a constant power struggle between the legislative, executive, and judicial branches.

In this view, the Duma's 23 February 1994 decision to grant amnesty, by a veto-proof resolution, to the August 1991 coup leaders and, more important, to the September–October 1993 occupants of the White House, including Aleksandr Rutskoi and Ruslan Khasbulatov, is instructive in assessing Russia's progress toward interbranch cooperation.[34] This decision was

28. Hoffmann, 48.
29. Sergeyev and Biryukov, *Russia's Road to Democracy,* 89.
30. Nikonov, interview of 3 February 1994.
31. As the parliament is itself a product of the constitution.
32. Klamkin, interview of 4 February 1994.
33. Marchenko, interview of 31 January 1994.
34. The text of the amnesty is available in *Rossiiskaya Gazeta,* 26 February 1994, 5;

likely unconstitutional.[35] The power to grant amnesty is given to the parliament by article 103(1)(f) of the constitution; this case, however, looked like a pardon (its beneficiaries had not yet been tried and convicted), a power given to the president under article 89(c). Erik Hoffmann thus registers his concern with the Duma's violation of the constitution "only two months" after its passage.[36]

Yet President Yeltsin's response to this transgression and the ensuing events should also be remembered. Initially Yeltsin attempted to forcibly prevent his opponents' release, which led two of his political allies, prosecutor general Aleksei I. Kazannik and chief of secret police Nikolai Golushko, to resign in protest. Subsequently, though he continued to express his disagreement with the parliament's decision, Yeltsin came to accept it. Even Sergei Shakhrai, a close Yeltsin associate who voted for the amnesty, managed to retain his senior position in the Government and in Yeltsin's entourage. Yeltsin gave in to the Duma, he declared, since his primary interest was in "maintaining and expanding common ground for interaction and cooperation in the state and society."

"Today in Russia," Yeltsin told the parliament only days later, "democracy means above all stability, order and cooperation."[37] In only two months, thus, the substantive values of constitutionalism had begun to emerge, notwithstanding little compliance with its procedural directives. And while the latter should not be discounted, the former is of the essence.

As this case demonstrates, much of the responsibility for heightened cooperation has fallen upon the president, whose stature and singularity make him less prone to populist pressures than the Duma. Yet President Yeltsin long operated extra-constitutionally, just as he did while Party boss of Sverdlovsk. By the terms of the 1993 constitution, moreover, the president

---

translation available in *FBIS-SOV-94-040,* 1 March 1994, 32. Notably, the amnesty resolution also included a "Memorandum of Accord," calling for interbranch cooperation.

35. But see Donald D. Barry, "Amnesty Under the Russian Constitution: Evolution of the Provision and Its Use in February 1994," *Parker School Journal of East European Law* 1, no. 4 (1994): 455. Barry argues that the constitution's provision on amnesty is broad enough to allow for the Duma's decision.

36. Hoffmann, 42.

37. Steven Erlanger, "Yeltsin Denounces Amnesty but Concedes to Parliament," *New York Times,* 5 March 1994, A5.

stands above the separation of powers,[38] relatively unchecked by the legislature; he must therefore take care not to overstep the already broad
prerogatives of the office, but to live within its constitutional limitations.

The president, elected as he must be with a broad popular mandate, has a
unique ability to press forward the reform and restructuring Russia will
remain in need of for the next decade. This will require that the president
maintain a steady course and not float back and forth "like Mary Poppins in
the wind,"[39] as have Presidents Gorbachev and Yeltsin. Presidential cooperation with the Duma is likewise crucial to constitutionalism's development. The scholarly Aleksandr Yakovlev's work as President Yeltsin's
representative to the Duma and Federation Council set a powerful precedent
for improved executive-legislative relations. Yakovlev's primary function, one
he served well, was to facilitate political compromise.[40] He described this
important role as that of "a catalyst for compromise, designed to more
clearly define the relations of the president and the Duma, enhancing their
interactions and thus avoiding another 'war of laws.' "[41]

The president now stands in a position to move one way or the other,
either tilling Russian soil for a season of democracy or taking Russia back
down the authoritarian path of its history. It has yet to be proven that, in
Justice Zorkin's pessimistic view, "if the choice was once between democracy
and totalitarianism, it is now between authoritarianism and authoritarianism."[42] President Yeltsin and his successors can still disprove this claim by
avoiding the accumulation of too much power in their own hands. True, the
constitution grants them broad emergency powers and authority to rule by
decree; yet they should avoid this approach, as it is sure to derail the
development of constitutionalism.[43]

Each branch must make every effort to press the others to remain within
their prescribed roles and "give up their traditional practices, for the liberal
norms of the constitution." Thus, suggests Yakovlev, the president must
"consistently try to shift the parliament onto pure legislative ground."[44] The

38. International Reform Foundation, "We Need a Different Constitution, and It Must Be
Adopted Without Haste," *Nezavisimaya Gazeta,* 7 December 1993.
39. Topornin, presentation of 27–28 July 1993.
40. Huskey, "The State-Legal Administration," 129.
41. Yakovlev, interview of 5 February 1994.
42. Zorkin, interview of 2 February 1994.
43. Foster-Simons, "The Soviet Legislature," 115.
44. Yakovlev, interview of 5 February 1994.

reverse, meanwhile, must hold true as well. This opportunity arose soon after the election of the first Duma with reference to the article 83(l) authority of the president to dismiss foreign ambassadors "after consultations" with the Duma's Foreign Relations Committee. Yet before the removal of Vladimir Lukin as ambassador to the United States,[45] Yeltsin did not contact the committee. At its first session, the committee consequently drafted a memorandum to the president informing him that the documents concerning Lukin's dismissal had somehow failed to reach them but that they supported his decision nonetheless. They knew, of course, that Yeltsin had simply ignored his duty to consult them, but they set, in this way, a precedent for the future. Such precedents, as they persist, will strongly encourage all parties to act "within their strict limits."[46]

As interbranch relations develop, a further cooperative atmosphere will begin to emerge. This was already evident in February 1994 in the practical and substantive cooperation of the president and the Duma on economic reforms. No doubt the 29 April 1994 Treaty on Social Accord (though belittled as lacking substantive bite and provisions for its enforcement) was an important step in this direction.[47] Its disavowal of political violence and its proscription of calls for early elections and major constitutional changes proved to be critical to constitutional stability. Most of the central parties in Russian politics agreed to the treaty, and it held up quite effectively.[48] A marked decrease in political contention and a more probing focus on critical questions about crime and the economy have been apparent since its adoption. The Duma's passage of the 1995 budget, though much delayed, and the Law on the Constitutional Court were concrete products of this cooperation. The former, in fact, was passed with greater ease than was the 1996 budget of the United States, the debate over which shut the latter government down on two occasions.

As the Duma came halfway, deputies noted Yeltsin's increasing willingness to cooperate as well.[49] Ivan Rybkin and Vladimir Shumeiko, heads of the Duma and Federation Council, respectively, were invited to become mem-

45. Lukin resigned, in fact, to become chairman of the Duma's Foreign Relations Committee.

46. Yakovlev, interview of 5 February 1994.

47. Signed into force on 28 April 1994, the treaty is available in translation in *FBIS-SOV-94-083*, 29 April 1994, 18.

48. Michael Specter, "Yeltsin Wins Peace Accord in Parliament," *New York Times*, 29 April 1994, A5.

49. Hoffmann, 31.

bers of Yeltsin's National Security Council in January 1995.[50] Further,
Yeltsin resisted pressures to veto the Duma's controversial Law on the Status
of Deputies (May 1994) and instead heeded adviser Giorgi Satarov's advice
to prioritize political stability.[51] Most recently, the president's bitter differences with the parliament over the war in Chechnya were resolved along the
lines of compromise and the law.

A 22 June 1995 no-confidence vote by the Duma, expected to be followed
by a second, confirming vote two weeks later, thus inspired Yeltsin's efforts
to appease the Duma by sacking three of his most hawkish ministers[52] and
pressing for an end to hostilities and a negotiated settlement. Unlike in
October 1993, the parliament's opposition to the president led not to chaos,
but to compromise and progress.

The Government and presidential apparatus must also continue to cooperate. They compose a dual executive, with the Government, until now,
largely in control of the economy, and the president in charge of political
matters and military and foreign policy. This sharing of powers, however,
remains unstable. "Unlike other political systems with dual executives,
Russia has thus far failed to develop an accepted division of labor between
presidential and Government institutions."[53]

This relationship must therefore be closely monitored and more clearly
defined in order to prevent a future rift. This necessity was quite clear to
Prime Minister Viktor Chernomyrdin, from whom future prime ministers
can learn valuable lessons. In a speech to the Government in early 1994, he
declared that "some people are trying vainly to drive a wedge between the
president and the government. This will fail. . . . He is the leader of the
nation, elected by the people, and I am not going to stab him in the back."[54]
The trend of cooperation that emerged during 1994 and 1995 between
Prime Minister Chernomyrdin, Federation Council chairman Shumeiko, and
Duma chairman Rybkin demonstrates that a broader environment of cooperation is possible. This must be maintained by the new government.

Erik Hoffmann cautions that it may be too early for such cooperation. If

50. The inclusion of Rybkin and Shumeiko has been characterized by some as an effort to
co-opt them, and specifically to frame them as supporters of Yeltsin's unpopular decision to
invade Chechnya in December 1994. Even if true, there is still much to be said for a state of
politics that encourages their inclusion, motivated by political ends though it may be.

51. Huskey, "The State-Legal Administration," 129.

52. Namely director of the Federal Security Service (successor to the KGB) Sergei Stepashin,
Internal Affairs Minister Viktor Yerin, and Deputy Prime Minister Nikolai Yegorov.

53. Huskey, "The State-Legal Administration," 124.

54. Erlanger, "Yeltsin Denounces Amnesty," A5.

the more liberal executive concentrates all its efforts on attempting to work with the more conservative legislature rather than pressing for reforms itself, it may achieve neither cooperation nor progress. This worst-case scenario, suggests Hoffmann, may become a reality in the divisive political climate of the moment and should not be risked.[55] Yet Hoffmann's assessment fails to lend enough weight to the cooperation that increasingly appeared as the norm by the second year of the first Duma. If so much progress may so quickly be made, the time may well have passed for a government of necessity and come for one of law.

Interaction of the various branches' personnel will help to sustain a cooperative atmosphere, as will improved communication within each branch of government.[56] "Such cooperation at the grass roots is the way constitutionalism is made."[57] As the mass of mid-level bureaucrats learn to work together, they will force cooperation at higher levels. Gradually Russia's own unique meta-institutional system will consolidate; it may not exactly resemble any of the traditional systems now in existence, but it will be appropriate to the Russian political environment.

Eventually it may become necessary to formulate a "little constitution," analogous to that Poland adopted in 1992,[58] which will clearly delineate, and thereby codify, how institutional relations are functioning in practice, not merely how they are prescribed in the constitution. For now, however, this document is unnecessary; an evolutionary process of development seems both adequate and preferable. An adviser to Yeltsin, Emil Paen, thus admits that the "present character of institutions is temporary and will change."[59] And if even Oleg Rumyantsev, Yeltsin's sharpest constitutional critic, now aspires to a republic that is "three-fourths presidential," a climate for cooperative constitutional reform clearly exists.[60] Such a gradual constitutional maturation will allow increasingly fine-tuned versions of Russia's

---

55. See Hoffmann, 29, 50–55.

56. Problems of interbranch communication were apparent in Russian decision making on the former Yugoslavia and on NATO's Partnership for Peace program during 1994 and 1995. On several occasions, mixed messages from the various concerned ministries made for tense moments in Russia's relations with NATO and the West.

57. Nikonov, interview of 3 February 1994.

58. Louisa Vinton, "Poland's 'Little Constitution' Clarifies Walesa's Power," *RFE/RL Research Report* 1 (4 September 1992): 19.

59. Paen, interview of 28 January 1994.

60. Rumyantsev, comments, 101.

political institutions to develop and endure, expanding their legitimacy and authority with their very persistence.[61]

Political parties can play a vital role in this process. As they grow stronger, they can help educate the public about the issues while instilling greater discipline and professionalism among the elites. To enhance their own appeal, parties will develop innovative solutions and press the government to select the most effective ones. This is essential, as the ineffectiveness of governmental institutions and policies during the last decade has been most responsible for reducing their legitimacy and authority in the public eye. In the campaign and aftermath of the December 1995 parliamentary and June 1996 presidential elections, a new stage of party development has been reached. Previously, "free elections [had] produced too many parties with too little effective political organization."[62] Parties must now work to unite the discipline of the old order with the legality and constitutionalism of the new.[63] Consistent party-line voting, though occasionally harmful (as with the voting patterns of nationalist and fascist deputies), is critically necessary to the ordering of the system. Thus has the Communist Party proven so successful, maintaining party discipline and unity and thereby scoring impressive electoral victories, while the democrats have divided their paltry share of the electorate with three uncooperative and unfriendly parties led by Grigory Yavlinsky, Yegor Gaidar, and Boris Fyodorov, Russia's three pre-eminent reformers. Their willingness to cooperate only in the most extreme circumstances, in the end, greatly undermines their collective influence.

Party building will surely be a painstaking task, as the public is now more focused on their own business than on politics. Yet it is no less crucial for its difficulty. With the recent round of national elections behind them, the parties should take their efforts beyond urban areas to the provinces, where they still "mean nothing" to the people.[64] By focusing on local and regional elections, parties can arouse public interest in the political issues of the day and thereby acquire greater political clout throughout the country.[65]

61. Sergei Stankevich, "Why I Will Vote Aye," *Rossiiskaya Gazeta*, 11 December 1993.

62. Rose, "Postcommunism and the Problem of Trust," 25–26.

63. Burlatski, interview of 1 February 1994.

64. Zorkin, interview of 2 February 1994. His involvement in the formation of a new opposition party in late 1994 may explain his avid interest in party politics during our interview.

65. Parties rooted in local politics, furthermore, are more likely to be liberal or centrist, rather than conservative. Donna Bahry and Lucan Way, "Citizen Activism in the Russian Transition," *Post-Soviet Affairs* 10 (October–December 1994): 364.

Which is not to say that elections are the answer to all that ails Russian politics. While some, such as Aleksandr Yakovlev, place great faith in the educative power of elections, others express doubts in this regard. David Lempert argues that Russians still need to develop the habits of democracy and thus may need more than occasional elections at this stage. With elections alone, he suggests, the norm of democratic rule becomes: "I vote, You vote, He/She votes, We vote. They rule."[66]

Furthermore, elections must be carefully regulated to avoid domination by the influence of old regime elites and the wealth of nouveaux riches criminal businessmen. When effectively regulated and supplemented by additional mechanisms of democratic control, however, elections can serve a valuable function. This is especially true given a constitution that lacks "serious guarantees against authoritarianism" and the ability to constrain its executive branch without active public support for the legislature and vocal opposition to the concentration of power in the hands of the president.[67]

Ultimately, strong political parties will likely be a key factor in the emergence of constitutionalism. With weak political parties, even the avoidance of authoritarianism does not guarantee democracy. Instead, corporatism will develop. In such a scenario, a variety of large official and semi-official organizations will dominate Russian civil society. This scenario, with "no political parties, but political departments of big corporations," may best describe the direction of Russia preceding the 1995 and 1996 elections. Should this persist, subsequent elections can be expected to be increasingly commercial and undemocratic, degenerating finally into "a public auction or sale."[68] Politics will no longer be a public commodity, but a private one. To avoid such a crisis, the branches of government must continue to work together to carry forward effective reforms that will garner the support of the masses and, with time, make them an indispensable part of the political process.

Rhetoric

Essential to any move toward compromise and cooperation is the rhetoric that surrounds and defines it. A public rhetoric of constitutionalism must

66. Lempert, "The Proposed Constitution of Ukraine," 294 n. 33. See also Lempert, "Changing Russian Political Culture," 636.

67. Burlatski, interview of 1 February 1994.

68. Olshanski, interview of 2 February 1994. Arguably, this degradation has already taken place.

thus be encouraged and more thoroughly integrated into the constitutional and political process. Officials should make a particular effort to speak to the constitution and its norms as much as possible. As Vladimir Entin insisted during the *perestroika* period, "modern Soviet law needs *glasnost* for its legitimation."[69]

A public discourse of constitutionalism is critical to the emergence of the constitution as a reality of Russian life. Such rhetoric does not consist of words disconnected from reality, as epitomized by the inflated exhortations of Leonid Brezhnev and Konstantin Chernenko. On account of seventy years of such nonsense, "the difference between reality and appearance became institutionalized in Russia."[70] Rather, constitutional and legal issues must fill the mouths, and therefore occupy the minds, of government officials. At first these efforts may be conscious and the result of artifice and design; yet gradually such thinking will become natural and take on substantive meaning.

Even if most of Russia's political activity still "happens above or below or in other spheres than the constitution," Vyacheslav Nikonov suggests government officials should present the constitution as critical to their work.[71] Only then will constitutional terms of reference begin to permeate public discourse, strengthening the foundations of civil society. Rhetoric's positive power is evidenced through consideration of the proven influence of negative polemic. The ill effects of the Bolsheviks' bitter denunciation of democracy early this century thus can still be felt in the suspicious mind-set with which most Russians have approached the democratization of their country.[72] More recently, from 1991 to 1993, the liberal movement's virulent attacks on the standing 1978 Russian constitution were a grave error that undermined its own cause more than any other.

Yeltsin once asked *Izvestiia*, attacking the 1978 constitution: "How can we demand that the Constitution be respected when the process of creating it has been fraught with infringements of the law?"[73] Yet subsequently, these very words would be read back to Yeltsin with regard to his own constitution.

---

69. Entin, "Law and Glasnost," 103.

70. Biryukov, interview of 18 November 1993.

71. Nikonov, interview of 3 February 1994.

72. Sergeyev and Biryukov, *Russia's Road to Democracy*, 45. Increasingly, however, public suspicion is also based on democracy's failure to halt Russia's growing crime wave and to raise the standard of living.

73. *Izvestiia*, 17 November 1993, quoted in Semler, "The End of the First Russian Republic," 110.

Thus the liberals' "severe criticism, often unjust, fed legal cynicism towards all legal norms," says Vladimir Lafitski, "including those later espoused in vain by the liberals themselves."[74] The tradition of which Lafitski was a part—that of the Supreme Soviet's Constitutional Commission—more appropriately, and quite consciously, attempted to use constitutional talk to build legal consciousness.

Constitutional propaganda, in the Russian sense of the word, must strive to place not only the president and parliament but the constitution as well at the center of public discourse. Though indirect in their influence, words remain quite powerful. Thus was Yeltsin's call for "trust . . . forgiveness," and "real collaboration" in his 24 February 1994 State of the Union address so important to the evolution of constitutionalism, especially following, as it did, the Duma's recent amnesty of his most bitter opponents.[75] Real collaboration, Yeltsin's words suggested to the public, truly might be possible.

The television broadcast of this address and other positive political activities will only enhance their educative function. Televising the early sessions of the Soviet Congress of People's Deputies thus allowed for "constant communication" between the people and their representatives.[76] Likewise, the coverage of candidate debates during the March 1989 election of deputies invited the public to join in the political process. The return to this practice during the recent cycle of national elections should be extended to local districts as elections are carried out this level.

As such efforts continue, a "reciprocal process" of public-elite interaction will emerge.[77] Official rhetoric should focus increasingly on constitutionalism, as with the State Legal Administration's expanding efforts to educate the public about the substantive meaning and relevance of pending laws.[78] With this, the public will develop a greater awareness of constitutionalism and will in turn put more sustained pressure on their representatives to abide by the law, to translate their words into deeds, and to press on with their legislative work. In this dialectic manner, suggests Yakovlev, "by changing social institutions and roles, we will hopefully change the behavior of those who agree to fill those roles."[79]

74. Lafitski, interview of 31 January 1994.

75. Address to the Federal Assembly, Moscow Television, 24 February 1994; translation available in *FBIS Daily Report: Central Eurasia,* 24 February 1994.

76. Entin, "Law and Glasnost," 111.

77. Migranyan, interview of 4 February 1994.

78. Huskey, "The State-Legal Administration," 132.

79. Yakovlev, interview of 5 February 1994.

The rhetoric of human rights, which has been important since the rise of the Russian dissident movement in the 1960s and especially during the latter half of the 1980s, must be actively invoked, as human rights remain "the biggest issue in Russian legal consciousness."[80] For the general public, the concept of universal human rights is still the most understandable aspect of constitutionalism, so a concerted emphasis on their place and protection in the new Russia will likely command public attention. Russia continues to have a mixed record in this area; though substantial human rights protections have been adopted on paper, concrete mechanisms for the defense and restitution of rights remain weak. However, the institutions that do exist, such as the newly created post of "ombudsman for human rights,"[81] can play a vital role as they interact with the public. Sergei Kovalov has thus described the ombudsman and other human-rights institutions' most important task as shifting public consciousness from a sense of granted rights to one of inalienable rights.[82]

Kovalov was a Soviet political prisoner who later served as chairman of the Human Rights Committee of the Russian Supreme Soviet and now actively leads the effort to bring human rights to the forefront of government policy. After his appointment as head of Yeltsin's informal human-rights commission and as the Duma's human-rights ombudsman, Kovalov filled these posts until the spring of 1995, when he began to do his job too well, calling attention to the gross violations of human rights in Chechnya; unsurprisingly, this led to his abrupt removal from office. The president and parliament must again unite to reinvigorate this important institution.

With the end of the linkage of individual rights and duties, inculcated in article 125 of the 1936 constitution (the exercise of individual liberties had "to strengthen the socialist system") and article 50 of the 1977 constitution (rights had to be exercised "in accordance with the people's interests"), the shift in public psychology toward inalienable rights can begin. As rights are increasingly understood as inviolable, in turn, the people's sense of their place in the system and their authority within it will grow stronger.

The mass media must recognize its responsibility in the emergence of constitutional rhetoric as well. The Russian press, which is gradually freeing itself from the few remaining constraints that have survived the Soviet period (a process the political elites must continue to support),[83] must become a

---

80. Yegorov, interview of 2 February 1994.

81. Article 103, section 1(e).

82. Sergei Kovalov, member of the Russian Supreme Soviet, 5 August 1993.

83. The presidential apparatus still has some control over the media, as it controls the

dispassionate educator of public mores. Notwithstanding a massive decline in readership, the press, which remains far more widely read in Russia than in the West, can affect public consciousness dramatically. This was apparent at the start of *perestroika,* when papers released from censorship had an "unprecedented influence on the public."[84]

The mass media is therefore among the central players in the development of constitutionalism.[85] Rather than pandering to the degraded standards of communication increasingly common on the street, the media should strive to uphold civil conduct and the highest standards of public discourse. "It is time," Yakovlev urges, "for the media to become less negative, more positive, [and] more creative."[86] The media must increase and improve its coverage of constitutional issues. Former television shows on the law, such as *Man and the Law* and *600 Seconds,* proved extremely popular and can serve as models for new programs designed to capture public interest while also increasing public understanding of and participation in the political and legal process.

This is not to suggest that the media should shy away from incisive coverage of government corruption and other controversial political and social issues; such coverage is, in fact, essential. Journalists must simply approach these issues with the highest standards of integrity and quality. By breaking away from long traditions of political bias and from a tendency toward one-sided discussion of issues, problems that have survived the worst excesses of Soviet *Pravda,* the Russian mass media can offer its audiences a rational analysis of issues that will foster the emergence of civil society and constitutional order in Russia.

This was apparent in the significant impact independent television had in shaping public opinion on the Chechen war. By televising the realities of the conflict, the media forced the Yeltsin administration to be honest and forthcoming in its official reports on the war, a critical element of constitutionalism with little previous history in Russia. While detrimental to the short-term stability of the Yeltsin presidency, the long-term contribution of the media with reference to Chechnya was truly historic.

---

allocation of paper subsidies and television broadcasting. A disturbing recent trend in efforts to control the media was manifest in the July 1995 criminal suit brought against NTV, an independent television network, for libel of the president.

84. Sergeyev and Biryukov, *Russia's Road to Democracy,* 87; see 87–90.

85. N. P. Koldaeva, "Separation of Powers in the USSR: Emerging Theory," in Butler, *Perestroika and the Rule of Law,* 128.

86. Yakovlev, *The Bear That Wouldn't Dance,* 235.

Federalism

Federalism has long been at the heart of Russia's constitutional order, though often more in name than in reality. Since the earliest years of Soviet rule, the Union's shape and character have been hotly debated and carefully constructed to serve the regime's political goals. Federalism remains central for modern Russia, with its eighty-nine constituent subjects—twenty-one ethnic republics and varying numbers of other entities, including autonomous republics, *krai*, and oblasts.[87] For Vladimir Kudriavtsev, in fact, "all else means nothing when compared with the federal question."[88]

Although President Yeltsin's nationalities' adviser Emil Paen once argued that federalism was no longer an issue after the adoption of the 1993 constitution, it is more meaningful to think of its relevance as having changed, not disappeared.[89] As evidenced by the huge impact of the war in Chechnya on Russian national politics and on public attitudes toward President Yeltsin's regime (cutting his approval in half), the federal question remains a crucial aspect of the constitutional order and may significantly contribute to the development of constitutionalism from below or to the dislocation of Russia.

The 1993 constitution most significantly impacted on federalism with its equalization of the status of the various constituent subjects.[90] Article 5(4) thus declares that "all subjects of the Russian Federation, in relation to the federal bodies of state power, are legally equal among themselves." In a significant break with past practice, the ethnic republics no longer enjoy a privileged status, as regards taxation and natural-resource control, vis-á-vis the more numerous non-ethnic regions. Unlike the regions, the republics have retained the right to have their own constitutions under article 5(2),[91] and language rights under article 68(2), but they have lost their "sovereign" status as well as "dual citizenship" authority. More important in latter-day Russia, the republics' autonomous control over taxation and natural resources has been dramatically reduced.

---

87. For a further consideration of the politics of particular ethnic groups, see Sharlet, "Russia's 'Ethnic' Republics," 39–46.

88. Kudriavtsev, interview of 31 January 1994.

89. Paen, interview of 28 January 1994. On Russian federalism generally, see Hoffmann, 43–45.

90. While Yeltsin's July draft also included an equality provision, inclusion in the earlier draft of the Federation Treaty, with its provisions for varying treatment, directly contradicted this notion.

91. The regions may have charters.

The latter aspects of an effective fiscal federalism are of the highest priority for Russia today. As trade barriers are raised across the country, the federal government must exercise its authority to keep the nation economically united. This is critical to the Federation's economic viability as well as that of its constituent parts.

The final draft of the constitution dropped the Federation Treaty from its text. Actually a combination of three separate treaties, the Federation Treaty was hastily negotiated in March 1992 in preparation for the Sixth Congress of People's Deputies in April 1992 and was to be included as part of any new constitution.[92] Most important, the decentralizing Federation Treaty constitutionalized the disparate treatment of the Federation's regions and republics. It also required over one hundred laws to execute it, few of which were ever passed.[93] Its vagueness, thus, had often "proven more of a hindrance than a guide to resolving the questions involving local power."[94] Consequently, Yeltsin was probably wise to excise it from the constitution.[95] This decision to drop the treaty and to give the constitution a more centrist tone had its consequences, however. In twelve republics, majorities failed to be secured in support of the revised constitution in the December referendum. This was to be expected, though, and is not an obstacle to a new federal order.

On the basis of this constitution, notwithstanding provisions such as article 72, with its long list of poorly defined areas of joint jurisdiction, federalism can play a constructive role in the development of constitutionalism. Russia may now create a true federation that will encourage experimentation and diversity together with cooperation and unity, the hallmarks of effective federal unions such as the United States. This nation recognized two hundred years ago that a unitary national government does not have the flexibility to discover and implement the best approaches to the myriad issues that face its diverse constituencies. Thus did it concede considerable political power and independence to state and local governments.

Russia, in the midst of recreating itself, should do no less. It must "move the authority of norm decision making down the chain of command to the

92. See Aleksandr Yakovlev, "To Build the Russian Federation," *Parker School Journal of East European Law* 1, no. 1 (1994): 1–22.

93. Sharlet, "Russian Constitutional Crisis," 322.

94. Semler, "Summer in Russia," 21.

95. The demotion of the Federation Treaty from a constitutional to a subconstitutional document (by section II, article 1 of the constitution) leaves its present status and juridical force unclear.

oblasts and *krai*," developing regional centers like St. Petersburg, Nizhni Novgorod, and Yaroslavl to their full potential.[96] Resources, including both international assistance and domestic tax revenues, should be channeled into the development of local governments, where moderate and practical politics and policies will dominate, and where the shift to constitutional modes of governance must take place.[97] As the constitution dictates, local control must not be interpreted to mean regional sovereignty—including the right to unilateral secession and the supremacy of regional constitutions—as this represents the abandonment of stability for flexibility. As even Elena Lukasheva, a human-rights scholar, warns: "If Russia had gone on this path of letting the regions separate, nothing good would have come of it."[98] The creation of new constitutional norms would have been impossible in such an environment. Decisions on the status of the subjects of the Federation must instead be made in a consultative manner through which they become binding. Should each subject have the authority to change its status at will, as the city of Sverdlovsk attempted to do, absurdly declaring itself the Urals Republic in June 1994,[99] the existing constitutional order would become a mockery.[100]

The separate agreements signed by the central government with Tatarstan[101] and Bashkortostan[102] soon after the constitution's adoption were thus problematic. There are strong arguments that practical politics require some concession to the divergent conditions and economic status of the various subjects, and that bilateral agreements may address this while reducing the unitarism of the present constitutional order. Care should be taken, however, to avoid extreme asymmetries in the status of subjects and a resulting race to the bottom, with regional sovereignty or de facto independence soon on the negotiating table.[103]

The inevitable consequence of such exceptions is represented by Chechnya's

96. Yakovlev, interview of 5 February 1994.

97. The establishment of civic organizations such as the League of Russian Cities, a recently formed consultative group, are evidence that this process has begun.

98. Lukasheva, interview of 11 August 1993.

99. A declaration that met with a swift response from the federal government, which annulled the decision and removed the regional governor from office. Sharlet, "The Prospects for Federalism," 122.

100. See Sharlet, "The Prospects for Federalism," 122.

101. Reached after three years of negotiations, on 15 February 1994.

102. Signed on 25 May 1994, this agreement acknowledged Bashkortostan's "sovereignty" but failed to define this term in any detail.

103. Sharlet, "The Prospects for Federalism," 126.

later demands for even greater autonomy than that granted to Tatarstan and Bashkortostan, demands that erupted into brutal violence in December 1994 and into the deadly conflict between Russian and Chechen troops that ravaged the region for nearly two years. The domino effect of these side agreements also inspired the demands of Tatarstan and Bashkortostan's neighbor, the Urals oblast of Perm (once simply a city), that it be treated equally with its neighbors. Arguing that it was paying more taxes and had less control over its resources than Tatarstan and Bashkortostan, Perm suspended its agreement to the April 1994 Treaty on Social Accord on 18 August 1994, provoking the drafting of yet another side agreement with it later that month.

Such inconsistency and potential instability in the federal order has been institutionalized in a presidential commission specifically responsible for the negotiation of such bilateral power-sharing treaties.[104] The potential ill effects of this are great. The centrifugal pressure in Russia must be kept in check by reducing flagrant inconsistencies in the status of the various subjects, rather than adding to them. These differences, after all, were the source of federal discontent in the first place.[105] Only by binding all subjects by the terms of the constitution will an effective federal state thus emerge. In this respect, the constitution's leveling of the federal order must be made a reality.

As meta-relations stabilize and local institutions expand their authority and become more effective, constructive relations between the federal elites and regional officials must be encouraged. The Federation Council, comprised of two representatives from each of the eighty-nine subjects, can help make this possible, acting as a bridge between the federal government and the local parliaments and executives whom they represent.[106] The activities of local officials are more familiar to the people and can play a far greater role in educating the public about the relevance of constitutional structures, both national and local, to their own daily lives. Standing in the middle of the chain of political authority extending from the citizen to the national bodies of power in Moscow, the regional elites have a "uniquely powerful role to play at this point in the history of Russia."[107]

---

104. Robert Sharlet, "The New Russian Constitution and Its Political Impact," *Problems of Post-Communism* 42 (January–February 1995): 7.

105. In 1993, 0.1 percent of the tax revenues of Tatarstan went to the federal government, while 60 percent of those of Krasnoyarsk did. Troyitski, interview of 20 July 1993.

106. Zorkin, interview of 2 February 1994.

107. Klamkin, interview of 4 February 1994.

"Mass psychology will develop not from the highest levels of power, but vice versa, from the lowest. History shows us no other way."[108] Accordingly, an effective federal system must encourage the public to recognize the parallels between their local police marshal and the president as wielders of executive authority, and to see their town councils as local forms of the Duma and Federation Council. This orientation will inspire an understanding, otherwise impossible to achieve, of these national bodies' operations. In short, the lowest rungs on the ladder of political authority must become "places of education . . . which create a real political base for the entire constitutional order."[109]

Local power is critical to constitutionalism's emergence from below. The period of *perestroika* from 1985 to 1988, reflects Nina Belyaeva, was an initial "era of system reconstruction controlled by Gorbachev," only after which lasting change began to emerge—from below.[110] This shift was necessary if the people were ever to understand and respect the law. In the new Russia, the evolution of constitutionalism continues to "depend on solving grass-roots political problems."[111]

"Most real things are still at the bottom level—the Russia of the towns and villages is where the real Russia begins and ends."[112] Until now, a focus on the center has limited legal consciousness to a respect for who is on top and, only by association, for what are seen as derivatives of this individual— the constitution and its institutions. With growing local authority, alternative nodes of power will develop and expand the scope of constitutionalism.

The public, in touch with local issues and their local representatives, will come to better understand the importance and potential impact of voter participation. They hardly do today. Local elections are essential to remedying this state of affairs. Beginning at the community level, where people best understand the tasks and responsibilities of their governors, the public will learn to "choose better leaders with better character," ensuring effective governance at all levels.[113]

Of course, federalism has its side effects: occasional extremism, and even the possibility of ethnic tension and conflict. In regions where the old guard is powerfully entrenched, calls will be heard for the precedence of conser-

108. Olshanski, interview of 2 February 1994.
109. Burlatski, interview of 1 February 1994.
110. Belyaeva, "Russian Democracy," 8.
111. Mishin, interview of 14 August 1993.
112. Marchenko, interview of 31 January 1994.
113. Zorkin, interview of 2 February 1994.

vative local over reformist national laws. Furthermore, as manifest by the rise of Zhirinovsky and General Aleksandr Lebed, and by the return of Aleksandr Rutskoi to the political field, the rise of a violent nationalism in reaction to the decentralization of authority remains a serious threat. As Carl Linden notes: "Nationalism and democracy were . . . born twins, one after the other, fraternal but not identical. With the kinship also comes antithesis. Yeltsin has striven to build the new Russia on the affinity, and his nationalist (and neo-communist) opponents on the counterpoint, between them; the first relies on a civic patriotism, and the second on imperial patriotism."[114]

That the latter will prove victorious over the former is not yet a foregone conclusion, contrary to media tales of the rise of the right. An enlightened patriotism thus remains a real possibility and potential substitute for virulent nationalism in Russia.

Moreover, the constitutional order's increasing legitimacy and strong roots at all levels of government will make it far easier for the national government to resist these tendencies. Nongovernmental bodies now entering the political playing field will also help stabilize public views by connecting them to the actual processes of governance and by developing special relations with public organs similar to those that have evolved over the years in western democracies.[115] This will also help prevent the type of rift between the political elites and the masses that radical reforms in Russia have traditionally created through their noninclusive formulation and character.[116]

Beyond such arguments for decentralization, however, lies the recognition that a decade of weak federalism and a centralized approach have clearly proven inadequate. With a more effective federal approach, the center and the regions will each have their legitimate scope of authority, within which they may better fulfill their duties and responsibilities, thereby furthering the process of reform and reconstruction. The growing recognition of the advantages of this approach is manifest by the wide range of flexibility for local adjustment that the 1994 National Education Program allows.

Changes are still necessary in the regions. Many have been dominated by their executive officials since the dissolution of the local soviets in October

---

114. Linden, "The Dialectic of Russian Politics," 11.
115. Ametistov, interview of 4 February 1994.
116. Walter Murphy, professor of politics, Princeton University. Comments at presentation of Nikolai Biryukov, Princeton University, 15 November 1993.

1993. Many regional constitutions continue to contradict the federal constitution. Yet these issues can be resolved with time. The willingness of the Federation Council, earlier expected to become a passive tool of the president, to instead resist pressure from him is evidence of the fact that federalism has survived the transition to the Second Russian Republic and may yet thrive.[117] This unexpected resistance has included decisions to repeatedly reject Yeltsin's choice of Aleksei Ilyushenko as procurator general through 1994 and 1995 and to actively oppose, together with the Duma, Yeltsin's invasion of Chechnya.

If change is ever to come to Russia, it will be from the bottom. If constitutionalism is ever to emerge, it will be from below. As Blair Ruble succinctly notes: "It is precisely at the level of a single provincial town that the potential for a new democratic Russia is most unmistakable."[118]

Corruption

Particularly threatening to constitutionalism's future in Russia is the public perception of political corruption as part and parcel of the reform process, a problem whose existence prior to December 1993 has only been aggravated since.[119] This issue is thus central to our discussion. Given the dangers that growing government corruption poses, it can no longer be ignored if constitutionalism is to take root either within Russian politics or in society at large.

Corruption is hardly new to Russia. Within a year of their revolution, the Bolsheviks had to address this problem by issuing their November 1918 decree, "On the Strict Observance of the Law." Government corruption continued to be prevalent and familiar to the public throughout Soviet rule; however, state domination of the mass media deprived it of the persistent attention it has received of late.[120] The public expected little better of the

117. Huskey, "The State-Legal Administration," 121 n. 22.

118. Cited in Hoffmann, 44.

119. The rise of organized crime, and its linkage to political corruption, is explored infra, in the "Economy" section.

120. Public enthusiasm for Leonid Brezhnev's rhetoric of law and order, and especially for Andropov's discipline campaign, directed as it was against government corruption as well as worker absenteeism, suggests both a public awareness of and an interest in corruption in the Soviet years.

Soviet bureaucracy and since the economy was generally stable and the quality of life adequate for most, corruption was a relatively minor concern. With notable exceptions, such as the vigorously prosecuted Great Caviar Scandal, which achieved national notoriety in the early 1980s, political corruption did not elicit a public outcry; it simply inspired a plentitude of Russia's renowned anecdotes. One such tale spoke of General Secretary Leonid Brezhnev taking his mother, who was visiting Moscow from her Ukrainian home, to visit his many dachas by private helicopter. "Beautiful," she tells him, having seen them all. "But Lonya, what will happen if the Communists come back?"

Were they to come back today, the Communists would probably find few surprises. Other than the sums exchanged, little has substantially changed in terms of bureaucratic corruption. As Yeltsin's former press secretary, Pavel Voschanov, has aptly remarked: "The criminal party has left the stage, but the criminal state has remained."[121] Yet public perceptions and expectations have shifted 180 degrees since 1985; accusations of corruption have become the most damaging political attack on any party or person. This was exemplified in the wave of public outcry over corruption that began with former security minister Viktor Barannikov's July 1993 allegations (made after his forced resignation from the Government) of deep-seated corruption in the highest ranks of the Yeltsin administration.[122] These charges were followed by a series of counteraccusations and responses that targeted a wide spectrum of officials, including several apparently innocent bystanders whose only fault was their political position. This flurry of activity during the summer and fall of 1993 affected public trust in the government no less than had the Watergate scandal in the United States twenty years earlier.

The conflict Barannikov began may have made political corruption and its consequences, both direct and indirect, the most powerful threat to constitutionalism today. In the midst of this battle, Vladimir Kudriavtsev expressed his fear that "this war of words could undermine all that we have done, leading the people back into the past."[123]

Though the people "did not believe in [government] power even before," adds his colleague Elena Lukasheva, "now their belief or lack of belief actually means something."[124] Mass legal consciousness and faith in the

---

121. Quoted in Michael Dobbs, "Mobsters in Red Square," *Washington Post Book World,* 13 August 1995, 4.
122. Marchenko, interview of 31 January 1994.
123. Kudriavtsev, interview of 17 August 1993.
124. Lukasheva, interview of 1 February 1994.

system are now critical to the Russian political order. In Russia's fledgling democratic system, only consistent public support will ensure the stability and success of political and legal transitions. As Erik Hoffmann reflects,

> Some national legislators' and executives' desire for personal aggrandizement and the rampant corruption in Russian society are a lethal mix. Money and power go hand in hand in virtually all political systems, but the temptations for Russian officials to use elected and appointed positions for personal gain and the opportunities for mafiosi to buy political offices and preferential treatment are enormous.[125]

If corrupt practices in government persist, they will inevitably spread to the nongovernmental *intelligentsia,* destroying respect for the law among the entire class of elites. As one worker struggles by on his meager official salary but watches daily as his coworker arrives in a new Mercedes, the appeal of the rule of law is likely to die a quick death. Money will displace the law, and even rank, as the final arbiter of power. Corrupt practices will spread both across and along the chain of command, becoming a malignancy impossible to excise. "Such a thorough infiltration into the society means that it ceases to be a crime problem and becomes a political phenomenon."[126] With more than 46,000 government officials in Russia prosecuted on charges relating to corruption and abuse of office in 1993, this is already true.[127] As one newspaper commented: "Only lazy people do not take bribes these days."[128]

Rather than a speculative doomsday scenario, this is the daily reality of Italy and Japan today, where corruption has frayed the very fabric of the political order. In these settings the removal of corruption cannot be distinguished from the dismemberment of the entire political system.[129] Yet

---

125. Hoffmann, 43.
126. Shelley, "Organized Crime," 56.
127. Handelman, *Comrade Criminal,* 285. Registration of a bank is now reported to cost eighty thousand dollars, while a 15 percent commission is necessary for receipt of an oil-export license. Ariel Cohen, "Crime Without Punishment," *Journal of Democracy* 6 (April 1995): 36.
128. Quoted in Handelman, *Comrade Criminal,* 286.
129. Arguably, Russia could do worse than become another Italy or Japan. The former and latter, however, were not built by corruption but developed notwithstanding it. Russia is unlikely to be so lucky. See Martin Malia, "Russia's Democratic Future: Hope Against Hope," *Problems of Post-Communism* 41 (Fall 1994): 33 ("This is not the parasitical mafia of long-developed economies; it is almost a functional aspect of [the] market . . .").

Russia may produce an even uglier scenario if recent events typify the norm.

The July 1993 killing of a parliamentary deputy by known members of organized crime, allegedly as reprisal for a failed business deal, was ignored by most. Such things, thought the resigned public, will happen. This was followed by the April 1994 murder of Andrei Aizderdzis, another member of the Duma and a former entrepreneur with ties to several criminal organizations involved in banking and metals export. Most important, however, he had recently financed publication of a list of 260 prominent "shadow businessmen" in Russia.[130]

Only days later, when thirty-three-year-old Deputy Sergei Skorochkin drew forth his Kalashnikov to exchange shots with mobsters who had attacked him, killing one of his assailants, Russians began to wonder about their deputies. Skorochkin thereafter revealed his former ties to a crime gang that had financed his election campaign and was now demanding extortion money in return.[131] In the final chapter of this tale, Russians were not surprised, in March 1995, to learn that the police had discovered Skorochkin's body in the woods outside Moscow, handcuffed and with a bullet in his head.[132]

Thus has it become increasingly clear that a "symbiotic relationship exists between organized crime and post-Soviet national, local, and municipal governments." In its most absurdist form, this is manifest in the financing of political campaigns, such as that of Skorochkin, by organized crime groups.[133] At its worst extreme, however, we have the election of Sergei Mavrodi to the Duma in a 1995 midterm bielection. Mavrodi, whose campaign consisted in large part of the distribution of money and goods to voters, ran for parliament for the singular perk of immunity from prosecution. This is unsurprising, as he faced serious fraud charges arising from the failure of his multimillion-dollar stock fund, MMM, a Ponzi scheme that collapsed on itself in late 1994.[134]

---

130. Handelman, *Comrade Criminal,* 312.

131. Handelman, *Comrade Criminal,* 312.

132. This pattern shows no signs of abatement. On 26 November 1995, Deputy Sergei Markidonov was murdered by his own bodyguard while campaigning for reelection in his Siberian hometown. Less than two weeks later, on 8 December, Mikhail Lezhnev, another Duma candidate, was shot to death on the doorstep of his home.

133. Shelley, "Organized Crime," 57.

134. Also featured prominently in Mavrodi's campaign was his pledge to his shareholders (36,000 in the electoral district) that he would repay their losses if he was elected. One would imagine that this may have played some part in his victory, with some 40,000 votes. With his election, however, Mavrodi blithely declared that he would not be participating in the sessions

In this world of money politics, the lines between truth and deception, between right and wrong, have become blurred. No longer does anyone appear to be above or beyond the reach of corruption's invisible hand. Absent regulatory and disciplinary measures, individual bureaucrats begin to feel that anything is possible, if not permissible. And as new players enter the system, they too are caught up in its privileges and perquisites, creating a self-cycling process impossible to turn around. Former Party elites, having taken the money and run, are now Russia's crime lords;[135] criminals, meanwhile, enter politics to protect themselves from prosecution. Thus, in the December 1995 parliamentary elections there were eighty-seven criminals and suspected criminals up for election.

Corruption breeds inefficiency and ineffectiveness, great dangers for Russia. Estimates suggest crime cartels have raised prices between 20 and 30 percent. Privatization has been hindered, if not entirely co-opted, on account of criminal efforts to prevent public participation in property auctions and to solicit investment into fraudulent funds and enterprises. Such ill-gotten gains then flow out of the country, instead of being reinvested in Russia's sustained economic growth.

Yet even more threatening is corruption's impact on public attitudes toward constitutive government and the law. Amidst a barrage of media coverage of government corruption, how meaningful is the rhetoric of law? When common citizens hear regularly that their congressman or cabinet minister has engaged in theft or circumvention of the law, why should they not do likewise? If officials are embezzling millions of dollars, why not forge a benefit check or remove a few coins from the till? Glaring accusations of corruption, such as those made in July 1993 by Vice President Aleksandr Rutskoi against former first deputy prime minister (and later chairman of the Federation Council) Vladimir Shumeiko and Yeltsin's press spokesman Mikhail Poltoranin, loosen the fabric of the entire social and political order[136] and produce an environment in which "no one trusts the government, but only himself." Even if the charges were true, suggests Vladimir

---

very much, as he was a businessman, not a politician, and that he had run only to secure his immunity from prosecution. "Honestly speaking," he told a journalist, "I do not think I will be attending the Duma very often." "Constitution Watch-Russia," *East European Constitutional Review* 4 (Winter 1995): 29.

The refusal of the Duma, however, to seat him, an act of moral—if not much legal—merit, deprived him of his hoped-for goal.

135. Former communist *apparatchiki* comprise 80 percent of Russia's wealthiest citizens.
136. Semler, "Summer in Russia," 22.

Lafitski, who views them with a sympathetic eye, the vituperative politics that shaped their presentation by Yeltsin's opponents did more damage than good.[137]

More recently, public and media backlash against political corruption reached Prime Minister Chernomyrdin, who was accused of amassing huge wealth through his political support for the gas industry he formerly worked in, and Ivan Rybkin, chairman of the Duma, who was accused of using government funds to buy patio furniture and ship it back to Russia after an official visit to the United States.[138] Whether true or not, such charges are undermining faith in the entire class of political elites and in the constitutional system with which they are associated.

Even if corruption remains limited, there is no realistic way to distinguish the exception from the rule. If one minister has cheated, the public will assume that all the others are doing so as well but are simply too smart to get caught. "If you admit that there is corruption at the top levels, sooner or later someone will think to ask why the system allowed bad people to be at the top in the first place."[139] This state of affairs delegitimates the work of every official, corrupt or otherwise. That liberal politicians, including former Moscow mayor Gavriil Popov and President Yeltsin, appear to have *once* accepted financial support from shadow businessmen in their campaigns for office casts doubt not only on their election, but on all they later do.[140]

A drive to root out corruption is therefore critical. Here too, today's leaders have positive legacies to build on. Foremost among these is Andropov's drive to discipline the bureaucracy, one in which "thousands of government officials were dismissed, demoted, subjected to disciplinary procedures, or charged with crimes." Even though he acted before the political openness and public engagement of recent years, Andropov managed to find the political support for his efforts among the people themselves. "His campaign for discipline struck a responsive chord with a public weary of the mediocrity of everyday life and craving effective leadership to deal with the country's problems."[141]

Reading *mediocrity* as *chaos*, Sharlet's words support the view that public enthusiasm can be generated for a campaign against corruption today as

137. Lafitski, interview of 31 January 1994.
138. Alessandra Stanley, "Russia's New Rulers Govern, and Live, in Neo-Soviet Style," *New York Times*, 23 May 1995, A8.
139. Belyaeva, "Russian Democracy," 7.
140. Handelman, *Comrade Criminal*, 311.
141. Sharlet, *Soviet Constitutional Crisis*, 72–73.

well. During the Gorbachev period, the widely publicized bribery prosecution of Yuri Churbanov, Leonid Brezhnev's son-in-law, is further evidence of the public's interest in political malfeasance and its curtailment. The public character of this latter-day show trial may also hold lessons for subsequent efforts to stamp out corruption.

Channeling the force of public opinion, political will at the top can be concentrated in a rejuvenated Commission on Corruption, established in October 1992 but politicized soon after by its chairman, former vice president Aleksandr Rutskoi, and thereby delegitimized. This body, with a broad investigative mandate and its own staff and investigative personnel, should be designated by Yeltsin and the Duma as the sole forum for identifying political corruption; this will enhance its authority and legitimacy and allow for the quick disposal of spurious claims against innocent officials. The sensitive nature of this issue renders accusations damaging regardless of their veracity. Yeltsin was thus forced to dismiss Shumeiko and Poltoranin, though charges were never brought against them, because of the damage done by the biased prosecutor general's public investigation. The commission, finally, must also be provided with adequate security and benefits to ensure the safety and reliability of its personnel. Only thus can it be a vigorous, effective, and neutral force against corruption.

Those at the very top of the pyramid of power must lend their explicit support to the drive against corruption. Law-enforcement efforts to root out corruption are doomed to fail without such support. This has become apparent to many staunch opponents of corruption in the law-enforcement community, whose efforts in the late 1980s and early 1990s were stymied when they began to reach too high on the lines of power. To reach the source of the corruption they battled, they needed support from those highest on the ladder. Yet this was not forthcoming, and they finally gave up their fight as tilting against windmills.[142] Andropov's efforts proved successful, on the other hand, for just the reason the latter efforts failed; their impetus came from the very top.[143]

142. Handelman, *Comrade Criminal*, 2.
143. There are, of course, threats beyond mere frustration that haunt those committed to battle corruption. Witness the unsolved October 1994 murder of Dmitri Kholodov, a reporter for *Moskovski Komsomolets*, when a briefcase he was told contained evidence of military corruption exploded. Kholodov was actively investigating military corruption and was preparing to testify before the Duma as to his findings. Thankfully, the public outcry that followed Kholodov's murder led to the dismissal of several corrupt military officers, though prosecutions against them did not follow.

To the extent possible, government salaries must be raised to reasonably competitive rates, if officials are actually to resist "the lure of *bizness*."[144] As official paychecks can never realistically keep up with those of the black market, however, financial temptations will persist; especially harsh criminal penalties for corruption, including heavy fines and imprisonment, must therefore also be legislated. Till now penalties have been weak and ineffectual; only 9 percent of those convicted of embezzlement or abuse of position, for example, were sent to prison in 1993.[145] Penalties must thus be stiffened and enforced.

Pending legislation designed to improve the detection of corrupt practices, by requiring the disclosure of assets, among other things, should be promptly adopted and built upon with legislation focused on the ex post facto prosecution of corruption. Till now such prosecutions have been few and far between. They must now be vigorously pursued. The proliferation of Lempert's mechanisms of citizen democracy, including public oversight committees, will place a further check on governmental practices and thereby reduce corruption.[146] The March 1995 announcement of executive decrees limiting administrative agencies' authority to grant special tax and customs exemptions, a major source of corruption, is another sign of progress.

Customary expectations of government perks and privileges must also be adjusted. Though these were standard practice in the tsarist bureaucracy, the Bolshevik Revolution introduced a particularly virulent system of official privilege.[147] This was what government service was all about. Thus, a desire to stay in Moscow for the remaining two years of their term, with the entitlements of deputies, motivated Supreme Soviet deputies' uncompromising attitude in 1993 toward early elections.[148] While these perks and privileges were scaled back dramatically after the August 1991 failed coup, they have gradually returned into common practice.

Thus have special license plates immunizing their holders from traffic citations been reissued to high government officials, after being dispensed with when Yeltsin first came to power in 1991. Similarly have closed hospitals and supermarkets, with unpublished budgets, also been reopened for the government elite. These privileges, along with others including country homes, free travel, and pension raises, are being doled out by both

144. Handelman, *Comrade Criminal*, 287.
145. Handelman, *Comrade Criminal*, 286.
146. See Lempert, "The Proposed Constitution of Ukraine."
147. Lukasheva, interview of 1 February 1994.
148. Kovaldin, interview of 21 July 1993.

the presidential and parliamentary administrations; both share responsibility for their ill effects.

A dramatic and bureaucratically unpopular reduction in privileges must be linked with new regulations on government administration in Russia. These should be designed and adopted by the Duma. Such legislation, regulating itself as well as the broader bureaucracy, will greatly enhance the Duma's authority in the public eye and give a sense of its prioritization of the nation's needs above its own, building public faith in Russia's political institutions. Established western norms and regulatory codes can help guide this effort.

After several declared "wars on crime" during the last several years, deeds must now displace words as the focus of Russian officialdom.[149] Failure to take concrete and effective steps to curtail political corruption now has the potential to jeopardize and undermine the entire post-Communist reform project.

A personal observation may lend some insight into the travails of political ethics in Russia today. Having taken a member of the State Duma to lunch at Pizza Hut, popular among deputies for its proximity to the parliament's offices, I began to pay the bill. This gave rise to a lengthy discussion. Since he had taken the time to see me during what was only the second week of the Duma's very first session, I felt I owed him at least this much in thanks. "No, no!" he protested, only half in jest. "It will look like an American bribe."

"Don't worry," I retorted, "you haven't had time to pass a law on this yet."

"True," he responded, "but then think of the precedent you are setting."
I willingly split the bill down the middle.

Ultimately, efforts to curtail corruption and enhance the flexibility and openness of Russian governmental institutions will require downsizing the bureaucracy. Turning the tide of Gorbachev's reductions, the apparat has exploded in size since the collapse of the August coup. In the words of Eugene Huskey, an expert on Russian state institutions, the presidential administration has become "a bureaucratic leviathan." In 1992 alone, the Russian federal bureaucracy grew more than twice in size, bringing in 194,000 new personnel.[150] Inevitably, such a top-heavy structure will slow

---

149. These include Yeltsin's January 1993 anti-crime package; his 23 February 1994 speech to the Duma on crime; and his June 1994 Anti-Crime Decree.

150. Eugene Huskey, "The Presidency in Russian Politics: A Study of the State-Legal Administration." Unpublished manuscript, 1 n. 35, n. 78.

the process of reform. Knowing full well that more power to the people means less power for itself, the bureaucracy may even attempt to resist meaningful reforms.[151] Thus "it is these holdover legions that first resisted and then virtually halted the Yeltsin-Gaidar reforms."[152] The "*chinovniki* [bureaucrats, with a negative connotation] are rarely oriented toward the defense of human rights or any constitutional norms."[153]

Reductions will not be easy since the system still relies on the same close-knit *nomenklatura* structure it always has.[154] In downsizing the bureaucracy, "one fires a member of a 'family circle' and not just an isolated individual."[155] Notwithstanding these difficulties, however, major reductions will generate positive results: bureaucratic professionalism will increase, improved morale and engaged commitment will follow, and the danger of widespread corruption will begin to recede.

THE LAW

The Constitutional Court

> "A great deal must be done to return the court's legitimacy. I am afraid this will take a long time. And with all that has happened, it will not be easy."[156]

The troubled history of Russia's courts dates back to Tsarina Catherine II's failed attempt to establish a Court of Conscience in 1775. Yet the continued awareness of their importance was evident almost 150 years later, when the Bolsheviks announced their Decree no. 1, "On the Courts," only two weeks after the revolution.[157] Present-day ambivalences toward the courts thus have a long legacy in Russian history. In this light, their modern struggle to

151. Marchenko, interview of 31 January 1994. In the main, the apparat has cooperated with reforms since their positions make them the best equipped to reap the benefits of economic liberalization. See Jerry F. Hough, "Russia: On the Road to Thermidor," *Problems of Post-Communism* 41 (Fall 1994): 30.

152. Malia, "Russia's Democratic Future," 34.

153. Lukasheva, interview of 1 February 1994.

154. See Juviler, "Russia Turned Upside Down," 39.

155. Huskey, "The State-Legal Administration," 137; see 136–38.

156. Ametistov, interview of 4 February 1994.

157. 24 November 1917. "*O Sude*," *Sobranie Uzakonenii 1917–1918*, no. 4, item 150.

establish their place in the political order is unsurprising. Yet acceptance of the supremacy of law and maintenance of interbranch cooperation under the terms of the constitution continue to depend on the development and maturation of the judicial branch.

Developing effective judicial institutions may well be the ultimate key to an effective constitutional transition.[158] It is a sad testimony to the continuing weakness of the third branch, therefore, that its latter-day Court of Conscience—the Constitutional Court—languished in suspension for nearly eighteen months after President Yeltsin "temporarily" suspended it in his infamous Decree no. 1400 of 21 September 1993 and his subsequent Decree no. 1612 of 7 October 1993, on the court especially.[159] Yeltsin's allies insisted this suspension was merely a recommendation to which the court agreed. Yet this seems implausible. At that time more than ever, Yeltsin was not in the habit of making "recommendations." Either way, it was not until nine months later, after some serious question as to the court's survival,[160] that article 125 of the constitution, which reestablished the court, was finally put into effect by the Duma's Law on the Constitutional Court of 12 July 1994.[161] Another nine months would pass, however, before the court finally convened in February 1995.

From October 1994 to February 1995, Yeltsin nominated a series of individuals to the court to fill the six vacancies created by its expansion to nineteen members. Notably, this itself violated the Law on the Court, which required that the six vacancies be filled within thirty days of the adoption of the law. Instead, it took nearly two hundred. Most of his nominees were rejected, however, by the Federation Council, whose consent by an absolute majority is necessary for appointment. While much of the council's opposition to certain candidates was motivated by their close association with the president rather than by any substantive concern with their judicial temperament or qualifications, this approach did serve to promote the creation of a

---

158. Paen, interview of 28 January 1994.

159. *Vedomosti RF,* no. 41, item 3,921 (1993).

160. During October and early November, Yeltsin appeared to be moving toward a decision to merge the Constitutional Court with the Russian Supreme Court, making it simply a special collegium of the latter institution. Broad support for the continued existence of the court by parties across Russian politics, including Yeltsin's allies on the court itself, prevented this. While weakened somewhat by changes made to the July 1993 draft by the reconvened Constitutional Conference in October and November, the court survived into the final draft, adopted in December of that year. See Sharlet, "Russian Constitutional Crisis," 332.

161. *Rossiiskaya Gazeta,* 23 July 1994, 4–7.

court that is politically neutral on the whole. The appointment of two justices with prior judicial experience, moreover, is further evidence of the effectiveness of this process.

With the election of its officers (chair, vice chair, and secretary) in late February 1995 and its adoption of its rules of procedure in March, the new court was ready to hear its first case, as it did on 16 March 1995. Like many of the cases the court would choose to hear in the aftermath of its long suspension and tenuous return to the constitutional playing field, this first one was essentially a technical inquiry. Involving the interpretation and reconciliation of two provisions of the constitution (articles 105 and 106) on the number of days available to the Federation Council to consider bills forwarded to it by the Duma, the case was one of little controversy and even less public interest.

With certain exceptions this would be true of the court's subsequent cases as well, at least during its first two years back in operation. Yet most of its cases also involved some issue of citizen's rights, including the right to strike, to housing (the impermissibility of eviction), to criminal appeals, and to rehabilitation (for victims of Stalinist repression). Consistently, the court ruled with aggrieved plaintiffs in said cases, painting a clear picture, one obscured by the first court, of itself as a haven for citizen's rights.

Tied to the court's concentration on such cases, with low visibility but great impact on individuals, has been the court's avoidance of so-called political questions. The one exception to this rule was their 31 July 1995 decision in the Chechnya case. Therein, after several weeks of hearings, a sharply divided court[162] decided against the Duma and Federation Council, which had challenged Yeltsin's decision to invade Chechnya without their express authorization. While the technical nature of the ruling is beyond the scope of this discussion, it is notable that the two provisions of Yeltsin's decrees the court did invalidate concerned civil rights—namely, the right of the media to cover the war, which Yeltsin had attempted to curtail in order to limit news of the high casualties, and the right to free movement, which the army had made efforts to limit.

Unsurprisingly, the court was attacked for this decision and accused of being biased toward the president, but in the broader context of all its early decisions, it has not shown any such bias. More important, it has managed to maintain its authority and public respect by otherwise avoiding cases of this

---

162. Though, significantly, not divided along the political fault lines (of supporters and opponents of Yeltsin) that had been predicted.

nature. The jurisprudence of the new court, then, has been largely devoid of the prominent, high-stakes cases that the first court made its bread and butter.

Steps to prevent such incursions against the judicial branch as have occurred in the past are critical, as the courts' development is the "only way of progress toward constitutionalism." Without strong courts, every step forward will inevitably fall back.[163] Therefore, the foremost concern of every constitutionalist in Russia should be that the Constitutional Court "emerge from the shadow" to play a prominent role in the public eye, not by entering politics, but by becoming the defender of rights and liberties in Russia.[164]

After years of authoritarianism, the rebirth of public faith in government requires a highly visible, institutional guarantee of its limitation; an unenforceable promise that rights are "natural and inviolable" is insufficient. "It is necessary also to provide a machinery for protecting [those] rights against violation."[165] This is the court's function, one it has finally begun to fulfill.

Every effort must be made to ensure the complete independence of the Constitutional Court. While article 120(1) of the constitution declares that "judges are independent and subordinate only to the Constitution," such words could be found in the Soviet constitutions as well, yet they provided little protection for the judicial officers of that period. As former chairman of the court Valery Zorkin, one who ought to know, has stated: the court can be "effective only if there is a clear separation of powers."[166] Even the appearance of violations of its independence must be avoided. Given a long history of Soviet show trials dating back to the 1922 trial of the oppositionist Socialist Revolutionaries, the courts' legitimacy and authority are themselves now on trial in the public eye. Once seen as "little more than appendages of executive power,"[167] Russia's courts must now "not only be independent in fact, but [be] *seen* to be independent as well."[168]

Yeltsin's forceful comments on the Constitutional Court and its future "restraints," made soon after the December 1993 referendum, were thus untimely.[169] The accusations of executive subordination of a "puppet court"

163. Yegorov, interview of 2 February 1994.

164. Andrei Stepanov, "Grand Piano Lurking in the Bush," *Moskovski Komsomolets*, 5 January 1994.

165. Berman, "The Rule of Law and the Law-Based State," 51.

166. Zorkin, interview of 2 February 1994.

167. Eugene Huskey, "The Administration of Justice," 221.

168. Donald D. Barry, "The Quest for Judicial Independence," in Barry, *Toward the "Rule of Law" in Russia?* 259.

169. As was Yeltsin's decision to give a pay raise to the justices in the midst of their deliberations on the Communist Party case, in which his own decrees were at issue.

that followed, even if limited to the opposition press, aroused public doubt just at the time popular support for the court was most necessary.[170] Thankfully, this has not proven to be true. While the court has not directly faced off with the president in any of its cases, it has shown no tendency to improperly defer to the president's will either.

Both the president and parliament must realize, Justice Zorkin urges, that it is "in their interest for the court to be independent."[171] They must learn to abide by what the court decides and to live within these constraints. Even President Yeltsin managed to do so with the early decisions of the court, such as its annulment in 1991 of his decree merging the KGB and the internal police. With a neutral court now in place, its fellow branches must hold fast to this position. Official pledges by the presidential apparatus and parliamentary structures to refrain from attempts to influence the court will encourage public confidence. The provision of adequate salary benefits to the justices of the Constitutional Court and the judges of the lower courts is also critical, as are grants of life tenure to senior judges.

Thus, the compromise decision to fill the six vacancies on the new nineteen-judge court with twelve-year appointees forbidden to serve second terms was unfortunate.[172] Beyond the oddity of placing thirteen judges with life tenure on the same bench as six "junior" justices with twelve-year terms, the latter will clearly be far more open to political pressure than their peers; this applies especially to the several newly appointed justices who are younger and can be expected to continue a career in Russian politics after their terms expire. Continued control of the justices' benefits and living amenities by bureaucrats in the presidential administration must also end. This is a dangerous mechanism of extrinsic pressure on the court[173] and must be replaced with a system in which adequate salary benefits will allow justices to handle their own personal finances.

The court remains a potent public symbol and "much now depends on how it will behave."[174] If, as it did under the interim chairmanship of Vladimir Tumanov in 1995 and 1996, it draws a sharp line with the past,

170. Viktor Trushkov, "Russia Said Goodbye to Democracy, Curtailed As It Was," *Pravda*, 29 January 1994.

171. Zorkin, interview of 2 February 1994.

172. Mandatory retirement at the age of seventy (sixty-five for the original thirteen justices) is yet another questionable provision.

173. Just such a curtailment of benefits was used against former chairman Zorkin to pressure him to comply with the president's will in 1993.

174. Nikonov, interview of 3 February 1994.

Russian constitutionalism can progress; otherwise, Russia is sure to move backwards. Under article 125(3) of the constitution and the 12 July 1994 Law on the Constitutional Court, the court has greater authority to address normative acts than it previously did. It is now authorized to interpret the constitution directly and to hear individual rights cases prior to their adjudication in the lower courts.[175] It is also, unlike the first court, able to hear cases either in plenary sessions or in one of two chambers.

Yet it is, says Justice Ernst Ametistov, "limited so that it is not higher than the other powers."[176] It cannot hear cases at its own initiative and is generally bound by the order in which petitions are received and by a variety of other, highly detailed, regulations set out in the Law on the Court. Like its predecessor, the Constitutional Court must be as activist as possible; but unlike the 1991–93 court, it must remain within the bounds of its jurisdiction and authority. It should not avoid every issue that has political overtones; it would then be simply a weak junior partner in the constitutional order, one with little clout or substantive authority. Yet it must take great care to avoid, as mandated by article 4(2) of the 12 July 1994 law, the openly political questions that undermined its authority in 1993.

Where the court might wish to defend abstract principles of justice, the separation of powers, or the particular course of political development it perceives as best for Russia, but it is appropriately prevented from doing so by its procedural guidelines, it must stay its hand, publicly voicing, with reference to the constitution, its inability to act. In this way it may fulfill both its strict and broad responsibilities to the constitutional order of Russia, upholding the letter of the law while educating the public in its spirit.

Essential to this educational aspect of the court's work is a clarification of the status and function of precedent in the decisions of the Constitutional Court. Until now stare decisis has not been given any clear place in the Russian judiciary.[177] As a common law principle, its role has been limited in the Romanist legal system of Russia. Yet increasingly precedent seems to be gaining a foothold in the Russian judiciary, including in the Constitutional Court's sister court, the Supreme Court of Russia. Its place, however, needs to be better defined, especially in light of the growing use of juries, for whom

175. In terms of American jurisprudence, the court is no longer bound by any "case or controversy" requirement.

176. Ametistov, interview of 4 February 1994.

177. Ernst Ametistov, comments at Mentor Group Conference on Russian Constitutional Affairs, 14–18 November 1994. Conference report, 77. Hereafter Ametistov, comments.

standing precedent can serve as a useful guide.[178] The enactment of an enforcement statute for Constitutional Court decisions is also critical.[179]

Assessing the mandate of the present court, Justice Ametistov discovers an "adequate place of operation for us."[180] As noted, the court is now explicitly empowered to interpret the constitution. In addition, under article 104(1) of the latter, the court has the power to initiate legislation. Thus did the court itself put forth the 12 July 1994 law on its operations, which the Duma revised and passed. Certain new limitations on the court have also proven beneficial. These have prevented it from drowning beneath a flood of cases. The removal of much of its mandatory original jurisdiction is prominent among these changes. Standing has also been narrowed, with individual legislators unable to bring suits to the court and the court's consideration of issues at its own initiative proscribed. Finally, its competence over sub-legislative acts has likewise been limited.

The Constitutional Court, and the courts more generally, should continue to focus their attention on the promotion and protection of civil and political rights. By giving the constitution and its guarantee of fundamental rights substance in the public eye, rights cases will have a significant impact on legal consciousness. Such cases must become the main feature of an "awareness campaign to educate the population at large in the intricacies, the nature and the characteristic features of constitutional justice."[181] In addressing these cases, the court does well to refer to international norms, thereby raising Russia's constitutional standards. Having previously done so with the Universal Declaration of Human Rights and various conventions of the International Labor Organization, the court must make this a hallmark of its work.

Given the potential impact of individual rights cases, it is troubling that certain justices continue to see individual complaints as distractions and not as serious work. Rather, these complaints and concerns should be at the heart of the court's adjudication. Individuals' ability to go before the court when their constitutional rights and freedoms have been violated, citing article 125(4) and the court's original and apparently mandatory jurisdiction

178. See John N. Hazard, "Is Russian Case Law Becoming Significant As a Source of Law?" and "Russian Judicial Precedent Revisited," respectively, in *Parker School Journal of East European Law* 1, no. 1 (1994): 46; and 1, no. 4 (1994): 471.

179. Sharlet, "Russian Constitutional Crisis," 334.

180. Ametistov, interview of 4 February 1994.

181. Vitrouk, comments, 51.

over such cases (like that of the Federal Constitutional Court of Germany), is an important step in this direction. Appeals to the court should be strongly encouraged among a citizenry still inadequately aware of their own rights in the constitutional order. While this may burden the court at first, the development of clear precedents will alleviate some of this pressure with the passage of time.

The Russian Constitutional Court is far from perfect. Its inexperience, troubled surroundings, and inadequate support are serious obstacles to its success. Yet a similarly constituted German Constitutional Court, with a similarly weak early jurisprudence and analogous limitations, managed to become the preeminent constitutional court in both the common and civil law worlds. In light of this, there is hope for the Russian court as well.

Lower Courts

The judicial branch, however, does not begin or end with the Constitutional Court. Arguably, the heart of the judiciary is at the other extreme, in the local People's Courts all over the country. The strengthening of these courts of first instance and the broader system of appellate courts, a process that has gained momentum as the national political order has stabilized itself, is critical if constitutionalism is to emerge and if Russia's highest courts[182] are not to drown under a flood of cases beyond the limits of their time and staffing.[183] As the court system takes root at the local level, moreover, it can play a critical role in the constitutional stabilization of the country. While some have questioned how effective Russian courts can be given the present instability in the country, Hoffmann appropriately reminds us that courts "can perform diverse and changing functions, especially in unstable polities that lack dominant authority patterns."[184] Thus may the courts in Russia help to encourage reform rather than to ensure conservation.

Ultimately, the greatest lessons in constitutionalism will be taught and learned at the lowest levels of the judicial system. Though until now the public "did not regard these [courts] as part of the constitutional system," they must come to do so.[185] Legal consciousness will then emerge with

182. The Constitutional Court, the Supreme Court, and the High *Arbitrazh* Court.
183. Vlasihin, interview of 10 August 1993.
184. Hoffmann, 22.
185. Nikonov, interview of 3 February 1994.

public exposure to and "practice with court business, which will show people that they can have their rights defended there." Only then will the people truly respect the courts and the laws they interpret and apply.[186]

Until now the courts have always been weak and ineffectual, hobbled by their inferiority to the all-powerful procurators[187] and the resulting disinterest of the public in their work. With few resources and little political clout, the courts were correctly viewed by the public as being of little use to them. That most judges were female was thus considered evidence of both women's and the courts' low status in the Soviet Union.[188] The dangers of the courts' weakness were recognized as long ago as August 1991, when laws depoliticizing the procuracy and sharply delimiting its powers were adopted, and Yeltsin decreed that all property holdings of Communist Party local committees (*partikom*) be transferred to local and regional courts to improve their dilapidated facilities and to raise the poor salaries that made "telephone justice"[189] possible.

As many have noted, the courts' physical condition has long symbolized their place in the system. A new judicial order thus deserves a new judicial climate. Adequate funds must be provided to end the continued financial weakness of the lower courts and to enable them to be more than a feeble cousin in the legal system. Otherwise, "not subordination, but a kind of dependence" on those with the purse strings will continue to exist—a dependence that may be difficult to distinguish from the judicial handicaps of the past.[190] Sadly, however, years after Yeltsin's decree, there has been little if any improvement in the status of the judiciary.[191]

186. Ametistov, interview of 4 February 1994. Notably, though the Constitutional Court alone is authorized to interpret the constitution, the court cannot judge the interpretation and application of normative acts by the executive branch, an area that is the sole prerogative of the lower courts. The latter thus have an important complementary function to fulfill in the Russian judicial system.

187. A tsarist institution adopted by the Soviets, the procuracy combined judge, policeman, and prosecutor into one individual, with all the resulting abuse of power one would expect. See Handelman, *Comrade Criminal*, 280–81.

188. Mikhail S. Paleev, "The Establishment of an Independent Judiciary in Russia," *Parker School Journal of East European Law* 1, nos. 5–6 (1994): 650.

189. This was the practice, common under Soviet rule, of Party officials calling judges to encourage them to decide certain political cases in a particular way.

190. Yakovlev, *The Bear That Wouldn't Dance*, 75.

191. According to Vyacheslav Nikonov, there is no record of even a single property or asset transfer to the courts before February 1994. See Yuri Feofanov, "Rejection of Justice," and Valery Savitsky, "What Kind of Court and Procuracy?" in Barry, *Toward the "Rule of Law" in Russia?* 373–76, 377–84.

This distressing state of affairs must be alleviated if constitutionalism is to emerge from the Russian judiciary. For it is with these courts of the first instance that the general public has substantive contact. It is in the small-claims courts and even criminal courts that the people will act on and defend their rights. Here, and here alone, are they likely to experience equal protection under the law and observe the due-process norms of their constitution at work. Thus, in many respects, the facilities of the local People's Courts are even more important than those of Russia's three high courts, for it is in the former that the people will meet the law.

As the Duma improves Russia's still contradictory and convoluted legal codes, including its codes on land use and criminal procedure, the courts must strive to systematically and fairly apply these. These codes, in regulating the activities of both private and public institutions, will help define the constitutional limits of government authority as well as the rights of citizens vis-á-vis the government.[192] In private adjudications, they will help instill a sense of the law as an effective ordering tool in society, one that encourages stability and predictability in societal relations.

This will lend consistency to the legal order, a critical element of a developed legal culture. This is essential if public respect for, and even appreciation of, the law is ever to take root in Russia. Under Soviet instrumentalism, the law failed to fulfill this important function of providing predictability to citizens' lives. The Soviet criminal code exemplifies this limitation, with its abstract, and thus unhelpful, description of all "socially dangerous" acts as criminal. Yet this was perceived until quite recently as a benefit, and not a failing, of the system. A 1989 government tract thus boasted that "soviet law has never had a formal approach to [defining crime]. That is why an action or lack of action which, formally speaking, has features of an act described in the criminal code, but is not socially dangerous because of its insignificance, cannot be recognized as a crime."[193]

Odd as it may seem, this view was in keeping with the broader understanding of the function of the courts in applying the law. Thus, "under socialism, the role of law was understood in its relation to the state. Its purpose was to discipline people and create some kind of bureaucratic consistency in the administration of state affairs. Contrary to Weber's bureaucratic law model, this legal system was not predictable."[194] It is thus

192. Barenboim, interview of 3 February 1994.
193. Quoted in Handelman, *Comrade Criminal,* 275.
194. Sajo and Losonci, "Rule by Law," 333.

critical that Russia's courts shift gears and strive to create substantive consistency and predictability in the law, rather than a mere formalistic consistency. Equally important, and related, is the need for judges to begin to think about the law not in relation to the state, but in relation to the individual. The law must thus be understood to be about rights, and not simply about discipline.

The coming into force of the Civil Code in January 1995 was a major step toward stability and predictability. New copyright, patent, and leasing laws; legislation on shareholder rights; and corporation laws addressing issues such as fraud and misuse of credit must also be enacted. The Duma should expedite its work on improving Russia's land laws. As economic reform continues and personal and real property holdings are spread among a broader spectrum of the public, the courts' resolution of contractual and other business disputes can serve as a powerful leading edge in judicial development. Judicial effectiveness and efficiency in this area, mandated by the market, will raise standards across the board and thereby improve the entire legal system.

Delays in the hearing of cases, with 16 percent of criminal cases and 13 percent of civil cases heard late in 1993, represents an area in which the needs of the business community can help to improve the administration of justice. With timeliness critical in business disputes, courts' work on such cases will force them to improve their efficiency and to demand the greater resources necessary for the effective hearing of their dockets. In this way, the impetus of the business community may prove invaluable to the improvement of the work of Russia's courts.[195] The defense of narrower business rights in the courts may thus help set a precedent for the protection of broader civil and political ones.[196]

If the Central Bank's quasi-legal rouble confiscation in July 1993 had a significant negative impact on legal consciousness, the reverse ought to also hold true: if economic rights are protected by the courts, the public should gradually accept that the law can protect them beyond the economic arena as well. The judicial defensibility of economic rights, then, is essential.[197]

---

195. In this regard, Yeltsin's July 1994 creation of the Russian School of Private Law is a hopeful sign. See Peter Solomon, "The Limits of Legal Order in Post-Soviet Russia," *Post-Soviet Affairs* 11 (April–June 1995): 92.

196. Vlasihin, interview of 10 August 1993.

197. Oleg Rumyantsev, speech to Supreme Soviet, 10 October 1991. Translated by the author.

The development of local arbitration[198] courts, which handle a large proportion of Russia's business-related litigation, should also be noted. From 1990 to 1993, the number of private cases against the government brought in St. Petersburg's arbitration courts rose from 27 to 151. In most of these, the plaintiffs proved victorious.[199] With the adoption of legislation on the arbitration courts by the Duma in April 1995, it can be hoped that the development of these courts will continue.[200] The jurisdiction of these courts, furthermore, should be extended as far as their resources will allow.

In contrast to their historic practice, care must now be taken by the courts to comply with the rules of judicial procedure. This is sure to be difficult. For decades procedure has been *mere* procedure in Russia. Thus is it troubling, but unsurprising, that even a jurist such as Aleksandr Yakovlev discounts the need for rigid adherence to procedure.[201] Yet if the courts are to promote constitutional and political reform, they must walk clearly on the path of the law. On the mine field of present-day Russian politics, only this can ensure their integrity and stability.

Adherence to proper procedure is especially critical in light of the many changes in the courtroom that are now under way. Most important, litigation is becoming increasingly party-driven. As this trend has been largely ad hoc, however, the limitations on judges remain unclear. It is thus especially important that the latter limit themselves. For example, while judges are still authorized to themselves question parties and witnesses, as is the jury (though only through written inquiries submitted to the bench), this should be limited to the most exceptional circumstances.

In criminal prosecutions, which have seen the most change in recent years, judicial self-restraint is most essential. Traditionally the courts prosecuted defendants, reviewed the evidence against them, and, finally, sentenced them. This has naturally changed, and for the better. The Code of Criminal Procedure, while imperfect, now provides for a fair hearing before a neutral adjudicator. Defendants now have a presumption of innocence (article 49 of the constitution) and a privilege against self-incrimination, have the right to remain silent (article 51), and are protected by the right to counsel (article 48) and an exclusionary rule (article 50). The courts must take seriously their

198. Though denominated as such, these are actually regular courts that simply specialize in business disputes.

199. Solomon, "The Limits of Legal Order," 91.

200. *Sobranie Zakonodatel'stva RF* 1995, no. 18, item 1589; no. 19, item 1709.

201. Yakovlev, *The Bear That Wouldn't Dance,* 82.

obligation to protect these rights.[202] The long history of investigative and prosecutorial abuses by the procurators will make this a challenge, but one necessarily faced up to.

Though juries are not an element of the civil-law system, but rather of the Anglo-American tradition of the common law, they are, as Alexis de Tocqueville has suggested, among the most beneficial tools of direct democracy available in the creation of civil society. This may be especially true for Russia, where legal professionals, corrupted by the Soviet political system, will be extremely difficult to reform. Juries are particularly important in criminal prosecutions, in which they act as a counterweight to the overly powerful procurators and their huge investigative apparatus. Jury duty also serves an educative function. Such a radical change in judicial procedure, finally, may be necessary for Russia to make a clean break with past legal processes. Lacking the external occupation or complete illegality that made judicial reform possible in Japan and Germany, Russia's legal system has largely stagnated since Gorbachev's reforms, including proposals to allow jury trials, faltered in the late 1980s. Thus did Gorbachev himself first propose the introduction of juries in 1988 and 1989. Juries "may not be an ideal structure, but in any event [they are] better than what existed earlier."[203]

Nor are jury trials entirely alien to Russia. They were, in fact, one of the most significant innovations of the 1864 judicial reforms. Even under Soviet rule, two "lay assessors" sat alongside the professional judge.[204] While usually under a compulsion to agree with their senior partner,[205] these lay assessors functioned on the same principle of peer review as do full-size citizen juries. Support for the use of juries, moreover, is quite common in the media and in academic circles.[206]

Given a hesitant public that "does not believe in juries quite yet,"[207] and the limited effectiveness of jurors with a narrow sense of the law, initial

202. Habeas corpus legislation (*Vedomosti RSFSR*, no. 20, item 1084 [1992]) should also continue to be liberally applied by the courts, in keeping with recent patterns. Thus were seventy thousand habeas cases heard in 1994, of which 19.4 percent led to releases. See Solomon, "The Limits of Legal Order," 100.

203. R. Z. Livshits, "Jus and Lex: Evolution of Views," in Butler, *Perestroika and the Rule of Law*, 32.

204. This system was dispensed with in 1992, but it may now be making a comeback in the arbitration courts.

205. Hence their derisive designation as "nodders."

206. See M. D. A. Freeman, "The Rule of Law—Conservative, Liberal, Marxist and Neo-Marxist: Wherein Lies the Attraction?" in Butler, *Perestroika and the Rule of Law*, 41.

207. Marchenko, interview of 31 January 1994.

efforts to introduce juries have had mixed results. Yet Russian juries have, as a whole, shown greater maturity and worked far more effectively than anticipated.[208] Provided for by law on 16 July 1993, and adopted as part of a comprehensive amendment of the criminal code,[209] jury trials were initially introduced in nine regional courts. At the insistence of the procurators, who vehemently opposed the jury system, jury trials were made available only for the most serious crimes. From December 1993 to October 1994, 108 jury trials were held in which a significant decline in convictions was noted. Even more significant, however, was many juries' willingness to convict defendants on lesser charges than were sought by prosecutors, suggesting an independence of mind few expected of Russian juries.[210]

The introduction of juries, though apparently incompatible with a rigid inquisitorial system, has thus been a worthwhile experiment. As their use is expanded, however, care should be taken that constitutional rights to equal protection not be violated, as they were during a first set of experimental jury trials the Supreme Court and the Justice Ministry sponsored in 1992.[211] More prosaic questions also arise. One legal journalist appropriately wondered whether there was even a place for juries to sit.[212] Eventually, however, one can hope that juries will no longer be "an extraordinary form of legal procedure, but a civilized way of fairly deciding the most difficult legal conflicts."[213]

Russia continues to lack a cadre of legal personnel to ensure the fluid and effective operation of the legal system. This situation has slowly improved since the creation of the first national bar association, the Union of Advocates of the USSR, in February 1989. On the whole, however, the professionalism of attorneys remains quite low, possibly even lower than that of the tsarist defense bar. This is a vital issue, for able judicial officers and attorneys are essential to the progressive judicial reforms now being implemented. Until the judicial system is stabilized, attorneys will daily set precedents by their own decisions and acts, making their professional standards critical.

With this in mind it may make sense, only partially tongue in cheek, to

208. Ametistov, interview of 16 August 1993.
209. *Vedomosti RF,* no. 33, item 1313 (1993).
210. Solomon, "The Limits of Legal Order," 103–4.
211. Vlasihin, interview of 10 August 1993.
212. *"Pravo i sila," Moskovski Komsomolets,* 18 May 1991, 2.
213. Valery Savitsky, "What Kind of Court and Procuracy?" in Barry, *Toward the "Rule of Law" in Russia?* 379.

amend former U.S. vice president Dan Quayle's suggestion that the United States export western lawyers to Japan, including Russia as an additional recipient. These attorneys can assist with both the practice of and training in the law. Generally there has been "a lack of Western support in developing law." The most ambitious venture to date, the American Bar Association's Central and East European Law Initiative, proposed to lead its target nations out of their "legal Dark Ages."[214] Its limited efforts in Russia, however, have proven inadequate to Russia's needs.

Western experts can also help develop a new curriculum for Russian legal education. Russian professors have long taught only what the law is, ignoring what it can and should be.[215] Thus lawyers have not stood in the forefront of reform, as they would generally be expected to.[216] Progress is being made in improving Russian legal education, with better materials and more demanding requirements, but much remains to be done and funding is still far from adequate.[217] Higher educational standards are especially important for judges, who until now have not been "well trained to deal with complicated matters."[218] In fact, "judges were, and remain even in the post-Soviet era, among the least qualified jurists."[219] This dilemma was recognized as early as 1989 with the Law on the Status of Judges, which bolstered the qualifications for judicial service.[220] In Russia itself, the Concept of Judicial Reform (1991) and the Law on the Status of Judges of the Russian Federation (1992)[221] were adopted to improve the standards of judges and to improve the conditions and quality of their work. Together these provided for a more secure tenure for judges, for immunity from

214. James H. Andrews, "Helping Law Come In from the Cold," *Christian Science Monitor,* 21 March 1994, 15.

215. Lempert, "Changing Russian Political Culture," 637. Of course, this is an approach some legal employers, bewailing the complete ignorance of many law-school graduates, would like American law schools to adopt as well.

216. Tellingly, only forty to forty-five members of the first USSR Supreme Soviet were lawyers. Yakovlev, *The Bear That Wouldn't Dance,* 48.

217. Huskey, "The Administration of Justice," 227–28.

218. Nikonov, interview of 3 February 1994.

219. Huskey, "The Administration of Justice," 223. The numbers of judges must also increase. On 1 June 1988, there were 15,781 judges in the USSR, roughly the same as in the Federal Republic of Germany, which has only one-fourth of Russia's population. Huskey, "The Administration of Justice," 228. The appointment of judges remains in the hands of the president, who receives recommendations from judicial panels that he generally follows.

220. *Vedomosti SSR,* no. 9, item 223 (1989).

221. Respectively, at *Vedomosti RSFSR,* no. 30, item 1435 (1991); and *Vedomosti RF,* no. 30, item 1792 (1992).

prosecution, and for their structural independence (by removing them from executive control). They also mandated political neutrality and provided for an adequate salary. These standards should continue to be raised.

Improvement in the standards of judges and lawyers, however, is unrealistic in the absence of an influx of new blood into the law. The legal profession must come to have broader appeal. Though speaking of conditions in 1931, Eugene Huskey could have been describing Russia today: "Law faculties were on the verge of extinction, as students abandoned a dying discipline."[222] The best and the brightest in Russia are increasingly selecting business (and often illegal business) as their career field, and law schools are consequently stumbling. This brain drain must end. Improving the standing and prominence of those in the legal field may alter the "leftover principle" of career selection, by which the worst and not the best choose the law.[223] For only a new generation of talented and able judicial officers and actors can "know true independence from the other powers" and help secure a new constitutional order.[224]

Judicial security must also be reassessed. Several attacks on judges and bombings of courthouses are a warning that the courts must be protected if they are to effectively prosecute the wave of organized crime now ravaging Russia. Safety from political threats, however, also remains an issue, with resources still scarce and the provision to judges of gas, electricity, and paper, among other things, still in the hands of the bureaucracy. Combined with the present-day practice of appointing judges to a five-year probationary term before granting them life tenure, these are serious concerns.

Thus, judicial independence must be protected against new forms of control, for dependence on the political bureaucracy rather than on the Party may prove equally detrimental.[225] In fact, it may be impossible to discern any difference.[226] Yet without longer terms and a more manageable workload, this dependence will persist. Even more threatening to judicial independence, however, may be the popular pressures of mass demonstrations and recall proceedings that are becoming increasingly common. Such practices, contrasted with "telephone justice" as "megaphone justice," must be controlled. "These unwelcome and unintended consequences of political

222. Huskey, "From Legal Nihilism," 28.
223. Huskey, "The Administration of Justice," 228.
224. Satarov, interview of 4 February 1994.
225. Huskey, "From Legal Nihilism," 37.
226. Hiroshi Oda, "The Law-Based State and the CPSU," in Barry, *Toward the "Rule of Law" in Russia?* 166.

reform remind us that changes in legal structures and procedures have to be accompanied by equally far-reaching changes in legal culture."[227] Public respect for the sanctity of judicial proceedings and determinations must therefore be heightened.

In any political system, the courts are the institutions most closely attuned to the constitutional order and its norms, as they are the living embodiment of the law and its authority. Accordingly, the United States associates its most elaborate rituals with the court system and its robed judges presiding over solemn proceedings. The courts are seen by the populace as being above politics and short-term concerns. They must now achieve this status in Russia, holding "*zakoni* [the laws] to the constitutional standards of *pravo* [the law]" as they have not been in the past.[228] Then will the public see the courts as serving justice[229] and themselves learn to challenge injustices, not to suffer them.

Because of their long historical absence from the Russian political scene, the courts are especially well suited to guide the transformation of Russian legal consciousness. Their cameo appearances have been few and far between, and the courts consequently have taken little hold in mass consciousness as players on the political landscape. Even as late as 1990, Chief Justice Yevgeny A. Smolentsev described his Supreme Court's function as simply "giving guidance to lower courts [in order] to assure uniformity."[230]

This flavor of novelty to most Russians may be the courts' best weapon. Unjaded by political bickering in the way the parliament and president are, the courts must cherish this "innocence" and use it to attract the public's confidence in ways no other institution can. As Marx aspired to end the alienation of the masses from the means of production, legal reformers must now end the masses' alienation from the legal process. Should they do so, the public will turn to the lower courts just as they turned to the Constitutional Court with their letters in 1992 and 1993. This process has already begun. Thus did complaints rise from 3,941 in 1991 to 6,366 in 1992, to 8,300 in 1993, with satisfaction of claims up from two-thirds to three-fourths.[231] The

227. Huskey, "The Administration of Justice," 225.
228. Burlatski, interview of 1 February 1994.
229. This may also help break the public's habit, dating back to 1918 and the Russian Civil War, of turning to administrative agencies and the bureaucracy rather than to the courts for legal remedies. Huskey, "From Legal Nihilism," 25.
230. Thornburgh, "The Soviet Union and the Rule of Law," 21.
231. Solomon, "The Limits of Legal Order," 99. Sadly, however, the procuracy still receives ten times as many complaints as do the courts.

courts can serve as educative forums in which the public may learn respect for the law and its legitimate institutions. They will thereby create constitutionalism by "joining the constitution with a whole system of law" connected to and emerging from the people.[232]

This will not be easy. As Justice Ametistov joked to Peter Juviler during his visit to the United States Supreme Court: "If only we had your problems!"[233] Yet in the new constitution, for the first time in Russian history, there exists the basic framework to create a functional judiciary and a new constitutional order. This must now be made a reality.

The Constitution of the Russian Federation

Despite its turbulent and troubled history, the Constitution of the Russian Federation has become critical to the creation and consolidation of Russian constitutionalism. With its adoption on 12 December 1993, it became "the framework for the politics of transition."[234] Unlike the 1978 Constitution of the Russian Republic,[235] a "generally pragmatic statement of already existing practice and principles,"[236] the 1993 constitution balances description with prescription. It lays out the structure of the existing political order but also aspires to a new political culture. While Robert Sharlet understandably expresses his concern with utopian and transformist constitutions, classifying the early Soviet constitutions as such,[237] the 1993 constitution is not of this genre. Rather, it accepts reality while aspiring to something greater. Such a "transformational" approach is acceptable, if not necessary, for Russia today.[238]

"To put it quite mildly," muses constitutional scholar Vyacheslav Nikonov, "this is a rather strange constitution."[239] It contains both technical and substantive flaws as well as a wide range of contradictions and discrepancies. Though established by article 10, the separation of powers survives in a rather muted form. In a structure of "superpresidentialism," the president

232. Satarov, interview of 4 February 1994.
233. Related to the author by Peter Juviler.
234. Sharlet, "Russian Constitutional Crisis," 315.
235. It should be recalled that the Soviet Constitution of 1977 was essentially copied by Russia and the other republics in 1978.
236. Sharlet, *Soviet Constitutional Crisis,* 18.
237. Sharlet, *Soviet Constitutional Crisis,* 21.
238. Hoffmann, 20.
239. Nikonov, interview of 3 February 1994.

stands above the constitution's checks and balances,[240] with the power to rule by decree, at least insofar as the parliament fails to reach certain areas with legislation.[241] Lawmaking and law-executing functions are thus partially fused. The penumbra of presidential power that emanates from article 80 is not entirely dissimilar from the Party Hegemony clause of article 6 of the Brezhnev constitution. Yeltsin's power to dissolve the Duma and to dismiss the government under article 117(3), as well as his apparent authority to suspend or terminate judges, casts a further shadow on the principle of the separation of powers. Even the most fundamental rights, such as article 29's "freedom of thought,"[242] can be abridged in times of crisis—including when the president declares a state of emergency and rules by executive decree, under article 88. Even more threatening may be article 55(3)'s open-ended allowance for the compromise of civil and human rights.

A variety of "serious ambiguities and omissions" can be found in the constitution. There may, for example, be a new "war of laws" centered around the vague legal terminology used therein. The interrelationship and relative authority of laws (*zakoni*), resolutions (*postanovleniia*), decrees (*ukazi*), normative acts (*normativnye akti*), and other legal acts must be clarified.[243] An explicit hierarchy of laws must be established if the legal order is to be stable. Other areas in which ambiguity may lead to conflict are the multiple nodes of legislative initiative set out in article 104 and the unclear policy-making process outlined in articles 105–108. Finally, most detrimental to the development of constitutionalism may be the lack of substantive clarification of federalism and the internecine conflict this may ignite. Together, these factors could be quite destructive.

Yet assessing the constitution only at the textual level or in comparison with western norms of constitutionalism that have developed over long periods reveals little about its actual value in Russia today.[244] Instead, one must judge the constitution in the context of present-day Russia.[245] In this framework, a weak presidency might prove impotent. Yeltsin adviser An-

240. Stephen Holmes, "Superpresidentialism and Its Problems," *East European Constitutional Review* 2 and 3 (Fall 1993 and Winter 1994): 123.

241. And maybe even in such areas, as long as his decrees do not contradict standing laws.

242. The judicial defensibility of which Vyacheslav Nikonov appropriately questions.

243. Hoffmann, 38.

244. See Sharlet, "The New Russian Constitution," 4–5. Sharlet suggests that we assess the constitution as both "fundamental law" and as "metaphor."

245. German Diligenski, "*Konstitutsiya nikogda ni prinimaetsa v abstraktom prostranstve*," *Russian Commentary* (24 November 1993): 2.

drannik Migranyan argues that the American separation of powers is too sophisticated for Russia, while a true parliamentary system would collapse in the absence of a party system or a more developed civil society. Given this predicament, the "omnipotence of the president as an elected tsar" is not entirely unusual, nor an impediment to the constitutionalization of Russian society.[246] Fyodor Burlatski (hardly a Yeltsin partisan) concurs that this might be a necessary stage, though he worries that "such an approach risks the future in the name of the present."[247]

Opponents argue that "a power system created for the needs of a particular moment" will permanently disfigure Russia's constitutional order.[248] This seems implausible. "There is no indication that either the leaders or the Soviet peoples have ever expected a constitution to be eternal, as do the leaders and the people of the United States."[249] The likelihood that much of the 1993 constitution, if not its entirety, will be replaced by the turn of the century and the end of Russia's transitional period makes its flaws and failings, even as regards presidential prerogative, far more palatable. As long as an adequate level of respect for such a lame-duck constitution can be maintained, moreover, this provisional status will not unduly threaten constitutionalism.

The actual realities of political life under the constitution since 1994, furthermore, have proven the distribution of power to be far more equitable and rational than it may have appeared on paper.[250] The parliament has not found itself holding the short end of the stick. During the tenure of the first Duma, united efforts by strong majorities to oppose the will of the president

---

246. Migranyan suggests that the emergence of the France's Fifth Republic out of the Fourth proves this point. "It is therefore vital," he argues, "that while the complicated process of moulding and reinforcing civil society is going on in the economic and spiritual sphere, strong authoritarian rule should be maintained in the political sector, so as to impose certain restrictions on the present stage of democratic change." Andrannik Migranyan, *Perestroika As Seen by a Political Scientist* (Moscow: Novosti, 1990), 7.

247. Burlatski, interview of 1 February 1994. See also Holmes, "Superpresidentialism" (124), arguing that a strong president is necessary, since no assembly could effectively carry out necessary reforms.

248. International Reform Foundation, "We Need a Different Constitution."

249. Hazard, "The Evolution of the Soviet Constitution," 93.

250. It should also be noted that some of the criticism of the Russian Constitution applies equally to the American Constitution. Thus have many expressed concern with the tendency of the upper house of the parliament, the Federation Council, to act as a brake on the legislative efforts of the Duma. Council members, furthermore, have been criticized for representing the localized interests of their regional electorate and not the interests of the entire nation. Yet this attack describes perfectly the role of the United States Senate, one for which it was established and has long been commended.

consistently bore fruit. Thus, while the Duma's 228-to-38 vote[251] calling on President Yeltsin to end the war in Chechnya was unavailing, their persistent pressure over the next six months would bring Yeltsin not only to focus more seriously on a political settlement, but to dismiss several of the most hawkish ministers in the government. The president and the Duma's sharp division over the election law for the 1995 parliamentary elections also concluded in a clear victory for the parliament on the two provisions in dispute.[252]

While some have criticized the amount of detail in the constitution, suggesting that this will freeze current political arrangements, several points should be remembered. Again, this constitution will probably be periodic. Regardless of this, Russia's traditional embrace of the civil law system makes such detail the norm, not the exception. Finally, "it must be borne in mind that Russia in recent years has been emerging from decades, even centuries of civil and legal darkness; hence their compelling need to write everything down in a country in the absence of a democratic political and legal culture within which language would normally resonate.[253]

Given Russia's present stage of transformation, such a constitution may therefore be most appropriate and advantageous to the development of constitutionalism. Notwithstanding its many flaws, then, it seems fair to agree with Yeltsin adviser Giorgi Satarov that "from a juridical perspective, the constitution is adequate for a democratic society."[254]

"The new Russian Constitution, imperfect as it may be, is an asset to Russia's very fragile democracy."[255] If there is any hope for progress, it rests with this document. Though the constitution was illegitimately "rammed through," an effort to actively undermine it would tear Russia apart.[256] Should the Duma call for a new constitutional assembly or attempt to radically amend the constitution, the political stability painstakingly built up since its adoption will be shattered. As "the new Constitution became a

---

251. On 23 December 1994, soon after the invasion of Chechnya.

252. The issues were: whether 50 percent of the electorate should be required to participate to render the Duma elections valid (Yeltsin's position) or whether this number should be lowered to 25 percent; and whether the existing proportion of Duma seats filled by party slates versus by individual candidates (50–50) should be maintained. Regarding the latter, Yeltsin actively pressed for an increase in the share of individual-candidate seats, as the parties allied with him were generally weaker than those of his opponents.

253. Sharlet, "Citizen and State," 121.

254. Satarov, interview of 4 February 1994.

255. Hoffmann, 30. See Zielonka, "New Institutions," 103.

256. Vladimir Zharinov, "Yeltsin's Historical Period: Coming to an End," *Nezavisimaya Gazeta*, 25 January 1994.

major battlefield rather than a negotiating table" during its drafting and adoption, its public image was significantly bruised.[257] Further denigration in the public eye could prove fatal—not only to the constitution, but to Russia itself.

Public statements attacking the constitution as illegitimate, such as the tract drafted by Vladimir Lafitski at the request of a coalition of major parties and published in *Pravda* in January 1994, are a serious danger. As a speaker at the last Soviet Congress of People's Deputies declared, responding to violent criticism of the Soviet Constitution, "there ought to be some basis of stability, law and order in society! The Constitution determines the degree of the authorities' legitimacy. Outrage against the former deprives the latter of all respect, removes the moral safety device of the society and gives a part of it a moral right to resist by any means."[258] Opponents and supporters of the constitution alike should look to Ukraine—and the tragic political and economic consequences of its continued dependence on its empty Soviet constitution[259]—as evidence of the preferability of the 1993 Russian constitution to its feeble predecessor.

The political elites' support, even if not affection, for the constitution is essential to its success. As Rumyantsev asserts, "it is not enough to have merely a written constitution—even with a written constitution, it is still possible to have no constitutional order at all."[260] It is the elites' backing that will allow the constitution to make the transition from form to substance. Only thus will it metamorphose, in the words of David Lempert, from "an unenforceable literary work" to "a mutually enforceable contract."[261]

As early as 1975, Elena Lukasheva warned of the tendency of Russian law to reduce jus to lex. This tendency, she suggested, must be resisted; instead "the law [*pravo*], as exemplified by the constitution, ought to be seen as a force above the laws [*zakoni*]."[262] Russia "must be bound not only by lex, for this is merely self-limitation which turns out to be insufficient."[263] If the constitution is to provide a set of consistently applied normative principles

257. Hoffmann, 46.
258. Quoted in Sergeyev and Biryukov, *Russia's Road to Democracy*, 192.
259. As well as its resistance to a serious program of economic reform until the 1995 election of President Leonid Kuchma.
260. Rumyantsev, comments, 91.
261. Lempert, "The Proposed Constitution of Ukraine," 271–72.
262. Lukasheva, interview of 1 February 1994.
263. Livshits, "Jus and Lex," 27.

that individuals can rely upon, this distinction of jus and lex is critical.[264] Instead of a solitary piece of the legal jigsaw puzzle that is Russia today, the constitution must come to be understood as basic, or fundamental, law. Daily life must no longer be primarily controlled by government decrees, but by the constitution and such legislative acts as are born of it.[265] Russia's laws, then, are subject to the constitution, not coextensive with it.[266]

Evidence of the constitution's potential to provide at least a temporary framework for constitutional reform is provided by Oleg Rumyantsev. Though victimized politically and physically during the events of late 1993 that brought the constitution into force, Rumyantsev still describes the document as "a step toward constitutional order in Russia," whose "principles create the possibility for Russia to accomplish its transition from state order to a truly constitutional order." Despite his many criticisms of its adoption and of Yeltsin's compliance with it, he looks to a process of amendment and reform, not of overthrow, as the solution. Moreover, he suggests that this must occur "not necessarily immediately, but in good time."[267]

The Federal Assembly's careful use of the amendment process, which requires a vote of three-fourths of the Federation Council and two-thirds of the Duma, as well as the support of two-thirds of the subject legislatures, is the best route forward. For now, such amendments ought to remain within the limitations set out in article 1(1) of the April 1994 Treaty on Social Accord, which pledges its signatories to propose only such limited changes as will promote, and not undermine, stability.[268] "Utilizing the constitution to rewrite political agreements is counterproductive to the goal of creating respect and belief in constitutionalism. If a constitution is easy to amend it loses its majestic special role. . . . In that process law, including the text of the constitution, easily becomes a matter of technicality."[269]

In 1991, Peter Juviler analogized the USSR Declaration of Rights and Freedoms to the Universal Declaration of Human Rights, suggesting that "it

---

264. See Lempert, "The Proposed Constitution of Ukraine," 273. Using Lempert's method of comparing individuals "at different points in the system," the lack of adequate legal consistency becomes apparent. Consider, moreover, the substantial place of politics in our consideration of legal issues.

265. Huskey, "Executive-Legislative Relations," 91.

266. The attempts of the State-Legal Administration to compile a database of all legal acts may demonstrate an increasing awareness of the need for legal consistency and predictability. Huskey, "The Presidency in Russian Politics," 126 and accompanying notes.

267. Rumyantsev, comments, 91, 99–101.

268. "*Dogovor ob obshchestvennom soglasii,*" *Izvestiia*, 30 April 1994, 4.

269. Sajo and Losonci, "Rule by Law," 328–29.

enacts no immediately operative law, but leaves a legacy for [the] next phases of the difficult democratic revolution."[270] This prospective purpose may hold true for the constitution as well. It has flaws and limited potential, but as even Rumyantsev acknowledges, it may well be "a step toward constitutional order in Russia."

Uncertain support for the constitution has heretofore limited its effectiveness. Erik Hoffmann suggests why:

> To date the Constitution has performed multiple, even dialectical, functions. It has debased and uplifted political discourse; it has exacerbated and ameliorated political conflict; and it has been a weapon in the struggle over fundamental political issues and a means of resolving them. Too few Russian politicians view the Constitution as a mutually beneficial pact or a treaty worth keeping. Too many Russian citizens view the Constitution as the millstone rather than the keystone of constitutionalism.[271]

The constitution's most important contribution may thus be its influence on public views of what the function of an effective and authoritative constitution should be. The Russian people have had little respect for such instruments since their very first constitution, Tsar Nicholas II's 1906 Basic Law, which set out certain rights and established a parliamentary Duma. In keeping with the letter, though none of the spirit, of this document, the Duma was elected and dissolved three times by the tsar before a fourth election produced a monarchist majority with which he was content.

Thus did a peasant saying of the time cynically describe the 17 October 1905 manifesto that announced the tsar's intention to draft a constitution: "*Tsar ispugalsa, izdal manifest. Myortvam svobodu, zhivuikh pod arest.*[272] This flawed constitutional debut only served to "exacerbate the [people's] disillusionment with the mechanisms of law."[273] Years later, this disenchantment lingers as the primary obstacle to constitutionalism in Russia.[274]

---

270. Juviler, "The Soviet Declaration of Individual Rights," 3.

271. Hoffmann, 47.

272. "The tsar got scared, and declared a manifest. Freedom to the dead, and the living under arrest."

273. Gianmaria Ajani, "The Rise and Fall of the Law-Based State in the Experience of Russian Legal Scholarship: Foreign Patterns and Domestic Style," in Barry, *Toward the "Rule of Law" in Russia?* 13.

274. While comical, the decision, seventy years after the 1906 constitution, to adopt a

Russia's constitutional cynicism must finally be exorcised by nurturing public understanding of the importance of the constitution. "*Yeltsin's* Constitution will have to become the *Russian* Constitution."[275] This will not happen through a rote reading of the constitution by Russia's citizenry; rather, it necessitates a deeper awareness of the constitution's function and the character of the laws it generates.[276] Few Americans have read their constitution, but they understand and accept its underlying principles. Thus the American mind is as much a product of the United States Constitution as the document is a fruit of the American mind.[277] In the final analysis, the Russian Constitution can most fundamentally and enduringly shape Russia's legal and political order with its impact on individuals' awareness of its purpose.[278]

Public support for the constitution, however, must not be prompted simply by the personal benefits of freedom and the rule of law.[279] While this may, and should, be an initial motivation, it is far from enough. The common attitude that there is "nothing about teachers, for example, in the constitution, so they do not support it," must change.[280] Instead the people must perceive the constitution as broadly bearing upon every individual's life through its guarantees of rights and freedoms, its administrative structures, and other provisions not explicitly directed at them but at the collective citizenry of Russia. The constitution must become the charter for a new community, one greater than the sum of its individual parts. Then will it become a true social contract. As the people's own constitution, this piece of paper will come to be respected "not as a manifestation of power, but as a manifestation of law."[281]

As Hoffmann correctly acknowledges, "constitutions do not always foster constitutionalism."[282] If the Russian Constitution is to live up to its own article 15 and become "the supreme law" of Russia, it must ground itself

---

forty-one-hour work week in article 41 of the 1977 constitution suggested the continuing lack of serious respect for such documents.

275. Hoffmann, 45.

276. Huskey, "Executive-Legislative Relations," 93.

277. Biryukov, interview of 18 November 1993.

278. For this to happen, the parliament must play its part in adopting the various pieces of implementing legislation the constitution requires for particular provisions to go into effect. Thus does article 22(2), placing control of arrest and detention in the hands of the judiciary, await the adoption of a new code of criminal procedure.

279. Public support remains relatively low, with roughly half the population supporting the constitution in 1994. Rose, "Russia As an Hour-Glass Society," 41.

280. Nikonov, interview of 3 February 1994.

281. Satarov, interview of 4 February 1994.

282. Hoffmann, 21.

among Russia's citizenry. Only then will it become a "reality for the country" and a powerful source of constitutionalism.[283]

Individual Rights

Article 2 of the 1993 constitution describes human rights as the supreme value of both the constitution and the Russian state. Articles 17 through 64 elaborate on this theme, outlining the myriad rights guaranteed under the constitution and making human rights the most prominent theme addressed therein. Protected under the constitution, among others, are the right to equality, to life, to human dignity, to freedom and human inviolability, to privacy, and to one's choice of nationality and language. Freedom of movement and speech are secured, as are freedom from torture and the right to property, housing, health, education, and legal assistance.

Inclusion of this broad range of protected rights, though notable, amounts more to words than to substance, for the fundamental relationship of state and individual in Russia remains largely unchanged. In the public eye, rights are still granted by the state, not held by the individual. They remain a marginal concern to the everyday citizen.

Rights consciousness is thus extremely weak. Among Russians surveyed in 1994, 43 percent indicated that they did not know if their rights had been violated in the past three years.[284] Yet individual citizens' awareness of what their rights are under the constitution and how to protect them is the essence of an effective constitutional order and the key to its development. Thus is the still-low number of individual complaints of rights' violations disheartening. Among those few who do appeal violations of their rights, moreover, as many appeal to local executive authorities, including the police, as to courts (17.6 percent and 17.5 percent, respectively).

That things have begun to change, however, is evidenced by the fact that while the statistics on actual appeals show relatively little recourse to the courts, speculative inquiries into who individuals *think* they would appeal to

---

283. Olshanski, interview of 2 February 1994.
284. Inga B. Mikhailovskaia, "Constitutional Rights in Russian Public Opinion," *East European Constitutional Review* 4 (Winter 1995): 74. Russians are thus equally divided on whether the clearly aconstitutional system of internal passports (*propiski*) represents an unconstitutional violation of freedom of movement.

if the need arose show that 38.7 percent of individuals would appeal to the courts, 22.2 percent to the mass media, and 16.2 percent to human-rights organizations, all figures greater than the 10.8 percent that would appeal to the executive bodies of power, as was the wont in the Soviet era.[285]

The traditional Soviet concept of citizen obligations linked to rights also survives in Russia today. It is enshrined in the constitution in articles 57–59, though in a more muted form than in previous constitutional documents;[286] but more important, it continues to pervade Russians' sense of their place in the system. The right of free speech is thus theirs, but only if they use it within bounds the state sees fit to allow them.

As it was during Imperial Russian and Soviet times, the relationship of the state and the individual is paternalistic rather than reciprocal. Citizens passively receive from the state and, in return, abide by its will. The individual's identity apart from the state and in opposition to the state is thus circumspect in both elite and mass consciousness.

Economic rights, long the centerpiece of Soviet constitutions, though rarely of much actual significance, exemplify the statist view of rights this gives rise to. The right to housing, to education, and to employment, among others, are rights to a particular good that individuals hold against the government. They represent something the government must do for the individual. With such rights, the state remains the subject and the individual the object. This pattern must be turned on its head. Individuals must come to see themselves as the moving force, and not the passive recipient, in Russian society. For only in this way can a truly democratic constitutional order emerge and persist.

Thankfully, though economic rights remain central in public consciousness,[287] some signs of a shift are apparent. The order of economic and social versus civil and political rights, for example, has been switched in the 1993 constitution from that in its predecessors. Economic rights have also been downplayed, as with the switch from a right to work to a "defense from unemployment" in article 37.

On other fronts, the growing talk of international human-rights norms, and their application by the courts, will serve to encourage a stronger sense

285. Mikhailovskaia, "Constitutional Rights," 74.

286. Articles 50 and 51 of the 1977 constitution thus limited citizens' rights to those that "serve the people's interests" or "strengthen the socialist state."

287. Russians still rank the rights to economic security and to personal security and safety as the most important rights, with only 2.6 percent of Russians listing freedom of speech as most important. Mikhailovskaia, "Constitutional Rights," 71–72.

of rights as inalienable. As the individually oriented rights of the Covenant on Civil and Political Rights, which is already binding under the constitution, and of the Council of Europe's Charter are increasingly applied to the lives of Russia's citizenry, their understanding of their autonomy vis-á-vis the state will grow. An additional, related source of progress toward a rights consciousness is the post of the ombudsman for human rights, established by article 103(e) of the constitution and long filled by human-rights activist Sergei Kovalov. Implicit in this historic position is the independence of citizens' rights from the state and its authority. The independent ombudsman thus is to serve as a voice for the people against the government. Though appointed by the government itself, the ombudsman is a visible manifestation of the individual's possession of rights external to the will or whim of the state. This, one hopes, may help to encourage citizens' understanding of their autonomous role in an emerging civil society.[288]

Until quite recently, rights meant exceedingly little to the Russian people. Their place, in fact, continues to be quite limited.[289] Yet "if citizens are not aware of their fundamental rights, and of the procedures available for protecting them, the realization of constitutional norms will depend exclusively on the functioning of state agencies."[290] The emergence of constitutionalism is virtually impossibile in such a climate. A concerted focus on rights, through human-rights education programs and awareness campaigns by both domestic and foreign human-rights organizations, is thus critical to Russia's constitutional and democratic future.

THE ECONOMY

In recent years it has become impossible to speak with academics or officials about constitutionalism without their immediately referring to the latter's dependence on economic developments. "The political and economic reali-

---

288. Kovalov's 5 July 1994 human-rights report for 1993, with its scathing attack on the government, was thus a historic document. Though commissioned by Yeltsin himself by Decree no. 1798 of 1 November 1993, this well-publicized report was a tangible sign to the public that a sphere of activity beyond the scope of state authority and influence could truly be said to exist. That human rights was at the heart of this only enhanced its beneficial effects.

289. See Inga Mikhailovskaya, "Why the Russian Public Will Support Reform," *East European Constitutional Review* 2 and 3 (Fall 1993 and Winter 1994): 31.

290. Mikhailovskaia, "Constitutional Rights," 70.

ties of a society where the basic commodities of life are in short supply make it hard to contemplate the supremacy of legal ideals."[291] Even legal experts with no training in economics inevitably raised the question of economic stability and reform in my conversations with them. Elena Lukasheva, a human-rights scholar, described economic reform as the "most important factor in the development of constitutionalism today." Yet only a few months before, a lengthy discussion with Professor Lukasheva yielded not a word on economics.[292]

The economic collapse of Ukraine (once touted the republic "most likely to succeed") and Russia's own continuing economic difficulties loom too large to be ignored in any discussion of Russia. The consequent shift in public interest away from politics and law became apparent during the June 1994 trial of the August 1991 coup plotters. "There could be few clearer tokens of the fundamental change in Russian politics—and its growing irrelevance—than the courtroom's empty seats. Here was a chance to explore what really happened during one of the most critical events in Russian history. But almost no one seemed to care."[293]

A heightened concern with the interrelationship of economic stabilization and constitutionalism is entirely appropriate.[294] It is in keeping with a tendency in Soviet political culture, born of Marxist social philosophy and its materialist interpretation of history, to lay the ills of society at the doorstep of economics.[295] Thus, "for all their political and ideological disagreement, almost everyone in Russia seems to believe that whatever problems exist can be traced to the economy."[296]

Yet while there is much disagreement about the pace and exact style of economic reform, everyone I interviewed, whether democrat or communist, free-marketeer or socialist, supported its basic premises (including the shift to a market economy). A 1993 survey revealed 62 percent of respondents to support either a quick or gradual transition to the market, with 21 percent unsure and only 17 percent against market reforms.[297]

291. Shelley, "Legal Consciousness," 63.

292. Lukasheva, interviews of 11 August 1993 and 1 February 1994.

293. Alessandra Stanley, "Oh, That Coup (Yawn): In the Land of Show Trials, Playing to an Empty House," *New York Times,* 26 June 1994, 5.

294. See Jon Elster, "The Necessity and Impossibility of Simultaneous Economic and Political Reform," in Greenberg, 267–74.

295. Sergeyev and Biryukov, *Russia's Road to Democracy,* 53.

296. Sergeyev and Biryukov, *Russia's Road to Democracy,* 55.

297. Jerry F. Hough, "The Russian Election of 1993: Public Attitudes Toward Economic Reform and Democratization," *Post-Soviet Affairs* 10 (January–March 1994): 6.

Notably, among the 62 percent were many who voted for the nationalist Liberal Democratic Party and the leftist Communists and Agrarians in national elections.[298] The same pattern holds true with privatization; the majority support it,[299] though they have concerns about the need to control its detrimental side effects.[300] The first Duma bore out these findings. Its members, all reformers under Soviet rule, by and large came out in support of market reforms, proving false the extremist predictions of December 1993.

That even those former Soviet-bloc states with Communist leaders are still moving toward the market demonstrates the common accord on this issue. All parties agree that decisive action is the most critical need of Russia today. "The government must choose its road and stick to it, whatever it is," advised a weary wage earner struggling to support his family amidst staggering inflation.[301] Continued uncertainty, then, is the greatest threat to public support for reform. Action in the economic arena is the key to sustaining support for the government. As long as something is happening, the public will endure. Stagnation, on the other hand, will no longer be accepted.

An effective constitutional order can best facilitate a stable and consistent policy of economic reform. Stability in the political and legal fields will profoundly influence stability in the economic sphere—and vice versa. Economic safeguards against totalitarianism, such as the market, therefore, should not precede, but accompany, political safeguards such as judicial review. If the public sees the government taking clear, consistent steps toward reform in the economic arena, it will accept and expect consonant behavior from the government in other areas as well.

This symbiotic relationship cannot be overemphasized. Yet as Hoffmann notes, "few people understand the symbiosis between a civil society and economy."[302] Just as Ukraine may represent the worst-case scenario of the interplay of economic and political chaos, the Baltics represent the best of

---

298. Hough, "The Russian Election of 1993," 15.

299. Hough, "The Russian Election of 1993," 8.

300. Hough, "The Russian Election of 1993," 15.

301. Elderly taxi driver in Moscow, 4 February 1994. As Gail Lapidus has pointed out, "In Yeltsin's case, inconsistency is a more serious problem than authoritarianism; indeed, according to some of the most reliable public opinion surveys available to us, popular support for Yeltsin's leadership tends to rise when he behaves more decisively and to decline when people perceive a tendency toward drift at the top." Gail W. Lapidus, "Two Years After the Collapse of the USSR: A Panel of Specialists," *Post-Soviet Affairs* 9 (October–December 1993): 288–89.

302. Hoffmann, 21.

such interdependence. In Lithuania, Latvia, and Estonia, a stronger economy bolstered political stabilization, which in turn encouraged the economy's continued growth. In Russia, where for most of the last decade political instability has limited decisive economic reform, economic growth may now be making political cooperation and stabilization increasingly possible. Little credence ought to be given to portrayals of efficiency and the rule of law as competing values between which Russia must choose. While particular situations might require that a choice be made to prioritize one immediate goal over the other, the intimate linkage of economic and political development at a broader level makes them not only compatible but interdependent.

The interplay of economics and politics for the worse is already all too familiar to Russians. From the Central Bank's 1993 confiscation of roubles to the chaotic struggle over the pace of privatization, and from the rouble zone debate to the 1995 budget battle, Russians watched as political divisions stymied effective economic decision making and as the weak economy sharpened the lines of the political conflict.

Preventing the repetition of such debacles requires that dispassionate decision making on the course of economic reform continue. The cooperative interaction of President Yeltsin and Prime Minister Chernomyrdin on the economy, which emerged in 1994, is a valuable precedent for their successors. The realities of Russia's economic collapse thus forced them to act decisively. In late 1993, 26 percent and 32 percent of Russians, respectively, said their immediate family's financial and economic position had somewhat worsened or essentially worsened since a year before.[303]

Yet while economic reform and stabilization have been erratic and often of little benefit to certain segments of the population, the broad picture since 1991 reveals substantial progress. It is useful, in this vein, to recall the massive shortages and shopping lines that were commonplace in 1991, the expansion of the budget deficit to at least 20 percent of gross domestic product, the December 1991 loan defaults by both the Soviet Union and Russia, and the production decline of more than 12.9 percent that year. In 1991 expectations of hyperinflation, a complete collapse of production, and even starvation, were quite common. Yet none of these nightmare scenarios became a reality.

Two years later, Russia's inflation rate of 840 percent per year seemed like

303. Hough, "The Russian Election of 1993," 1–37.

a godsend compared with that of neighboring Ukraine, the republic considered most secure at the Union's collapse, whose 1994 inflation rate stood at 8,940 percent. By 1995 the Russian rate had fallen yet further, into the low hundreds. While this is still inadequate for a stable polity, Russia has clearly done far better than expected.[304] Privatization, led by the reformist Anatoly Chubais, proved similarly successful, with more than half the economy, in terms of both GDP and employment,[305] privatized by 1994 and 40 million shareholders in the country by that year.[306]

The decentralization of the economy, and a concomitant shift from vertical to horizontal bargaining, as well as a growing liberalization of import-export laws, are further signs of progress.[307] Others include the establishment of 2,214 commercial banks by 1994,[308] over 70 commodities and stock exchanges, more than 650 investment funds, 6 foreign-currency exchanges, approximately 1,000 insurance companies, and a flourishing market in treasury bills that is actively furthering the capitalization of the economy.[309] As tens of thousands of small manufacturing businesses appear, shareholders in large enterprises are forcing managers to improve productivity or face dismissal. By 1994 real unemployment had also begun to rise, indicating the beginnings of a rationalization of the country's work force.[310]

304. A reaccounting in 1995, furthermore, revealed that GDP fell far less between 1990 and 1994 than was initially suspected—rather than one-half, it had shrunk by a more manageable one-third.

305. By 1995, 70 percent of medium and large enterprises, including several major defense industries and even formerly secret government businesses, and 80 percent of small companies, had been privatized.

306. Anders Aslund, "Prospects of the New Russian Market Economy," *Problems of Post-Communism* 41 (Fall 1994): 16–17. See Stephen Hall, "Privatization in Russia After July 1, 1994," *Parker School Journal of East European Law* 1, no. 4 (1994): 503; William E. Holland, "Privatization in Russia," *Parker School Journal of East European Law* 1, no. 2 (1994): 275; and Darrell Slider, "Privatization in Russia's Regions," *Post-Soviet Affairs* 10 (October–December 1994): 367.

The privatization process, of course, was far from perfect. Approximately thirty thousand crimes are believed to have been committed in association with privatization, the illicit gains of which went, in large part, to bribe officials to protect the criminally culpable. Privatization, furthermore, was often a closed family affair, with managers shutting others out of purportedly public auctions and themselves buying their companies at artificially low prices.

307. Aslund, "Prospects of the New Russian Market Economy," 17–18.

308. Peter J. Pettibone and Juliette M. Passer-Muslin, "Russian Banking and Currency Regulations," *Parker School Journal of East European Law* 1, nos. 5–6 (1994): 709.

309. Scott Horton and Mikhail Saakashvili, "The Stage Is Set for the Russian Securities Market," *Parker School Journal of East European Law* 2, no. 2 (1995): 245–46.

310. Aslund, "Prospects of the New Russian Market Economy," 18–19.

Negative indicators, however, are also visible. Thus, while inflation may be coming under control, a fall in production of 29 percent from 1993 to 1994 (including an especially disconcerting 10 to 12 percent fall in oil production[311]) and drops of up to 90 percent of certain goods,[312] could undermine any progress that might otherwise be made. Unemployment remains artificially low, especially in light of the massive fall in production just noted.[313] This is true only because cheap industrial credits and subsidies remain far too readily available.[314] Finally, gross fixed investment also fell through 1995.[315]

The plight of the individual Russian is especially discouraging, with prices continuing to rise, wealth being distributed inequitably, corruption and profiteering growing rampant, and the social safety net falling into tatters.[316] Yet, surprisingly for those in the West, many Russians still hope for progress and are willing to be patient with the transition a bit longer. As Martin Malia acknowledges,

> Pensions are now worthless, savings have been wiped out, perhaps 20 percent of the population lives below the poverty line, millions of workers have not been paid for six months—and yet no one is rioting in the streets. French fishermen and farmers build barricades for far less. The Russian population, instead, muddles through with second jobs and recourse to a large unreported shadow economy.[317]

Leaving aside the theoretical debate of the monetary policy–oriented shock therapists[318] and the gradualists,[319] it is clear that much remains to be done with the Russian economy. In light of all that has gone before, it is obvious that there is no going back on the price liberalization and industrial privatization that has already been carried out. Yet there is validity in the

311. Malia, "Russia's Democratic Future," 36. From 10.36 million barrels produced in 1990, oil production fell to 9.2 million in 1991, 7.9 million in 1992, 6.9 million in 1993, and 6.1 million in 1994.

312. See table in Hough, "Russia: On the Road to Thermidor," 27.

313. Hough, "Russia: On the Road to Thermidor," 28.

314. See Handelman, *Comrade Criminal*, 329 n. 16.

315. James R. Millar, "The Failure of Shock Therapy," *Problems of Post-Communism* 41 (Fall 1994): 23.

316. Millar, "The Failure of Shock Therapy," 23.

317. Malia, "Russia's Democratic Future," 36.

318. Advocates of a policy that, in reality, never existed beyond several months in early 1992.

319. See, for example, Aslund and Millar.

argument that "the policies called for by shock therapy [are] necessary conditions for economic stabilization in Russia, but they are not sufficient conditions. . . . Shock therapy focuses on financial and price issues, but it cannot succeed without institution-building, thorough-going privatization and demonopolization, and a well-conceived industrial policy."[320]

The necessary implementation of the latter policies does not require major shifts in economic policy but involves efforts to stabilize the economy and thereby encourage confidence in it. Thus, "something must be done to break the wage-price spiral caused by the expectation of continued inflation. The inflation today is driven not by supply shortages but by self-fulfilling expectations."[321] The individual Russian, the Wall Street investment banker, and the Russian bureaucrat must each come to be reassured, by the implementation of stable and consistent policy choices, that the economy has begun to settle down.

Among the policies that will further this goal are a concerted effort to divest state enterprises of their "subsidiary 'welfare' enterprises (e.g., housing, schools, recreation)."[322] Intimately connected to this is an effort both to reduce government subsidies[323] and to carefully control the disbursement and expenditure of the credits provided. Inter-enterprise debt, which had reached up to 130 trillion roubles, or 16 percent of GDP, by 1995, must also be brought into check.[324] Part and parcel of this effort is better financial management.

Those federal expenditures and revenues (such as gold sales) now left out of federal-budget calculations should be included. Only then can realistic adjustments be made toward an efficient fiscal policy. Design of a new regulatory regime is also necessary, especially for the securities markets, which will not attract foreign investment in the absence of strictly construed and applied regulations. The time has also come for concerted agricultural reform, possibly in keeping with the Chinese model, combining controlled prices for a minimum amount of product and market distribution of the rest. Similarly valuable may be the Hungarian experience, with sections of existing collective farms separately administered by managers trained in

320. Millar, "The Failure of Shock Therapy," 23.
321. Millar, "The Failure of Shock Therapy," 23.
322. Millar, "The Failure of Shock Therapy," 25.
323. By keeping the Central Bank lending rate in line with inflation.
324. Newton Davis, "Russian Bankruptcy and Enterprise Sell-Off: Creating a User-Friendly System," *Parker School Journal of East European Law* 2, no. 1 (1995): 73.

agronomy.[325] In light of the highly organized resistance to agricultural reform, this process will be gradual, but it must continue nonetheless.

More broadly, inflation must be lowered even further in keeping with the stabilization of the rouble that began in 1995; this will encourage both a greater influx of foreign capital and a higher retention and reinvestment of domestic capital.[326] While this policy is unattractive to nationalists who wish to keep Russia in Russian hands, privatization and public offerings must be used to attract western capital investment. If western investors are shut out of critical privatizations such as those in the oil industry, the meager $2 billion of foreign investment in Russia from 1992 to 1995 will remain the norm. This is far from adequate for Russia's needs. For western investors alone have the capital necessary for the modernization Russian industry direly needs. Investor pressures will also help to slow drops in production by increasing the productivity of existing enterprises and by expanding the business base to new areas and technologies. Linked with this, finally, must be a strict effort to control the budget deficit, thereby keeping interest rates low and expanding access to capital.[327]

Finally, efforts at both price reform[328] and ownership reform are critical. Difficult as it might be, only linked progress in both these areas will prevent Russia from repeatedly falling back into its old ways. In this regard, active efforts to encourage capitalization of corporate bodies by their restructuring as joint-stock companies will be helpful. By distributing ownership, joint-stock structures will engage a broader cross section of society in the economy, deepening the people's awareness and understanding of it and thereby adding to its stability.

President Yeltsin's efforts to get such reforms on track, beginning with his series of May 1994 decrees reducing subsidies and lowering business taxes, has produced much success, as has the general effort to limit industrial subsidies and control inflation.[329] The 1995 resignation of longtime Central Bank chairman Viktor Gerashenko, with his stubborn focus on production levels and disinterest in inflation, and the appointment of one, and then

325. Hough, "On the Road to Thermidor," 30.

326. A reduction in the confiscatory tax rates that have made evasion the norm is also necessary in this regard.

327. Aslund, "Prospects of the New Russian Market Economy," 20.

328. Including both price liberalization and a firm repudiation of price freezes. The importance of such policies is demonstrated by the grain and bread price liberalization of 1992, which resulted in 1993 becoming the first year in decades that grain imports were suspended.

329. Alessandra Stanley, "Yeltsin Prods Government on Economy," *New York Times,* 11 June 1994, A3.

another, tight-fisted monetarist in his stead,[330] has also enhanced the potential for reform.

Discussion and compromise, the key to effective policy making generally, must be especially encouraged in the economic arena. Most now agree that "to build a democratic legal regime without market structures is practically impossible,"[331] so occasional disagreement is not an insurmountable obstacle. In fact, the debate it will inspire may heighten public understanding of the challenges of economic reform.[332] As the Duma's eventual passage of Yeltsin's 1995 state budget without major damage to its market-oriented principles proved, limited disagreement will not inevitably forestall or hinder the progress of reform.

Economic stability also requires that criminality be dealt with firmly. Not since the Russian Civil War in 1918–21 has there "been such a lack of law"[333] in Russia, with "laws broken so often and so badly."[334] Stabilization of the economy does not and probably could not require that every black-market enterprise be shut down. This sub-rosa sector has become a massive segment of the economy[335] and may be keeping Russia on its feet. The extreme state of affairs of today, however, with "no economic rules of the game," must be moderated.[336]

The wild business climate has undermined respect for the political order. Lawlessness, in the public mind, is now seen as a by-product of democracy. "Today, many Russians equate democratic reforms not only with greater freedom of speech and religion but also with the loss of the external and internal empires, domestic political stalemate, economic hardship, ethnic rivalry, rising crime rates, and a wide range of professional and personal anxieties."[337] While an invalid correlation, as crime and corruption were endemic in Soviet society as well, public perception remains critical.[338]

330. Tatyana Paramonova and Sergei Dubinin.
331. Lukasheva, interview of 1 February 1994.
332. Belyaeva, "Russian Democracy," 9.
333. Piskotin, interview of 6 August 1993.
334. Ametistov, interview of 4 February 1994.
335. The criminal economy was estimated at one-third of Russia's turnover of goods and services in 1993. Steven Erlanger, "Russia's New Dictatorship of Crime," *New York Times,* 15 May 1994, 3. Mobsters, furthermore, may control up to 40 percent of the nation's wealth. Handelman, *Comrade Criminal,* 3.
336. Barenboim, interview of 3 February 1994. Western interest in this area is hyper-accentuated by threats of a trade in nuclear fuels and technologies. See Shelley, "Organized Crime," 58.
337. Hoffmann, 33.
338. See Handelman, *Comrade Criminal,* 9. Thus did 59 percent of respondents to a 1993

Russians' "inability to distinguish between criminal and legal profits" has now become an obstacle to economic stabilization.[339]

Violence dominates modern-day Russian industry and business.[340] Estimates suggest that up to 80 percent of businesses and banks pay approximately 20 percent of their income to organized crime.[341] As early as 1993, forty thousand enterprises were estimated to be completely under the control of organized criminal enterprises. "This is not the parasitical mafia of long-developed economies; it is almost a functional aspect of a market without rules, contracts, a usable currency, insurance, pensions, or an effective police force."[342] Today, "gangsters not only open bank accounts; they open banks."[343] Criminal dominance is quite complete. "Citizens have thus involuntarily traded one form of control for another."[344]

In such a climate, foreign investment cannot be expected to appear, nor will the flow of domestic capital offshore abate. Unschooled in the illegal practices necessary to compete with organized criminal enterprises, and often bound to avoid such practices, as American firms are by the Foreign Corrupt Practices Act, foreign investors simply withhold their investments.

Control must therefore be reasserted, even if by means more intrusive than civil libertarians would comfortably condone. The situation does not necessitate nor justify "any means necessary." Remembering that Stalin's purges began with limited curbs on certain liberties, the public is wary of sweeping crackdowns on crime. Yeltsin's 14 June 1994 anti-crime Decree no. 1226, "On Urgent Measures to Protect the Citizenry Against Banditry and Organized Crime," while acceptable in its goals, thus crossed the lines of legitimacy. It violated the constitution's articles 23(a) and 25 on inviolability

---

public-opinion survey consider state control of "private business" to be necessary for stabilization of the economy. Handelman, *Comrade Criminal*, 307.

339. Handelman, *Comrade Criminal*, 327.

340. With the June 1994 explosion of several car bombs in downtown Moscow, a hitherto unknown act of violence in Russia, it is no surprise to find that crime is consistently the public's greatest concern in opinion polls (Michael Specter, "Yeltsin's Anti-Crime Decree Sets Off a Storm of Outrage," *New York Times*, 19 June 1994, A14). The statistics for both petty and serious crimes show percent increases in three digits over the last several years (Shelley, "Organized Crime," 59). More thus lost their lives to crime in 1993 than during five years of the Afghan war.

341. This figure was determined by Pyotr S. Filippov, a former Yeltsin adviser, and published in a January 1994 report to Yeltsin. Its release created a significant furor about the failings of crime control.

342. Malia, "Russia's Democratic Future," 33.

343. Handelman, *Comrade Criminal*, 3.

344. Shelley, "Organized Crime," 56.

of the home, article 23(2) on privacy of communications, and article 22's limits on periods of detention. Similarly aconstitutional was the 22 June Hurricane Operation that executed the decree.

Twenty thousand Internal Ministry troops on the streets thus conducted searches without court sanction and placed 2,200 individuals under arrest, holding many for extended periods without charge.[345] These extreme incursions against public liberties simply alienated Yeltsin's liberal supporters and reinforced his opponents' accusations that he was a dictator. Thus did the media and nearly all parties in the Duma condemn the decree, the latter having voted in late June to call on Yeltsin to withdraw it, a directive he ignored, citing the critical need to control crime. Another Duma directive instructed the courts to apply existing legislation and not Yeltsin's decree; the police, however, continued to violate the constitution's norms, in keeping with the decree. Since only the right-wing Zhirinovsky supported the decree in the Duma, Yeltsin's and his advisers' misjudgment should have been apparent to them.

With the 1 March 1995 gangland-style murder of Vladislav Listyev, a popular television personality and newly appointed head of *Ostankino*,[346] and the huge public mourning and outcry that ensued, an unconstitutional overreaction by Yeltsin again followed. His dismissal of Moscow's chief prosecutor Gennady Ponomaryev and chief of police Vladimir Pankratov, together with his favorable references to Uzbekistan's harsh and constitutionally questionable crackdown on criminal activity, aroused fears that Listyev's murder would be used to justify the very sort of civil-liberty violations Listyev himself had battled against under both Gorbachev and Yeltsin.[347]

Public opinion, exasperated by an unabating crime wave, might well support such a return to the police state.[348] In a climate of chaos, order takes precedence over the law in the public psyche.[349] Yet this must be avoided. Instead, measures must be taken that are more constrained but that will still strike at the criminal element of the economy. Among these steps are the adoption of legislation analogous to the U.S. Racketeer Influenced Corrupt Organizations Act, laws against money laundering, and provisions for a witness-protection program. Baseline charges of "banditism," while suffi-

---

345. Handelman, *Comrade Criminal*, 292.
346. The main Russian television broadcast system.
347. Some have even suggested his murder may have been masterminded by conservatives intent on provoking a tightening of government control.
348. Handelman, *Comrade Criminal*, 277.
349. Shelley, "Legal Consciousness," 66.

ciently broad to cover a variety of criminal acts, do little to strike at the ultimate sources of crime, reaching only their agents in the field.

Though defeat of the mafia is bound to be a challenge, it remains feasible. The strength of the mafia may be greater in Russia than in many other industrial states, but it continues to lack the organization and depth of engagement enjoyed by its counterparts in Italy and the United States.[350] An initial step is to equip the Russian police to effectively counter the firepower of organized crime. No longer should officers be sent out carrying handguns and driving old Ladas, while their opponents wield Uzis in BMWs.[351] Law enforcement, thus, must become a credible threat to criminal actors.

With a stronger economy and more stable political order, initial control by force can be succeeded by more effective economic control. Schemes of business regulation, such as the financial disclosure and false-advertising laws adopted in 1994, and a more effective tax policy must also be introduced. Gaps in the Civil Code, which came into force in January 1995,[352] should be filled, its conservative restrictions on land use (such as its "purposeful use" requirement) should be removed, and its positive place in the design of ordinary contracts and other financial instruments should be promoted. The kind of government action represented by the Civil Code—a true instrument of social change, designed by a group of market- and democracy-oriented reformers—will gradually bring the entire spectrum of Russian business into the economy's legitimate sectors. It will strengthen the economic order and demonstrate the power of the law to eliminate chaos.

Like pro-reform big businesses and banks, small businesses will come to support the reform process as it provides them with greater security and the potential to expand in a stable and orderly marketplace.[353] In this climate of normalcy, economic *zakonost,* legality, will take root. Only in this circumstance, when there is a better "social, political, and economic situation" and "the police are doing right, and the courts are acting well," will constitutionalism finally emerge.[354]

---

350. See Arkady Vaksburg, *The Soviet Mafia* (London: Weidenfeld & Nicolson, 1991). See also Handelman, *Comrade Criminal,* 3 n. 3. The 1993 murder rate of less than 30,000 and firearm-offense rate of less than 22,000 are hardly a crime wave by American standards, but are quite high compared with the Soviet years.

351. Handelman, *Comrade Criminal,* 282–83.

352. *Vedomosti RF,* no. 32, item 3301 (1994).

353. Laws on shareholder rights are also critical, as is a strengthening of the Russian Securities and Exchange Commission, formed by Yeltsin's 4 November 1994 decree "On Measures for State Regulation of the Security Market" and initially headed by Anatoly Chubais.

354. Kudriavtsev, interview of 31 January 1994.

The legalization of private property was long debated and struggled over. Having finally received official sanction, land ownership should now be used as a tool in the creation of constitutionalism. Lost on 10 July 1918 with the first Soviet Constitution, and slowly returning to favor since 1990, private property must now become a reality rather than simply a concept for the Russian people. It was not by chance that legalization of the private ownership of land was the liberals' greatest struggle over the last ten years. This simple right, its opponents worried, represented the essence of every individual right, freedom, and protection under the law. Even those lacking a conservative political bent thus acknowledge the positive impact of ownership rights on public consciousness of other rights.

If "the process of real privatization" can make private property a reality for a broader spectrum of the Russian population, it will create "a better training ground for the people's sense of legal rights than any other."[355] People will become aware of their legal interests in ways almost impossible to teach otherwise.[356] This sense of personal prerogative is particularly important with reference to those rights held against the government. The Constitutional Court's decision of 9 June 1992 limiting the government's right to infringe individual property rights, even in the service of economic reforms, thus greatly furthered public consciousness of the legal order.[357]

"Private property rights and an independent judiciary have allowed thousands of small businesses to flourish in St. Petersburg [and elsewhere] by protecting their leases and other contracts from the interference of city agencies and would-be bribe-taking officials."[358] This is critical. For "a reluctance to safeguard property dooms all constitutional effort both politically and socially. The transformation of the legal system can only be partial without a wholehearted endorsement of free market institutions."[359]

The control of resources increasingly defines power in Russia.[360] The people's power and influence has remained limited because they have not experi-

355. Migranyan, interview of 4 February 1994.

356. Small private businesses also have a critical role in encouraging this rights awareness. Thus, "a new enterprise employing a handful of workers can help its employees to realize that their future lies with the market, and not with the state and its subsidies." Rose, "Postcommunism and the Problem of Trust," 29.

357. Ametistov, comments, 24. The decision ruled as unconstitutional the Council of Ministers' Resolutions no. 403, of 17 July 1991; and no. 43, of 24 January 1992.

358. Joel M. Ericson, "Russia Shows Life Signs Beyond Moscow," *New York Times* letter to the editor, 4 March 1994, A26.

359. Sajo and Losonci, "Rule by Law," 323.

360. Belyaeva, "Russian Democracy," 10.

enced ownership themselves. Thus the failure of even one individual to sue the Central Bank after its July 1993 confiscation of roubles convinced one Russian legal scholar that people "still do not take their rights seriously." Property rights, like all other rights, remained intangible.[361] The basic right of property can now serve a first-order educative function regarding all individual rights.

As the "market is intimately linked with the development of constitutional processes,"[362] its concrete functions and relationships can provide a tangible forum for the individual's defense against violation and intrusion, either from above or from the side. In this way, as individuals begin to regard their possessions as legally and enforceably theirs, their whole sense of the legal order and their place in it will be transformed. This is why businessmen often are the first to embrace legal reforms. There is probably some merit to Tocqueville's argument that "those who prize freedom only for the material benefits it offers have never kept it long,"[363] but as a transitional impetus for reform, a self-interested, and even material, view of rights in Russia may be of value.

The possession of property, and land ownership especially, will also create a strong interest in the maintenance of order and stability.[364] The actual allowance for private ownership of land, first proclaimed by presidential decree in October 1993, and then adopted as part of the new constitution in December, should thus be made a reality. A new land code, one expanding the limited allowances for outright ownership of land that now exist, is thus critical.

By "opening up the possibility for a sizable part of the population to be economically free to vote," a new middle class will emerge and "become the bulwark of democracy."[365] In a climate of widespread ownership, each citizen will have a stake in maintaining effective governance and the rule of law. Public institutions generally, and the courts in particular, will become crucial to the individual in a way that few Russians would describe them to be today. Market reforms, along with their concomitant dislocations, will thereby become linked to real social interests and no longer will public support for reform be dependent on government appeals to "patience, forbearance, sacrifice, and patriotism, motives totally unrelated to the logic of the market."[366]

---

361. Vlasihin, interview of 10 August 1993.

362. Lukasheva, interview of 1 February 1994.

363. "L'Ancien Régime et la révolution," in Alexis de Tocqueville, *Oeuvres Complètes* (Paris: Gallimard, 1952), 217. Quoted in Elster, "The Necessity and Impossibility," 269.

364. Needless to say, ownership reform is also an important key to raising managers' incentives to increase efficiency. Elster, "The Necessity and Impossibility," 269.

365. Yakovlev, interview of 5 February 1994.

366. Lena Kolarska-Bobinska, "The Role of the State: Contradictions in the Transition to Democracy," in Greenberg, 305.

The increasing focus of Russian officials and the general public on economic development, as evidenced by the cooperation emerging around these issues and by their growing coverage in the media, is a great leap forward in constitutionalism's development. Real results and substantive, as distinct from merely procedural, progress is now critical. "Although the pursuit of limited government and individual freedoms is admirable, the establishment and maintenance of such a government and the exercise of such freedoms in a prosperous and secure society are what really matter to a country's citizenry."[367]

Effective economic policies are therefore essential. When the voucher program ended in 1994, formal privatization was basically completed. Entrepreneurs and managers must now attract cash investments from both within the country and abroad to improve these industries and businesses. Steps must be taken to encourage such investment through equity markets, to improve industrial efficiency, and to constrain undue disparities of wealth. As valuable resources such as oil, aluminum, and diamonds, as well as individuals, are tapped, the pace of development will pick up and demonstrable progress in the economic arena will ensue.

In fact, this has already begun. After the shocking 27-percent drop in the value of the rouble on 11 October 1994 (Black Tuesday), a collapse triggered by a new wave of government subsidies in the weeks just prior, Prime Minister Chernomyrdin, who once wavered on tight fiscal management and the pace of reform, was converted to the cause of a tight, anti-inflationary fiscal policy. The parliament adopted a tough budget, bringing monthly inflation down to 7 percent by July 1995, from 18 percent in January of that year. This, in turn, spurred the prime minister's pledge to keep the rouble within a band of 4,300 to 4,900 roubles to the dollar, a commitment that has been kept. Of course, the parliamentary and presidential elections in December 1995 and June 1996 were an impetus for the loosening of such strict politics, but these encouraging signs[368] suggest there is hope for a long-term shift toward good economics, even among former Soviet bureaucrats.

---

367. Hoffmann, 22.

368. In an especially hopeful sign, by late 1994 domestic assets invested offshore had begun to remigrate back into the Russian economy. Other positive indicators: from 10 percent of GDP in 1994, the budget deficit fell to 6 percent in 1995; inflation, meanwhile, from a high of 2,500 percent in 1992, had fallen to approximately 110 percent by 1995, and to 60 percent by 1996. Finally, by 1996 OECD indicators suggested that the Russian economy had begun to grow, possibly by as much as 10 percent.

EXTERNAL INFLUENCES

A few concluding comments are necessary on the policies of external states and their potential impact on the emergence of constitutionalism in Russia.[369] This influence was limited during the years of Russian and Soviet isolation. The world, however, is now intimately engaged in the economic and political affairs of Russia and is, for better or worse, a part of the developmental equation. Noting the potential benefits of heightened western exposure, Peter Juviler cites the Marquis de Custine's observation of tsarist Russia: "The political system of Russia could not survive twenty years' free communication with the rest of Europe."[370] While the West's potential contribution should not be exaggerated, neither should it be underestimated.[371]

On the whole, the impact of the West since 1985 has been positive. The West's "disproportionate influence" during this period, in fact, profoundly encouraged both the practices and the psychology of constitutionalism.[372] These external pressures have been particularly conducive to a strengthening of Russia's commitment to international legal norms and obligations.[373] This has long been true, as exemplified by the Soviet Union's adoption of the Helsinki Accords' Basket Three human-rights principles in article 29 of the 1977 constitution. During the last decade, western influence has helped undermine the imaginary dichotomy of a Soviet and a western legal culture and made plain the existence of a "global culture that it is Russia's destiny to be a part of."[374] This new understanding may in fact have been the West's greatest contribution to Russia to date.

The western democracies, however, must move beyond such general influences to address the nuts-and-bolts issues of Russia's new constitutional order. The West must "finally see the crisis in Russia"[375] and engage itself in

369. See George Ginsburgs, "Domestic Law and International Law: Importing Superior Standards," in Barry, *Toward the "Rule of Law" in Russia?* 179–95.

370. Marquis de Custine, *The Empire of the Czar: A Journey Through Eternal Russia* (New York: Doubleday Anchor Books, 1989), 139. Cited in Juviler, "Russia Turned Upside Down," 30. If the Marquis de Custine calculated correctly, we have only ten more years to wait.

371. See Lempert, "Changing Russian Political Culture," 636.

372. Anatoly A. Slussar, chief adviser to the president, Foreign Policy Association, and member of Soviet Diplomatic Corps, 4 February 1994. Hereafter Slussar, interview of 4 February 1994.

373. Kudriavtsev, interview of 17 August 1993.

374. Zorkin, interview of 2 February 1994.

375. Gleb Yakunin, member of Russian Supreme Soviet, Orthodox minister, and adviser to President Yeltsin, 20 July 1993. Hereafter Yakunin, interview of 20 July 1993.

"deeper and more concrete ways."[376] Russia stands in need of an "intellectual Marshall Plan" that will intimately connect it to the West's legal and political norms and encourage its evolution into a civilized legal culture.[377] Russia must become an equal partner in the community of industrialized democracies. In this respect, the western allies' failure to include Russian troops alongside those of the United States, Britain, and France in 1994 ceremonies celebrating the end of the occupation of Berlin was an egregious error.[378] As did the Organization for Economic Cooperation in postwar Europe, the West should design programs that bring Russians together with their western counterparts to address concrete problems and work on real projects. From building roads to maintaining electrical services, such efforts will create myriad fora in which the practical and functional knowledge Russia stands in need of can be readily taught and learned.

The same holds in the legal arena, where westerners can provide Russia with expertise in the mechanics and details of the law. This must begin with academia and does not involve simply translating legal textbooks, as financier and philanthropist George Soros did early in the reform process; rather, it involves true education. Research centers and scholarly gatherings can be organized at various academic levels. Germany's training of departing Russian military officers in business management may serve as a model. It provided valuable skills that will further Russia's long-term development and that otherwise would have never been available. Such efforts can tap into the "American legal and democratic experience," in which interest remains strong.[379]

Legal academics' "very strong vision of the American Constitution,"[380] though somewhat tarnished by overzealous American support for Yeltsin's extra-constitutional actions in September and October 1993, remains powerful and can be used to gradually raise the level of constitutional discourse. A paradox, however, exists in Russia's fascination with American law and the consequent limitations in their engagement of European legal scholars. Efforts to involve the latter must increase since their shared civil-law tradition, one unfamiliar to the United States, will allow Europeans to contribute uniquely to the development of constitutionalism. Nevertheless,

376. Slussar, interview of 4 February 1994.

377. Zorkin, interview of 2 February 1994.

378. Stephen Kinzer, "Bitter Goodbye: Russians Leave Germany," *New York Times,* 4 March 1994, A1.

379. Thornburgh, "The Soviet Union and the Rule of Law," 13.

380. Barenboim, interview of 3 February 1994.

leadership by the United States is critical, given the aforesaid Russian bias and greater American resources.

Increased professional contacts are also significant. Former attorney general Richard Thornburgh's visit in October 1989, "to discuss the meaning and importance of the rule of law," at the invitation of Soviet justice minister Venyamin F. Yakovlev, began this process.[381] This type of practical interaction of professional counterparts, and the knowledge of the functional details of governance it can provide, are important to the success of constitutionalism in Russia. For the "triumph of democracy in Russia will come in the details" of how the presidential veto and other "concrete techniques of interaction" operate in a real democracy. Russia does not need abstract words about the "end products of democracy, but rather answers about how to overcome its hardest problems."[382] Cooperative ventures are also advantageous, as was apparent in the enthusiastic welcome given to the FBI liaison office that opened in Moscow in June 1994 to help Russians battle organized crime. Such joint ventures can be of immense value in exchanging practical skills.

Although every western principle and practice will be Russified in its application, such modification will not detract from their collective beneficial impact. As Julio Faundez has noted,

> It could well be that in some cases the uncritical transplant of the liberal democratic model stems from a sincere belief not only in the virtues of the model, but in the possibility that, with patience and good will, citizens in other countries may learn how to use it. This idea appears to have inspired the recent Democratic Initiative Program launched by the U.S. Agency for International Development. These and similar initiatives seem to be based on the theory that democracy is a technology, like agriculture, with principles and practices that can be readily learned and replicated.[383]

Yet "mechanistic borrowing" of American legal concepts and instruments is of little use.[384] To begin with, these concepts are not perfect. More important, they have developed in an alien climate, the United States, and have

---

381. Thornburgh, "The Soviet Union and the Rule of Law," 13.
382. Yakovlev, interview of 5 February 1994.
383. Faundez, 357.
384. Sharlet, "Russian Constitutional Crisis," 318.

been adapted in ways that are incompatible with Russia's own circumstances.[385] Instead, by adjusting American legal principles and practices to
its own culture, Russia will develop a functional model more appropriate to
its own needs in building democracy and constitutionalism.[386] The Russian
diaspora, with its exposure both to Russia's needs and to western society, can
help convey western legal principles to Russia, as Armenians overseas have
done with Armenia. Armenian expatriates applied their extensive personal
and professional experiences in various democratic, constitutional nations
to their home state, greatly accelerating its political reform.[387]

Cultural and people-to-people contacts will also nurture the development
of legal consciousness. These interactions will encourage support for western
democratic and constitutional norms among the masses, who are now more
critical than ever. "When Russia was a dictatorship as part of the Soviet
Union, a good relationship with the man at the top was all that was
necessary. This is no longer enough."[388] The decision to hold the Goodwill
Games in St. Petersburg from July to August 1994 represents such efforts to
build non-political contacts between Russia and its fellow nations.

Western contributors to the development of constitutionalism in Russia
must remember that Russia has had even less experience with democratic
and constitutional principles than have Eastern Europe and the states. As
William Butler observes, "we are impatient, often more so than the Soviet
people themselves."[389] Yet patience with Russia's gradual adoption of these
principles is essential. No need can justify undue interference in Russia's
internal affairs. Thus, "American jurists and scholars who go to East Central
Europe to 'instruct' the peoples of the region on the true meaning of
constitutionalism too often act upon a series of universalist assumptions
that do not take into account the multiplicity of historical, ethnic, religious,
and political traditions and current realities at work in . . . different
nations."[390]

As an example, the West should certainly avoid situations such as U.S.
president Bill Clinton's 1993 discussion of former prime minister Yegor

385. See Lempert, "Changing Russian Political Culture," 636.

386. See Stanley N. Katz, *Constitutionalism in East Central Europe: Some Negative Lessons from the American Experience* (Providence, R.I.: Berghahn Books, 1994).

387. Paen, interview of 28 January 1994.

388. Richard Nixon, "Moscow, March '94: Chaos and Hope," *New York Times*, 25 March 1994, A29.

389. Butler, "Perestroika and the Rule of Law," 18.

390. Katz, *Constitutionalism in East Central Europe*, 10–11.

Gaidar's future with President Yeltsin, which inevitably confuse the public about the limits of western involvement in Russian politics.[391] Such "imperialistic" arrogance has already produced a backlash, with more than half of the Russians in a 1993 survey supporting the view that the "West has the goal of weakening Russia with its economic advice."[392] "Western tutors in democratization and marketization were at first welcomed and now are selectively tolerated."[393] Creating a renewed trust by making clear the advisory, and not directive, nature of western engagement is thus a priority.

The former Soviet republics can also contribute to one another's constitutional development. To begin with, the Baltic states may influence Russia in ways similar to the western democracies, since they are far more advanced in their progress toward democracy. A broader constitutionalization of relations between the former republics may also contribute to each one's political stability and individual constitutional development. If their interaction were to take on a more ordered and legalistic character, possibly under the auspices of the Commonwealth of Independent States, it would help to create a climate in which constitutionalism might more readily emerge within each respective state. Western attempts to peacefully resolve Russia's differences with the Baltic states over the withdrawal of troops and the rights of Russian minorities, illustrated during U.S. president Bill Clinton's July 1994 visit to the Baltics, can also contribute to this process.

Finally, foreign economic aid must no longer be seen as charity by either the Russians or the West. It should be provided as it was to postwar Japan, as a cooperative investment in a future more amenable to both donor and recipient.[394] With Poland, Hungary, Lithuania, and other former Soviet bloc states having already returned various proto-communist parties to power, western interest in a stable Russian democracy and market is extremely strong. Humanitarian aid must be distributed as best it can be, not because it will have any serious financial impact on the gigantic Russian economy but for its psychological reverberations. Foreign aid can thus serve as tangible evidence of western interest and will encourage and protect the Russian public's commitment to democratization and marketization. On the other hand, its absence will arouse disdain for the West and all it stands for. Thus did an elderly Muscovite became most agitated as he asked why the United

---

391. Olshanski, interview of 2 February 1994.
392. Hough, "The Russian Election of 1993," 6.
393. Hoffmann, 33.
394. Biryukov, interview of 18 November 1993.

States was not helping Russia more: "Don't they realize we are important?"[395]

Aid must be given more strategically and intelligently. It should not be dispersed as a gift to one individual, however openly the West might proclaim its political support for him or her. "Treating President Yeltsin as a politician rather than as the symbol of everything good would make it harder for Russians to complain that America is interfering in its domestic affairs."[396] By its orientation, western aid should serve to "strengthen the process instead of particular persons."[397] It should also be targeted at political and economic processes at the bottom rather than the top. This shift toward a fine-tuning of foreign assistance is part of an "emerging . . . new concept of aid to Russia which consists [of] supporting and promoting various democratic institutions directly, through mechanisms of grass-roots democracy and self-government."[398] This bottom-up approach is more conducive to lasting change in the country and should be expanded upon.

By tactful engagement, the global community may encourage Russian progress toward constitutionalism and avoid the pitfalls of actual or apparent interference. Thus can it contribute to a critical process in which its own interests are nearly as great as those of the Russian people. In the end, however, the creation of constitutionalism "is a job that East Central Europeans must do for themselves, nurturing their most promising local traditions and institutions. Americans must watch sympathetically, if anxiously, all the while resisting the temptation to urge their own historic accomplishments upon nations creating their own, unique constitutional moments."[399]

395. Elderly taxi driver in Moscow, 4 February 1994.
396. Dimitri Simes, "Is Yeltsin Losing His Grip?" *New York Times,* 6 March 1994, 15.
397. Zorkin, interview of 2 February 1994.
398. Nina Belyaeva, "Humanitarian Aid and Charity," *Interlegal Bulletin,* August 1993.
399. Katz, *Constitutionalism in East Central Europe,* 19.

CONCLUSION

My generation has done all it could to move our country to constitutionalism and democracy. The future lies in the hands of a new
generation.

—Mikhail Gorbachev[1]

"Our country is no longer what it was," reflects Fyodor Burlatski. "A new
Russia faces a new future."[2] The 1980s and 1990s have been a time of
massive historical change. A new set of core values has emerged at the
foundation of a radically altered sociopolitical system. Yet these values have
failed to implant themselves in the Russian psyche until now. Many of the
basic psychological and structural aspects of Russia's transformation thus
remain incomplete. As Gleb Yakunin laments, "the new order is still not a
reality for Russia."[3]

What, then, does Russia's development to date add up to? What role may
particular individuals and institutions play in leading Russia's further evolution toward constitutionalism? And what, finally, is the realistic likelihood
of constitutionalism's emergence in the near future?

"WHAT IS TO BE DONE?"

Nearly a century ago, Vladimir Ilyich Ulyanov, now remembered as Lenin,
put forth the question "What is to be done?" and answered with his call for

1. Mikhail Gorbachev, interview of 17 August 1993.
2. Burlatski, interview of 1 February 1994.
3. Yakunin, interview of 20 July 1993.

a proletarian revolution in Russia. Today Russia faces this query once more, only now the answers are more difficult. The destructive transformation Lenin espoused was relatively simple to achieve. Russia's modern politics of construction, in contrast, involves more than force and good timing. Most important, it requires not the labor of an elite party but the broad engagement of individuals and institutions at all levels of society. While even such universal participation will not guarantee the persistence and flowering of Russia's embryonic constitutional democracy, it is surely its best hope.

Public engagement in political and constitutional processes also requires that Russia dispense with its proclivity for fatalism, a tendency that has long stifled progress. Russians' traditional sense of themselves as caught in the river of history, unable to choose their own destiny, must finally be disavowed.[4] Instead, they must recognize and be confident that the concrete steps of today will determine the shape of their future.

In assessing the creation of legal consciousness, and even constitutional structures, it is difficult to highlight isolated policy decisions or individual actors as singularly influential. As I have attempted to do in the foregoing, one must weigh and balance the influence of a wide range of complex factors, each acting upon one another and upon constitutional development. A particular policy or individual will not bring constitutionalism to Russia, only an entire climate of positive social, economic, and political interactions.

Yet we must outline the tasks and responsibilities of particular individuals and institutions if principles are to be put into practice and ideals are to become realities. Political and societal actors must play a responsible role in the emergence of constitutionalism. The aggregate effort, in the end, will not be more than the sum of its parts. It will therefore be beneficial to conclude with a profile of the various agents of constitutionalism in Russia and their potential contribution to its emergence. What impact may they have, and how will this influence be actualized? This prescriptive focus on specific actors is critical if the theory of constitutionalism's evolution from below is to be applied in actual practice.

We may begin with the president, who is arguably the most influential individual, for better or for worse, in the emergence of constitutionalism. Any president's potential impact on constitutionalism is great, as is his or her responsibility for it. President Yeltsin, for example, long held onto "his Communist, Bolshevik instincts and, therefore, [did] not particularly *want*

---

4. Biryukov, interview of 18 November 1993.

to obey the written law."[5] Thus did he declare in his memoirs that "everyone knows that we Russians do not like to obey all sorts of rules, laws, instructions, and directives—any kind of previously established regimentation of behavior. We are a casual sort of people and rules cut us like a knife."[6] The impact of such personal characteristics of the president should not be disregarded.

Given Russia's instability, an erratic President Zhirinovsky, as distinct from a clear-headed President Chernomyrdin, can make all the difference— entirely for the worse. As Erik Hoffmann notes, "the flexibility of national governmental structures and functions is so great as to make the personalities of top officials critical variables in the state-building and policy-making processes."[7] It is thus critical that Russia's chief executive rein in any proclivity to act beyond the scope of his constitutional authority.

The president must rule in strict accordance with the constitution's provisions. If the most prominent figure in the constitutional order does not act to legitimize the current constitutional and institutional arrangements, who will?[8] Yet acts such as President Yeltsin's 1994 Omnibus Anti-Crime Legislation violate at least the spirit of the constitution, if not its letter as well. Similarly dubious was Yeltsin's dismissal of top regional executives in October 1994. His successor must avoid such conduct. "Presidential leadership can be decisive in creating a viable constitutional order—perhaps especially in the initial post-revolutionary, post-colonial, post-authoritarian, post-totalitarian stages of democratization and in major crisis situations that threaten the survival and identity of the nation (e.g., the American Civil War)."[9] By following rather than violating constitutional norms, the president sets a standard for every executive official in the country, potentially altering the very nature of Russian governance.

President Yeltsin's use of his executive-decree powers was especially problematic. Although this was a common practice throughout Yeltsin's years in power—with an average of 155 decrees issued monthly during 1993, and 184 in the two weeks after 21 September 1993 (and his infamous Decree no. 1400)[10]—executive rule is inappropriate to the constitutional

5. Nikonov, interview of 3 February 1994.
6. Quoted in Timothy J. Colton, "Superpresidentialism and Russia's Backward State," *Post-Soviet Affairs* 11 (April–June 1995): 146.
7. Hoffmann, 41.
8. Hoffmann, 41.
9. Hoffmann, 29.
10. Sharlet, "Russian Constitutional Crisis," 329.

democracy that Russia became in December 1993. Even if well intentioned, and even if permissible under article 90, which allows for presidential decrees that do not contradict existing legislation, such non-legislative acts should be seen as irregularities, not as instruments of daily governance. Until now, it has been "presidential decrees and Government orders that define, most clearly and fully, the rights and responsibilities of the state and its citizens."[11] Such means may appear more efficient but undermine the constitutional processes that will preserve Russia in the long run.

The most egregious example of Yeltsin's use of executive decrees, and that with the worst consequences for both himself and the nation, was the invasion of Chechnya. The terms of the invasion were set out in a series of executive decrees drafted in closed sessions of Yeltsin's Security Council. The voice of the public, as represented by the Duma, was completely ignored in this process. The debacle that followed and the humiliations of Yeltsin and his advisers, including the spectacle at Budennovsk and the collapse of Yeltsin's approval rating to 6 percent, might well have been avoided had democratic processes been allowed to run their course. They were not, however, with clear lessons for Yeltsin's successors.

The president and his minions must acknowledge the value of compromise and consensus in Russian politics. President Yeltsin's anxious hurry mini- mized the role of consultative deliberation and broad-based unanimity in political decision making. Yet "moving quickly," a traditional Russian saying cautions, "is only important when killing fleas." Rather than at- tempting to strong-arm the fellow branches into conformity with his will, the president must take pains to gain their support. This process is critical to the maturation of Russia's constitutional structures. The president must broaden his vision to include the big picture of Russian development and must recognize his role as a nation builder, laying the foundations for a future Russia.

The president must also take care to stay within the authority granted him under the constitution in responding to opponents, especially in the media. The raid of the offices of the oppositionist *Segodnya* by Yeltsin's personal security team[12] (which drove the paper's owner, Vladimir Gusinsky, into voluntary exile in London) was thus a grave blow to the development of

11. Huskey, "The State-Legal Administration," 129.
12. Yeltsin's security entourage and its former leader, the secretive and apparently quite powerful General Aleksandr Korzhakov, exemplify the kind of behind-the-scenes threat to democracy that Russia must be particularly wary of.

constitutionalism and freedom of speech in Russia.[13] Reformers should not fear open debate. Ultimately they have the better arguments, making secrecy and antidemocratic approaches unnecessary.

Neither patience nor statesmanship were in great abundance during President Yeltsin's early years in public office. His more temperate pronouncements and actions after the December 1993 elections thus represented a major shift in Russian presidential politics. The centrality of the theme of cooperation in Yeltsin's 1994 State of the Union address, given to the Duma only one day after its politicized amnesty decision, was a positive step in this regard. The persisting benefits of the April 1994 Treaty on Social Accord and the work of its Conciliation Commission also exemplify the shift of Russian politics toward consensus.[14]

On the other hand, the ill-conceived and excessively brutal military campaign in Chechnya, coupled with official constraints on television coverage of the war and attempts to suppress information on it, again typify the negative behavior that has marred Yeltsin's entire tenure and must be avoided by his successors. Gorbachev's far more limited use of governmental violence in the Baltics in January 1991 badly tarnished even the admittedly authoritarian Soviet regime.[15] Yeltsin's invasion of Chechnya, then, could not help but discredit the vision of Russia as a constitutional democracy, which Yeltsin had claimed as his greatest legacy. The military's gross violations of human rights in Chechnya only darkened this cloud of doubt. To avoid the repetition of such missteps in the future, the president must focus his attention on human rights and end the polarity of inaction and overreaction that characterized the early years of the Russian presidency.[16]

One of the most immediate issues facing the president is the massive state bureaucracy.[17] He must act decisively to reduce the size of this bloated body, whose tendencies towards conservation are bound to stifle reform. That

13. Gusinsky would later reject an article on government corruption for fear of retaliation, instead sending it to the anti-establishment *Moscow News*. Stanley, "Russia's New Rulers Govern," A1.

14. See Hoffmann, 51–52.

15. See Juviler, "Human Rights After Perestroika," 6.

16. See Hoffmann, 40.

17. From 1989 to 1994 the bureaucracy grew 1.7 times, with local and regional governments accounting for two-thirds of the increase. Non-uniformed officials thus number 1.66 million (Huskey, "The State-Legal Administration," 139 n. 59). The bureaucracy is also becoming increasingly conservative. This is evidenced by the State-Legal Administration, the Security Council, and other government institutions that were established to help reform the government but have themselves become Russia's entrenched bureaucracies. Huskey, "The State-Legal Administration," 135.

Eugene Huskey, an expert in Soviet and Russian state institutions, would parallel the extensive "supervisory" functions of Yeltsin's presidential apparatus (including control of housing, medical care, and office space for all branches of the government) with those of the Communist Party is damning evidence of how great a problem this has become.[18] The 1994 budget supports this assessment; it allots only 180 billion roubles to the Duma and 76 billion to the Federation Council, but 214 billion to the president's Administration of Affairs and 286 billion for his Administration for Planning and Realization of Special Programs. This disparity provides further evidence of the presidency's bureaucratic bloat.[19]

The bureaucracy's continued domination of the political and social processes of Russia, which are better controlled by the public and its elected representatives, must come to an end. Practical measures are also necessary to reduce bureaucratic corruption by increasing the sanctions against such activity as well as the incentives to reveal it. Long-entrenched *apparatchiki* must be forced to relinquish their "inherited stereotypes of political behavior as deceptive and dishonest" and to begin to operate in ways appropriate to an open political system.[20] Such efforts to curtail the bureaucracy's influence should include a systematic transfer of responsibility to regional authorities better attuned to local needs. In addition to improving efficiency, this shift in authority will expand the Russian people's interaction with the bodies of power, deepening their understanding of how constitutional government works.

The state of the economy, however, is the most pressing issue facing the president. Its improvement will require a concentrated focus, till now elusive, on economic reform. While the government has general responsibility for economic policy, the president can strongly influence the character and speed of the reform process. President Yeltsin's 23 May 1994 decrees advancing economic reform, including revisions of Russia's tax laws and efforts to ensure inter-enterprise debt payments and loosen the strictures on exports, are ample evidence of this. The increasingly cooperative atmosphere around economic decision making that emerged from 1994 through 1995 is also reassuring. As President Yeltsin's pragmatic partnership with Prime Minister Viktor Chernomyrdin integrated the Duma as well during 1995, economic reform gained steam and the economy made progress. In March 1994 Vitaly Tretyakov, a liberal journalist, complained about Yeltsin's

18. Huskey, "The Presidency in Russian Politics," 7–8.
19. Huskey, "The State-Legal Administration," 116 n. 5.
20. Yakovlev, interview of 5 February 1994.

economic policy: "There is no program. No new course. No honest analysis of past mistakes and achievements. There is no policy. Nothing."[21] Through Yeltsin's efforts at cooperation, this vacuum finally began to be filled.

The Government's most significant task in the service of constitutionalism will be to establish a balance in the relations of the president and parliament, and to act as guardian of a zone of compromise between them. Particularly, if the Government can mediate between the president and the Duma to ensure the progress of economic reform, it will create the greatest bulwark for order and stability and make the emergence and persistence of an effective constitutional order far more realistic. It was heartening to see Prime Minister Chernomyrdin's success in this respect in 1995. If there is any argument for optimism about Russia's future, it lies in the gradual improvement of the Russian economy we appear to be witnessing. The rapid expansion in Prime Minister Chernomyrdin's authority from 1994 to 1995, finally, evidences the influence that a careful and conciliatory prime minister can wield in shaping Russia's future.

As for the parliament, it must stringently avoid confrontation with the president. Of course, the Duma should not allow the latter to become an autocrat, as the Soviet legislature did Gorbachev.[22] Comity ought not be exaggerated into a slavish accession to the president's will and caprice. It simply means that differences and disagreements should not be drawn out of proportion. Though the majority of deputies may not be aligned with the president in their political ideology, most support the essential premises of reform and recognize the need for its effectuation. Rather than acting to sabotage the policies of its fellow government institutions, the Duma should therefore strive to constructively influence the policy-making process.

In surveying the legislative record of the first Duma, it is heartening to discern such tendencies in its work.[23] Led by the conciliatory Ivan Rybkin, the first Duma was surprisingly willing to compromise and cooperate. In large part, the source of these positive efforts lies in the Duma's discovery that, notwithstanding the constitution's bias toward presidential power, it has real power. This was manifest in June and July 1995, when a parliamentary vote of no confidence drove Yeltsin to dismiss three of his most detested ministers. The Duma must use this power, however, as a force for construc-

21. Vitaly Tretyakov, quoted in Erlanger, "Russian Battle: Stage Is Reset," A10.
22. Foster-Simons, "The Soviet Legislature," 116–17.
23. The slow pace of the Duma's legislative calendar, though criticized by many, was to be expected during the transitional Duma's two years of existence.

tive change, not destructive attack. When even as potent a critic of the present order as Deputy Oleg Rumyantsev admonishes the Duma to act constructively and live up to its potential (as limited as he considers this to be), there is sound reason for optimism.[24]

The Duma's essential task is to draw the "underlying political forces" of Russia—the people and various nongovernmental bodies—into its work,[25] thereby ending the masses' alienation from the political discourse of Russia.[26] No longer, as in a 1995 survey, should 67 percent of Russians declare the central government to have "little or no effect on their daily lives."[27] Members of parliament, this suggests, can radically alter Russian politics by concentrating on winning their constituents' support through political education and awareness. Recent elections were important to this process, as elections are among the "best schools for the legal consciousness of the Russian people."[28] With the pace of local and regional elections picking up, coalition building and the consolidation of a small number of strong parties must begin in the Duma. Given widespread political apathy, public involvement in parties is sure to prove challenging. Nevertheless, local party-building activities can help to inspire public interest in the character and politics of their potential representatives.

Yet, the alleviation of public apathy ultimately lies in the effectiveness of government action. As the government improves the economy and builds institutions meaningful to the man or woman on the street, Russian citizens will regain interest and faith in these institutions. This is essential to further progress. The parliament must thus concentrate on the timely and efficient adoption of laws that substantively improve the lives of the Russian people. This is their constituents' anxious desire. "We want something different," said one May Day protester in 1994. "I know we can't go back. But we are not going forward. We are poor. We are afraid. And we need a government that cares about that. I don't know who I would vote for now. But I want this country to change."[29] Legislation addressing basic public needs, from the educational system to welfare reform, will often appear mundane to ambitious and heady parliamentarians, but only such laws and statutes will give

24. Rumyantsev, comments, 10.
25. Belyaeva, "Russian Democracy," 15.
26. Mishin, interview of 14 August 1993.
27. Rose, "Russia As an Hour-Glass Society," 41.
28. Yakovlev, interview of 5 February 1994.
29. Quoted in Michael Specter, "May Day in Moscow: Remembrance of Soviet Past," *New York Times,* 2 May 1994, A11.

the people a concrete sense of the law's relevance to their own lives. It was thus the Soviet Congress of People's Deputies' perception of many critical questions as "minor procedural issues and . . . trifling or even meaningless," rather than as bricks in "the foundation of a new political order," that brought about its own downfall.[30]

Legislative initiatives must address the statutory regulation of the government as well—curtailing corruption and regulating campaign financing, among other tasks. The impact of such measures on the legal consciousness of the public cannot be overestimated. With a government above the laws, it has been difficult to create a society willing to live by them.

It is especially critical that the Duma act to adopt the various federal constitutional laws mandated by the constitution, including a Law on Referenda (article 84[v]), on the Ombudsman (article 103[d]), on the Government (article 114[2]), and on the Court System (article 118[3]). Without these, the constitution remains incomplete. Every effort must also be made to ensure that the Duma's enactments will be effective. Although statutory effectiveness has been limited during the last decade, the selection of well-defined, reasonable objectives and the enumeration of concrete mechanisms for their realization will help improve this poor record.[31]

Among the Duma's highest priorities, then, is decisive action on economic reform. The Duma will acquire greater prestige and influence by joining in the drive to reform the economy than by any other decision it may make. Long delays, such as with its adoption of the 1995 budget nearly halfway through the fiscal year, must also be curtailed if the Duma is to contribute to the economy's regulation. Legislation for the elaboration and financing of a strengthened judicial system is similarly critical. New local courts must be established and existing ones supported and secured. Failing this, the constitutional order of Russia is doomed.

There will inevitably be bumps on the road to effective legislative activity in Russia. With relatively little precedent or history to guide it, the Duma faces a daunting task, but not an insurmountable one. Inadvertently locked out of his committee office without his briefcase and papers just before a critical vote of the full chamber, one Duma member thus smiled and suggested that the first American Congress probably ran into similar problems![32]

30. Sergeyev and Biryukov, *Russia's Road to Democracy,* 114–18, 163.

31. Legal redundancies and contradictions in the enactments of the Duma should also be rooted out.

32. Mikhail Fedorov, member of Federal Assembly (Duma), 1 February 1994.

As noted above, the judicial branch is essential as the guarantor of the Russian constitutional order. At first, the judiciary's impact on the development of constitutionalism will most prominently involve the Constitutional Court, whose mission and casework we have already considered. Beyond its own work, however, the Constitutional Court must press the president and parliament to accelerate the judicial-building process at the local and regional level. This will involve training new personnel to staff an expanded number of courts of first instance. Improvements in court procedures and staffing will allow for some expansion in the caseload of existing courts, but the number of courts remains far from adequate for a law-governed society. Only if courts are readily available will the public turn to them with their disputes.

Increased financing for courts must be found in the national budget. While higher court fees and local financing are commonly discussed solutions, these approaches will limit access to the courts and may impinge on their independence. Rather, the government should cut bureaucratic waste and invest its savings in the development of a more effective and broad-based judiciary. The Constitutional Court, in cooperation with the Supreme Court and the High *Arbitrazh* Court, Russia's two other senior courts, can help to enhance the operational efficiency and legitimacy of the lower courts by drafting procedural and substantive guidelines for them. Such a task would be analogous to that of the Judicial Conference of the United States and would facilitate the development of consistent norms of adjudication throughout the judicial system. Without such guidance, the process of judicial development will be unnecessarily slow and sporadic.

The courts must handle cases in a manner that will inspire public esteem and respect. They must build trust in a land where 83 percent of the populace distrusts political parties; 72 percent distrusts the parliament; and 71 percent distrusts the police, the courts, and other institutions of authority.[33] Every effort must therefore be made to avoid engagement in political contention and dispute. Instead, the courts should demonstrate a commitment to the constitution and the law above the politics of the hour. This requires strict adherence to procedural guidelines, which must no longer be seen as "mere" procedure but as the bedrock of the judicial system. That Yeltsin failed to submit his ominous Decree no. 1400 to even his own legal advisers (the State-Legal Administration), as is technically mandated, underscores the

---

33. Rose, "Russia As an Hour-Glass Society," 38.

value of careful procedures. Violations of procedure are the first step, if not the last, on the path to substantive violations.

Judicial independence must be fiercely defended against encroachment by the other branches. Yeltsin's November 1993 attempt to revise the Constitutional Court's 1992 decision in the Communist Party case represents such egregious conduct. More recently, the growing influence of Yeltsin's State-Legal Administration (*Gosudarstvenno-pravovoe upravlenie*—GPU) and its potential domination of legal and judicial activity in the country has been raised as a concern.[34] The president and parliament must respect the courts as a peer to be consulted with and deferred to, not as an antagonist to be stymied and undermined. Such a dramatic change of heart will not be easy given the legacies of Soviet rule, but the public's interest in and support for the work of the courts may help preserve their authority.

The courts must particularly focus on the defense of individual rights. Resolution of such cases in the local courts, where they often have personal significance to the local population, will foster both a sense of inalienable rights and an allegiance to the courts among the masses, building legal consciousness at the grass roots. The law will gradually become "the preferred means for peacefully mediating and negotiating political, economic and social disputes and conflicts."[35] Yet for this to happen, the law must consist of more than theory—which was already available a century ago but provided little solace to the average Russian. Russia's citizenry does not need good theories; it needs practical legal experience.

The dispersal of judicial authority away from the center is in keeping with a broader need for federalization. In all respects, strengthening constitutional structures and legal consciousness requires that greater power be transferred to regional and municipal governments, the institutions that can have the broadest impact on constitutionalism in the years ahead. Russia must begin a "painstaking process of building institutions at the local level," imitating continental Europe's evolution toward constitutionalism.[36] Only through intimate contact with it will the public come to appreciate how a political order based on law actually works. The alternative of

---

34. See Huskey, "The State-Legal Administration." In December 1994 Justice Minister Yuri Kalmykov resigned on account of the State-Legal Administration's gradual displacement of many of the functions of the Justice Ministry. "Constitution Watch—Russia," *East European Constitutional Review* 4 (Winter 1995): 24–25. Of late, however, its influence may be on the wane.

35. Sharlet, "Citizen and State," 110.

36. Biryukov, interview of 18 November 1993.

"democracy as a set of instructions from above" is ephemeral and thus less than ideal.[37]

Naturally, the constitution itself has a vital role to play[38] in restructuring both horizontal and vertical power relationships and in creating a common ground for compromise and consensus.[39] It remains unclear which of Giovanni Sartori's categories of constitutions—real, nominal, or facade—Russia's 1993 constitution will fall into.[40] However, if there is any hope for the real, it lies in putting aside what controversy remains around the constitution and striving to optimize, not minimize, its legitimacy. For it is surely not as bad as it may seem. Thus, the president's veto power, though much criticized as too great, duplicates that of the United States, with provision for a two-thirds' override by the parliament. In its early years, even the United States Constitution was controversial. Only with two hundred years of hindsight, if even now, does its authority and contribution seem "clear and apparent."[41]

A constitution cannot create and sustain a constitutional order alone. In Russia, "such documents have never had this effect."[42] The public has become far more conversant with the law during the last decade. The government has made dramatic progress in its transition from a single-party, command-administrative system to a democratic one. Various parliamentary institutions are educating the public and beginning to "involve the people in the political atmosphere."[43] Yet neither a finely worded document, nor powerful institutions, nor an abstract knowledge of the law can prevent a return to authoritarianism or ensure the appearance of constitutionalism. Institutions lacking social underpinnings will crumble, and knowledge without conviction will provide little guidance at all.

Achieving constitutional perfection is thus a marginal issue. The crucial question is "whether the Russian people are ready to live up to the constitution they already have."[44] Rather than perfect laws and institutions,

37. Walter Murphy, professor of politics, Princeton University. Comments at presentation of Nikolai Biruykov, Princeton University, 15 November 1993.

38. Though not itself an actor in the creation of constitutionalism, the role of the constitution, and public and elite attitudes toward it, are obviously critical factors to consider.

39. Klamkin, interview of 4 February 1994.

40. Giovanni Sartori, "Constitutionalism: A Preliminary Discussion," *American Political Science Review* 56 (December 1962): 861, 863, with accompanying notes.

41. Biryukov, interview of 18 November 1993.

42. Lukasheva, interview of 1 February 1994.

43. Migranyan, interview of 4 February 1994.

44. Klamkin, interview of 4 February 1994.

Russia needs a sense of respect for the law. For without the active support and understanding of the Russian people, even the best of laws will give rise to the state of affairs H. W. O. Okoth-Ogendo has associated with many African states—"constitutions without constitutionalism."[45] Today Russia has "a Constitution without citizens, because most Russians do not see their everyday concerns as integrated with the government established by the Constitution of the Russian Federation."[46]

There thus persists an "inertia in the life of Russian society."[47] The general public remains largely removed from the political and constitutional processes under way, and Russia's transformation remains in the hands of the elites. "It has turned out," laments one Russian, "to be their revolution, not ours."[48] Not until the *people* embrace the constitutional order, however, will constitutionalism take root in a fundamental and lasting way.[49] If a civil society is to emerge in Russia, sociopolitical forces beyond the government must be involved. Until now these parties have failed to fulfill their potential in the creation of constitutionalism. Religious groups, for example, have not functioned in Russia as they have in other countries, establishing powerful social action organizations and Christian-Democratic parties. Yet the potential impact of religion on Russian political development cannot be underestimated, as the Orthodox Church has always occupied a central place in public consciousness and national identity. In fact, among the political and social actors in Russia today, the church is most trusted by the general public.[50] Religious groups can thus help to define both Russians' political and personal views. Lacking other powerful sources of values, Russian society needs religion.[51]

The western democracies have also failed to pursue their opportunities to help build civil society in Russia. Sporadic educational, informational, and cultural exchanges have hardly addressed the depth of need. Given Russian fascination with everything western, from literature to commercial merchandise, thoughtful engagement by the United States and Europe can have a tremendous impact.

45. H. W. O. Okoth-Ogendo, "Constitutions Without Constitutionalism: Reflections on an African Political Paradox," in Greenberg, 65.
46. Rose, "Russia as an Hour-Glass Society," 36.
47. Yegorov, interview of 2 February 1994.
48. Vassily Aksyonov, "My Search for Russia's Revolution," *New York Times,* 22 November 1994, A23.
49. See Pastykov, " 'Noviye russkiye,' " 23.
50. Rose, "Russia As an Hour-Glass Society," 38.
51. Biryukov, interview of 18 November 1993.

The Russian media similarly could have done more to assist in the political and constitutional education of the people. Rather than focusing on financial gain, media entities ought to have pursued a more noble purpose, striving to increase public understanding of political and constitutional processes. Their sensationalism and muckraking journalism may have sold more copies, but given the broad availability of government subsidies, this was a less than critical concern.

Yet, as noted from the outset, the key to the emergence of constitutionalism in Russia is the people themselves. While each of the foregoing players has an important role to play, Russia's citizenry must become the central actor on the political stage. Only then will constitutionalism, democracy, and a free market—and ultimately a new civil society—emerge in Russia.

WHITHER THE RUSSIAN TROIKA?[52]

Despite the many failings of recent years, Russia has made demonstrable progress toward constitutionalism. As even Oleg Rumyantsev acknowledges, the last decade has witnessed "a miracle of constitutionalism."[53] The opening of the political system led to the "creation of a public sphere of power with more and more people playing active and passive political roles."[54] This began in 1987 with the earliest mass demonstrations, in which the people showed themselves to be increasingly unafraid of the state. "The

52. Russia, are you not speeding along like a fiery and matchless *troika?* Beneath you the road is smoke, the bridges thunder, and everything is left far behind. At your passage the onlooker stops amazed as by a divine miracle. "Was that not a flash of lightning?" he asks. What is this surge so full of terror? And what is this force unknown impelling these horses never seen before? Ah, you horses, horses—what horses! Your manes are whirlwinds! And are your veins not tingling like a quick ear? Descending from above you have caught the note of the familiar song; and at once, in unison, you strain your chests of bronze and, with your hooves barely skimming the earth, you are transformed into arrows, into straight lines winging through the air, and on you rush under divine inspiration. . . . Russia, where are you flying? Answer me! There is no answer. The bells are tinkling and filling the air with their wonderful pealing; the air is torn and thundering as it turns to wind; everything on earth comes flying past and, looking askance at her, other peoples and states move aside and make way. Nikolai Gogol, *Dead Souls* (New York: W. W. Norton, 1985), 270.

53. Rumyantsev, comments, 2.

54. Migranyan, interview of 4 February 1994.

result was a flourishing of civil society and an explosion of voluntary movements, citizens' fronts, independent newspapers, and civic groups of all kinds. . . . Once unleashed, this process could not be stopped or even controlled from above."[55] By 1990 over five hundred parties existed in the Soviet Union;[56] today, they are innumerable. Social and nongovernmental organizations have likewise blossomed since their legal inception in 1991.[57] This is the greatest evidence of the public's commitment to change and the potential impact of this commitment on the progress of reform. "What might or should have been is simply not relevant to [Russians'] difficult lives. The issue is not how Russia got here, but how it moves on."[58]

In December 1992, when the parliament's Constitutional Commission removed the section on civil society (articles 57–61) from its draft constitution, it underestimated, like most, the need for a new civil society in Russia.[59] After much delay, the time is ripe for the construction of a moral civil society in Russia that will substitute new principles of social organization for a defunct *partinost*. This transformation of thoughts and attitudes, as Justice Zorkin suggests, is the key to constitutionalism.[60] And while he himself may not have lived up to this aspiration, that he would describe it as his vision is itself promising.

"A united force of powers—the cultural, governmental, and intellectual elites—must begin the drive to constitutionalism."[61] Utilizing the rhetoric of rights, whether human, economic, or civil, such a coalition must provide the general public with a practical constitutional education through the media, governmental bodies, and academic institutions. Even under Josef Stalin, children across the country received weekly "constitution lessons." In this era, such lessons are necessary for all Russians. As they are absorbed, "constitutionalism will emerge from the people" and systematically encompass the whole of society.[62]

While no one would argue that civil society will come easily to Russia, few

55. Belyaeva, "Russian Democracy," 7–8.

56. *Radio Liberty Report on the Soviet Union* (8 March 1991), 29.

57. Nina Belyaeva, "What Is Possible for NGOs in Russia: A Discussion of the Current Laws," *Interlegal Insert* (Spring 1993).

58. Serge Schmemann, "Solzhenitsyn's 'Deepest Russia': Is It Still There?" *New York Times*, 30 May 1994, A2.

59. Albert P. Blaustein and Gisbert H. Flanz, eds., *Constitutions of the Countries of the World—Russian Federation Supplement* (Dobbs Ferry, N.Y.: Oceana Publications, 1993).

60. Zorkin, interview of 2 February 1994.

61. Klamkin, interview of 4 February 1994.

62. Klamkin, interview of 4 February 1994.

would contend that it is impossible to achieve. Were it so, "why was it possible to hear the Beatles on underground radio stations in the 1960s, to pay market prices for a doctor's or plumber's house call in the '70s, or to open a private health clinic in the '80s?"[63] In its history, Russia may thus find guidance—and inspiration. During the final decades of tsarist rule, for example, one can point to the abolition of serfdom, the judicial reforms of 1864, and even jury trials as precursors to the constitutional reforms now in progress. Legal journalist Arkady Vaksburg, bemoaning Russia's "lack of memory," reminds us: "Today we are starting with a blank slate when we argue whether or not a jury system is democratic, although this question was resolved in our country more than a hundred years ago."[64] Too long ignored both within Russia and without, this history should be refurbished as an educative tool in support of legal and constitutional reforms.

As constitutionalism rises from below, the central government's role will diminish and it will increasingly shift power to regional bodies of authority. New nongovernmental institutions, their growth fostered by the private funds increasingly available in the economy and by supportive tax-deduction laws for charitable contributions, will develop to satisfy the myriad needs left unfulfilled by the present order. Their work, in cooperation with local governments, will gradually integrate people into the political sphere, giving them a heightened sense of citizenship and commitment to the constitutional order. The creation of such associational groups, and their encouragement by legislation such as the 25 May 1995 Law on Public Associations, is thus essential. Only at this level of intermediate social institutions can a disperse civil society—still divided into hundreds of parties and unfocused in its activities—begin to coalesce and take on a coherent, enduring form.

As with Robert Putnam's bowling leagues in the United States, political and nonpolitical groupings, from choirs to sports clubs, can help reconstitute the society the Soviet Union took years to atomize into its individual components. "The Soviet regime not only blocked the emergence of genuine classes; it also undermined many of the other sources of interest and identity on which the institutions of civil society are built. The eclipse of Orthodox Christianity and other confessions over seven decades of repression, for

---

63. Ericson, A26.
64. See Juviler, "Russia Turned Upside Down," 31–32 and accompanying notes, including Arkady Vaksburg, "*Kakim dolzhno byt' pravovoye gosudarstvo?*" *Literaturnaya Gazeta,* 8 June 1988.

example, has greatly reduced the potential of religion and spiritual commitment as bases for political organization."[65]

An increase in individuals' awareness of their rights will further the personalization of the new constitutional order. A broad-based rights dialogue may thus be quite beneficial in creating constitutionalism. As an example, the increasing application of international legal norms and the tendency to place these above domestic norms, and even to allow citizens to appeal to them, will enhance rights consciousness and constitutionalism.[66] As an awareness of rights becomes intuitive, the public's engagement with the constitutional order and place in it will change.

"[A] legislative culture cannot be legislated or willed from on high. Since attitudinal change is a long-term, glacial process, a supportive legal culture . . . [must] be 'grown' over time." In the final analysis, the emergence of constitutionalism will not involve the passage of new laws or schemes of social engineering. Rather, it will require practical experience with the life of the law.[67] This experience—with individual rights, with nongovernmental organizations, with local government, and with the courts—will propel Russia far down the path of constitutionalism.

With the Chechen war and the massive opposition to it that emerged in early 1995 (with four out of five Russians against the war), an important step was taken by Russian society. For the first time, one could truly speak of Russian "public opinion," with all its implications about Russian society having a voice and place in the political culture. How fascinating, thus, that it was the Chechen émigré Sovietologist Abdurakhman Avtorkhanov who said thirty years ago that the Soviet Union was not an industrial society, not because it lacked industry, but because there was no society.[68] This, it seems, may have finally begun to change.

The process of political and constitutional development will climax in a "constitutionalization of the everyday relations of the Russian people" not unlike that once achieved by the ten commandments.[69] One can only hope that this journey will similarly lead Russia out of the desert in which it has long wandered and into the promised land of a democratic, constitutional future.

---

65. M. Steven Fish, "Russia's Fourth Transition," *Journal of Democracy* 5 (July 1994): 33.

66. Peter Juviler, draft of book in progress: "Human Rights and Democracy in Post-Soviet Systems: The Ordeal of Freedom," 1.

67. Sharlet, "The Fate of Individual Rights," 197–99.

68. Quoted in Paul A. Goble, "Chechnya and Its Consequences: A Preliminary Report," *Post-Soviet Affairs* 11 (January–March 1995): 25.

69. Olshanski, interview of 2 February 1994.

In the final analysis, however, can such hope be justified given the state of Russia at this juncture? Or is it simply a pious, yet naive, longing for a better world that underlies the optimistic assessment of the future found herein? Is constitutionalism, in Hoffmann's words, a "viable possibility"?[70] While Juviler's position of "responsible hope" seems most appropriate, the case for doubt is an easy one.[71] The Russian economy remains in dire straits, with production falling and artificially maintained employment levels now under threat. If 1994 closures and layoffs of 20,000 workers at ZIL and 35,000 at Uralmash,[72] two of Russia's best-run corporations, are indicative of future trends, the threat of massive social upheaval and chaos, if not civil war, is now a realistic possibility. Moreover, the consequences of Russia's state of arrest are not limited to the short term. Decades from now the demographic impact of the recent decline in birth rates and collapse in life expectancies will still be felt.[73] With a 1993 population decline of 71,600, and diseases such as diphtheria, hepatitis, and dysentery increasingly common in both urban and rural areas, the survival of any Russia at all, democratic or otherwise, may be threatened.[74]

These elements of disorder and chaos, along with increasing crime and government corruption, have become fuel for the assailants of constitutionalism. Thus must we consider the increasing likelihood of complete parliamentary domination by either the leftist parties (at best) or the increasingly fascist, nationalist parties; or, worst of all, the frightening possibility of a President Zhirinovsky. The public's increasing impatience with "politics as usual," with centrists and liberals in control, is pressuring Russian politicians of all stripes to adopt the extremists' strident rhetoric and, occasionally, even their policies. Such concessions, in turn, strengthen the empty claims of radicals, heightening their appeal and potential for electoral victory. Constitutionalism will likely be the first, but not the only, victim of such nightmare scenarios.

Yet a more balanced assessment reveals a somewhat brighter picture and more positive trajectory. Russian mentality truly has begun to change, with support for fundamental reform increasingly strong among the general

70. Hoffmann, 20.
71. See Hough, "Russia: On the Road to Thermidor," 26–31.
72. Michael Specter, "Soaring Unemployment Is Spreading Fear in Russia," *New York Times,* 8 May 1994, A3.
73. Michael Specter, "Climb in Russia's Death Rate Sets Off Population Implosion," *New York Times,* 6 March 1994, A1.
74. Handelman, *Comrade Criminal,* 333.

public.[75] "Russian elite and mass political culture are not immutably authoritarian, and the trend is toward values supportive of a civil society and civic culture."[76]

The reactionary Zhirinovsky and his misnamed Liberal Democratic Party, for all the attention they received after the December 1993 election, fared relatively poorly in local elections held in the spring of 1994, after several months of public exposure to Zhirinovsky's antics and emotional instability.[77] Likewise, the shifting fortunes of the Communists in the elections of 1995 and 1996. More important, "demons" such as Yuri Mezhkov, labeled a Zhirinovsky clone in the course of his successful campaign for the presidency of Crimea, have turned out, once in office, not to breathe such scalding fire or to have such sharp talons.

A similar contradiction is found in Russian foreign policy, supposedly hijacked by the extremists. Occasional inconsistencies aside, the Russian national-security establishment supported western initiatives in the former Yugoslavia, joined the Partnership for Peace, and cooperated fully with nuclear disarmament and even verification regimes during 1994, the year the media claimed that foreign policy was ceded to the right. The military, traditionally considered a threat to stability and constitutionalism,[78] may thus be helping Russia move toward stable international politics. On the whole, order and stability thus appear to be holding their own. Democratic consolidation appears to have begun.

A similar sense of hesitant optimism seems justified in the economic arena. The April 1994 Treaty on Social Accord, reviled as it was in certain circles, endured, and the resulting focus on economic reform is producing beneficial results. Critical western capital and investment has started to flow into the country, former prime minister Yegor Gaidar's nightmare of runaway inflation has failed to materialize, and massive Central Bank subsidies have finally been brought under control. The International Monetary Fund's 1995 and 1996 agreements to provide more than $15 billion in standby loans highly contingent on fiscal discipline and control of inflation may also portend future progress.

As everyone from record companies to candy makers sets up shop across

75. See Donna Bahry, "Society Transformed? Rethinking the Social Roots of Perestroika," *Slavic Review* 52, no. 3 (Fall 1993).

76. Hoffmann, 54.

77. Contrariwise, this could also represent a turn to more "solid" politicians on the right. See Handelman, *Comrade Criminal*, 308 n. 9.

78. Yuri N. Afanasyev, "Russia's Vicious Circle," *New York Times,* 28 February 1994, A17.

Russia, stoking local economies through hard-currency investments from both home and abroad, the threat of economic and social collapse has begun to subside and the political order has gained strength. In some respects, Russian public mentality is not all that different from that of the United States today. In a September 1995 public-opinion poll, citizens of both countries were troubled by the state of the economy and by rising crime rates and, in advance of presidential elections, were looking to former military leaders for decisive leadership.[79] Russians' greater optimism, as well as knowledge and discussion of substantive issues, may even put them in a better position to break free of their doldrums. This analogy should not be strained, but that it could even be drawn is evidence that progress has been made.

Though the conventional wisdom held that it would take several generations to learn the ways of democracy and the market, the Russian people—both old and young—proved unwilling to wait so long. The basics of reform—of privatization, of individual rights—have already been learned and can no longer be turned back by any government.[80]

Debates are sure to continue about the efficacy of certain economic or political approaches versus others and the social impact of each, but these quandaries are increasingly the concern of elites and intellectuals alone.[81] Around them "the busy, metallic cacophony of Russian life goes on unheeding."[82] Finally, Russia may be moving from a politics of revolution to one of evolution, a key step on its journey to constitutionalism.

Asked if he was hopeful for Russia at a gathering on the future of constitutionalism, political philosopher Nikolai Biryukov wondered aloud if his reason could be pessimistic, yet his instinct optimistic. This, insisted a more doubtful participant, was an "irrational optimism." Or, responded Walter Murphy, the renowned constitutional historian and an optimist, it might be a "*super*-rational optimism."

---

79. Michael Specter, "Russia's Voters Turn Cranky," *New York Times,* 1 October 1995, 4.

80. See Edward W. Walker, "Politics of Blame and Presidential Powers in Russia's New Constitution," *East European Constitutional Review* 2, 3 (Fall 1993 and Winter 1994): 118–19.

81. Young people especially are focused on the future and thus provide the greatest hope for it. See Table X in Mikhailovskaia, "Constitutional Rights," 75.

82. Stephen Erlanger, "If the Russians Can Talk Freely, What's to Write About?" *New York Times,* 29 May 1994, 3.

"Nothing in her history," admitted Biryukov, "will help Russia much. Yet obstacles of similar magnitude did not prevent the establishment of constitutionalism in Japan after World War II. So maybe we can surmount them too."[83] Even in the United States, he might have added, constitutional difficulties of the most fundamental kind persisted at least until the Civil War, if not to this very day.[84] And with open talk of the rule of law even in Communist China, who can tell what is possible?[85]

Speaking at the United States Capitol on 10 May 1994, Yelena Bonner, wife of the late Andrei Sakharov, likewise expressed her hope for Russia's future. "Later today there will be a solar eclipse. As you probably know, during an eclipse animals behave very strangely because they do not understand what is happening. I have a feeling that many people, in trying to understand the current situation in Russia and the other countries of the former Soviet Union, have this same animalistic fear. As human beings, we should realize that the sun will in fact shine again."[86]

Amidst many a reasonable doubt, there thus remains a ray of hope. Russia surely faces a difficult journey.[87] Yet the "miracle of constitutionalism" we have witnessed in Russia to date may not have run its course and the cycle of failed reform may have finally been broken. By the careful engagement of all parties, the successes of the past can now be built on and a new constitutional order made a reality. The history of Russian constitutionalism may yet prove to lie ahead—in the future of a new Russia.

83. Discussion at presentation of Nikolai Biryukov, Princeton University, 15 November 1993.

84. Sharlet, "Russian Constitutional Crisis," 314–15.

85. Steven Mufson, "Chinese Movement Seeks Rule of Law to Keep Government in Check," *Washington Post,* 5 March 1995, A25.

86. Yelena Bonner, excerpts from speech at U.S. Capitol, *Journal of Democracy* 5 (July 1994): 137.

87. Sharlet, *Soviet Constitutional Crisis,* 149 n. 88.

EPILOGUE

At the close of 1996, nearly twelve years after the appointment of Mikhail Gorbachev as General Secretary set the Soviet Union on the path of reform, Russia remains in the midst of a profound transformation. Predictions, even those thoughtfully made on the verge of publication, continue to turn on conditions too fleeting to warrant much reasonable reliance. Moreover, "progress" in Russia remains unpredictable, with one step forward sometimes preceding two steps back and other times another three steps forward. Thus may the proponents of nearly every view of Russia's future cite various statistics and news items in support of their position. As U.S. Supreme Court Justice Robert Jackson noted, reviewing the state of American jurisprudence on executive power in 1952, "A century and a half of partisan debate and scholarly speculation yields no net result, but only supplies more or less apt quotations from respected sources on each side of any question. They largely cancel each other." Perusal of even a handful of the preeminent serials on Russia's transition to the market reveals just this. Only this month, one can find any number of articles, full of careful citations, either bewailing the imminent collapse of the Russian economy or celebrating its turnaround and imminent expansion.

Yet notwithstanding the difficulty—and limitations—of such prognostications on Russia's future, I shall briefly attempt, with a bit of the hubris that has long characterized study of this "riddle, wrapped in a mystery, inside an enigma," my own glance into the immediate future. To my mind, neither an entirely optimistic nor a painfully dark view of Russia's future is appropriate. Russia continues to face serious developmental challenges in every arena. A stable future is far from secure. The positive accomplishments of recent years are undeniable, yet they could be undermined as quickly as they have been achieved.

Five years into Russia's constitutional revolution, however, its *trajectory* remains positive. While it may not yet have achieved all we in the West had hoped for, it has hardly sunk into its own Thermidor. Surely, however slowly, the ambitious aspirations to constitutionalism and legal culture laid out in the foregoing are moving out of the realm of imagination and within the reach of reality. It is increasingly difficult, in 1996, to maintain that Russia is heading toward civil war or wholesale economic collapse. Thus, the optimistic, if not naive, view of several years ago is fast becoming conventional wisdom.

Why, then, do many continue to insist on the dire state of the Russian economic and political order? At least in part, these contrary views may arise from inappropriate assessments of conditions in Russia. The Russian economy in 1996 is thus appropriately compared with the same economy in 1992, not with OECD indicators for similarly sized industrial economies. In the former comparison, one cannot but applaud Russia's great achievements, while in the latter, Russia does appear to stand on the verge of collapse. Yet Russia, remember, was one of the "socialist republics" of the Soviet Union only five years ago. Similarly, if one narrowly focuses on the massive powers of the Russian presidency today, one hesitates to call Russia any sort of democracy at all. Yet a comparison of Russian governance under Yeltsin versus his predecessors, or an assessment of the powers wielded by Yeltsin against those *seized* by U.S. presidents such as Abraham Lincoln and Franklin D. Roosevelt at moments of national crisis, suggests a more hopeful prognosis for Russian democracy. Such evaluations are more reasonable and allow us to better understand not only the myriad difficulties Russia still faces but also those victories for which it is rightly praised.

Russia is thus finally moving toward a normalization of the political order, as a Russian "politics as usual" takes shape. Democratic processes are becoming habitual. On 16 June and 3 July 1996, Russians participated in their ninth national plebiscite in seven years, reelecting Boris Yeltsin as their president. From their first exposure to democratic voting in 1989, for the only partially democratic Soviet Congress of Peoples' Deputies, and through another three parliamentary elections (1990, Russian Congress of Peoples' Deputies; 1993 and 1995, Duma), two Russian presidential elections (1991 and 1996), and three referendums (preservation of the Soviet Union [1991], support for the Russian president and reform program [1993], and the Constitution [1993]), these national political engagements have become an essential, and *expected*, part of public life.

Thus, from a 1989 participation rate of 87 percent, one artificially inflated by lingering Soviet perceptions of voting as obligatory, participation had sunk to a low of 54.3 percent by December 1993. Yet it is now on the rise, pushing 70 percent in the 1996 presidential election. Seventy million of 108 million registered voters thus engaged with the political system in 1996, even if only at this most elementary level of national elections. Such engagement is a major step for the country. Arguably, it suggests that the political order, long a realm beyond the reach, and even the interest, of the Russian people, today means something to them. Of course, participation can always be improved. The many who stayed away from the polling places, as well as the 4 million who cast their vote against both candidates, must also be drawn into the system. Yet again, equitable comparisons with Western voting patterns reveal a particularly engaged Russian public.

Such participation in the democratic process, the "voicing" (*golosovat*) of one's political choices, is playing a critical role in the democratic education of Russians. The consideration of candidates and their policies, the exercise of one's choice, and the translation of this into concrete political realities, though much debased as a democratic asset in the West, continues to mean the world to the Russian people. Such is politics as they have never known it—a politics that is their own. As this has persisted, democratic elections have taken on a character of permanence that will brook no return to the past. Elections, as an early surrogate for democracy, have thus become so intrinsic to the system that all now fall under their sway. Even Mikhail Gorbachev, after avoiding the electorate during nearly seven years at the helm of a superpower, thus finally faced the Russian people in 1996. At last, he too was forced to hear their voice. And with only 0.5 percent of the popular vote, what a tragic voice he heard.

Democratic processes are becoming more meaningful as well. President Yeltsin, faced with single-digit approval ratings only months before the June election, knew radical steps were necessary to renew public support for his presidency. He looked in this regard beyond the conservative, almost Soviet cadre that had gathered around him, to young liberals such as Anatoly Chubais, Igor Malashenko, and Vyacheslav Nikonov, knowing that their grasp of democratic politics was critical to his success. Largely at their advice, he dismissed senior officials such as Defense Minister Pavel Grachev and Head of Presidential Security Aleksandr Korshakov, who, though close to him, were loathed by the public. Finally, he brought the unpredictable Aleksandr Lebed into his camp in between the first and second rounds of the election, hoping thereby to draw Lebed's substantial first-round vote (15 percent) to himself in the two-way race between Communist Party candidate

Gennady Zyuganov and himself. The public voice, suddenly, had become instrumental in shaping the government. Of course, this can be criticized as mere political maneuvering, yet such maneuvering well mimics the democratic processes of the West. Regardless of this, such respect for the people's views remains a step in the right direction. At last in Russia, the people speak, and so it is done.

Yeltsin's reelection efforts, however, are less significant for what he did do than for what he did not do. Notwithstanding pressure from many in his circle to cancel, delay, or restructure the election, Yeltsin kept it on schedule and fair. There were extremely few accusations of fraud, and these few, such as in Dagestan, where an enormous shift from Zyuganov to Yeltsin between rounds was noted, were rather minor in terms of the entire electorate. That a redoubled effort to win popular support would be Yeltsin's response under pressure rather than an attempt to tinker with the results represents a huge alteration in the Russian political ethos. Twenty, or even ten, years ago, such a reaction would have been unimaginable. Here, then, is the essence of Russia's political transformation.

The political balance in the country is also stabilizing. A rough balance between pro- and anti-reform forces has thus emerged both among the general populous and among the elites at the national, regional, and local level. Russia's early democratic, "wild west" political period, with players coming and going, and deeply held views abandoned and adopted overnight, is at last coming to a close. In both the 1993 and 1995 Duma elections, the balance of pro- and anti-reform forces remained steady, though centrist reformers won the seats of liberal reformers, and communists seized much of the nationalist vote. Though more emphasized, the political base of the communists is thus no more stable than that of Yeltsin, who consistently garnered about 40 million votes in national plebiscites in 1991, 1993, and 1996. Both camps, thus, are increasingly stable in their composition, with roughly equal support. This balance is also being played out in the regions, where the governors' elections under way are going to reformers and conservatives in roughly equal proportion.

This is an ideal atmosphere for the development of more effective policies, as each camp struggles to present itself as best suited to lead Russia toward economic growth and political and social stability. This dynamic, with each side consistently presenting its own take on the myriad issues facing Russia, is already helping to break down the unipolar political mentality of the Russian public. Such political reeducation is critical to Russian political culture. Elite training in the merits and exercise of compromise is also best conducted within this framework of balanced competition. Thus, while many pulled much hair about the close presidential vote in the first round, with 35.28 percent for Yeltsin and 32.03 percent for Zyganov, Russia may ultimately be well served by this narrow gap.

The shape of the Duma is likewise stabilizing. Thirteen parties ran for the 225 party seats allotted in the first Duma, eight of which passed the 5 percent hurdle and were seated. Forty-three parties, on the other hand, ran in the 1995 election, yet only four surpassed 5 percent. These figures subsume two positive indications for Russia. The first is an increasing politicization of views, suggested by the growing number of parties emerging to represent divergent interests. The ten presidential candidates in 1996 and the rise from 1,567 to 2,688 candidates for the 225 single-member Duma seats confirm this trend. Yet the failure of most of these parties to secure membership in the Duma suggests an increasing tendency to ultimately vote for one of several dominant political parties. To begin with, this is conducive to political stability. A Duma of four parties is thus far more functional than one of eight or more. The emergence of large, cohesive parties will also help to encourage improved party discipline and will allow for more reasonable contrasting of policy choices. Focus on a small number of large parties, moreover, will allow these to more effectively reach out to the general public and, in order to garner support, to pursue coalition-building and an accommodation of views that will help move all parties to the center.

Extremism is thus being pushed to the far bounds of Russian politics. The hard-line communists—the Communist-Working Russian Party—secured only 4.53 percent of the December 1995 vote. Likewise, though Vladimir Zhirinovsky's right-wing Liberal Democratic Party fared better in the Duma elections than their counterparts on the left, Zhirinovsky's diminished stature as a national figure was revealed in the 5 percent he polled in the presidential elections, close to his showing in the 1991 presidential elections, when still a political unknown. Again, normalcy has begun to emerge.

The threat of nationalisms, such as that of Zhirinovsky, moreover, seems increasingly to be overdone. While nationalism is inevitably a real threat in a once-powerful country now viewed, both from within and without, as weak and impotent, fears of a nationalist uprising or rebirth of the Russian empire are exaggerated. Parties of this ilk are not winning substantial electoral victories, nor are the Russian people generally, or military officers specifically, rallying around virulently nationalist, expansionist policies.

In fact, the tide of public opinion is moving away from such views as the economy and political order stabilize and, more fundamentally, as the political demographics of Russia press ahead. For these sharply favor reform. The supporters of nationalism and communism are thus primarily older voters, and often pensioners. The base of the reform party is younger, more economically independent, and far better able to navigate the new political order. By the next round of national elections, consequently, the political divide will likely be over the pace and character of reform, not over its essential merits.

In fact, this may already be true, with most Russians now supporting democracy, and even the free market, in one form or another. The democratic phase of Russian history may thus be beginning. The next generation of democratic leaders has already emerged, as the reformers who endeavored in the twilight of Soviet rule pass from the scene. Though Yeltsin survived the June 1996 elections, Anatoly Sobchak, as prominent an early democrat as Yeltsin himself, thus lost his bid for reelection as mayor of St. Petersburg. In reality, even the passing of Yeltsin himself from the political playing field is no longer a serious concern.

While the horrors of a Russia without Yeltsin were unimaginable as recently as two years ago, Russia is now replete with candidates, any one of whom could serve the needs of Russian democracy quite well. Including Prime Minister Viktor Chernomyrdin, Chief of Staff Anatoly Chubais, Moscow Mayor Yuri Luzhkov, and even head of the Security Council Aleksandr Lebed,[1] each of these leaders has adequate appreciation of the need for economic reform (or, in the case of Lebed, at least the capacity to learn to appreciate it) and of the constraints of the law to keep Russia on a roughly straight path. None of them would substantially alter the state or direction of Russian political and economic development. Considered seriously, in fact, it is unlikely that even Communist Gennady Zyuganov would drastically alter the character of Russian politics and economics. While reform might slow under a President Zyuganov, renationalization is entirely unlikely; violations or the uprooting of the constitution, moreover, would be no more likely under Zyuganov than they have been under Yeltsin.

Yeltsin's failing health and concerns about his planned heart bypass surgery in late 1996 are thus substantially less critical than they may once have been. The fears of Presidents George Bush and Bill Clinton of a world

---

1. It is a testament to the unpredictability of Russian politics that, since I penned the foregoing, Lebed has become the *former* head of the Security Council, having been dismissed by Yeltsin in a television address. Yet it is a testament to the altered state of Russian politics that the popular former general, rather than drawing up designs for a coup, announced (at a press conference, no less) his intention to establish a new political organization to promote his views in future elections. "We will act," he declared, "but we will act only using constitutional means."

without Gorbachev or Yeltsin, respectively, are no longer well founded. Russian politics has entered a new phase. The most significant result of Yeltsin's illness may thus be a positive step in Russia's democratic development. Though long delayed, Yeltsin's eventual announcement in September 1996 that he would undergo heart bypass surgery could set a new precedent for openness that would surpass even that of the United States. Coupled with the insistence (by Lebed, in fact) that the constitution required Yeltsin, on account of his failing health, to relinquish certain powers to Chernomyrdin, and the president's subsequent acquiescence to this demand, the episode of Yeltsin's illness may best be remembered for the precedents of openness and legalism it established. Moreover, that all expect the arrangements established in the constitution to deal with the president's incapacity, with the prime minister leading the country for up to three months, until a new election is called, is itself high testament to the altered relationship of law and politics in Russia today.

A more serious health concern, in fact, is the general health of the country. From 1989 to 1994, the crude death rate in Russia rose 45 percent. Meanwhile, life expectancy for men dropped from sixty-five to fifty-eight years, close to that of Kenya. This drop, much of it alcohol-related, as well as recent outbreaks of diphtheria and cholera, even in urban areas, must be addressed. If anything has the potential to destroy Russia, it is they.

In the economic arena, progress is also visible. The stabilization of the economy that began in 1994 and 1995 has persisted through 1996. Serious structural problems continue to exist, but the trend, again, is positive. Inflation has fallen to 20 percent during 1996, with August inflation at zero. Having myself watched the collapse of the ruble from 1991 to 1994, this itself seems substantial evidence of economic stabilization. The contraction of the economy may thus have finally run its course, with positive growth in certain sectors of the economy, as enterprise development continues and new investment begins to flow.

Former communist managers, suddenly the real thing, have so far proven quite effective in operating their now privatized firms in the competitive marketplace. While many doubted their untested skills would suffice in the face of competitive practices, they have proven more than adequate. Taking their fiduciary duties quite seriously, they are improving efficiency and adapting to the strictures of supply and demand. Nomenklatura ties are thus increasingly being replaced by the ties of the market. Suffering the inefficiency of an old buddy does not look nearly as attractive when faced with a bottom line. Thus did a shock wave run through the Russian business community when word leaked last month of the state tax administration's threat of sanctions against *Gazprom*, Russia's largest firm and largest tax debtor, for its delinquencies. Suddenly, even the patronage of Prime Minister Chernomyrdin, long head of *Gazprom* and until now perceived as its patron saint, could not protect one. The market was coming into its own.

Excessively generous public subsidies continue to be a serious problem, though substantial reductions have been initiated. Thus, for example, was Yeltsin wise enough to break many of his bank-breaking campaign promises and thereby sustain the relatively low budget deficit achieved of late. Instead, he boldly made further cuts.

Such positive trends in the economy's development ought not to be ignored. They represent a critical element in the reconstitutionalization of Russian society. For the free market, once secured in Russia, will help to ensure freedom in all respects. Yet likewise may the failings of an unregulated and uncontrolled market undermine the achievements made by Russia to date. The criminal economy thus continues to imperil both economic and political stability. Between the transfer of illegally earned profits out of the country and the resulting failure to pay tax dues on them, crime is a huge drain on the Russian economy. Yet the dominance of criminal enterprise has increased criminal activity of every sort. In this respect, sadly, Russia remains a Hobbesian world of lives at once "nasty, brutish, and short." This is a threat to democracy itself. Thus, with each car-bomb explosion in downtown Moscow, the public becomes more receptive to strong-arm police activity and violations of civil liberties, measures reminiscent of Russia's still-recent past.

In the three circles of internal federal relations, relations with the so-called near abroad, and relations with the international community, Russia is likewise on a positive trajectory. Most important, the conflict in Chechnya finally ended in September 1996 with the withdrawal of Russian troops and a still-ambiguous compromise on the region's future. Aleksandr Lebed, charged by Yeltsin with ending the twenty-one-month war soon after the president's reelection, thus reached an agreement with the rebels allowing for a five-year delay before the final resolution of Chechnya's constitutional status. While still unstable, what is most critical about this end of the Chechen misadventure is that Russia managed to walk away from utter defeat. This willingness to accept its own limitations bodes well for Russia's future, as does the sense of compromise that underlay the agreement. It is evidence that Russia can follow the path of compromise and thereby avoid the prospect of civil war, a horror it has already once suffered and will do all in its power to avoid.

Russian relations with the near abroad are also in flux, though they have proven far less dramatic, and traumatic, than was once expected. For all the huff and puff that surrounded the question at the passing of the Soviet Union, the issue of Russians in the various former republics has proven to be far less problematic than was imagined. Since the resolution of minor difficulties in the Baltic states, little talk has been heard of any crisis of Russians "abroad." All, it appears, remain content with the status quo. As the former republics struggle with their own share of democracy and the market, they have managed to maintain stable relations with Russia. Such cohabitation, even among Russia and the Baltic states, bodes well for a stable regional politics.

Finally, as noted above, Russian nationalism has not resulted in more than the most minor of backlashes against the West. While the artificially inflated affection of the 1980s and early 1990s is gone, it has hardly been replaced by a threatening aggression. Notwithstanding much heated rhetoric, it appears likely that NATO expansion will move ahead in December 1996 without any serious confrontation with Russia. Rather than absolutist opposition, Russians simply do not wish to be left behind.

The pattern of progress laid out, and aspired to, throughout this work has thus persisted through yet another year of Russia's second revolution. Yet neither the trend toward political nor economic stabilization will, in the end, suffice to secure Russia's future as a democratic, free-market state. Ultimately, the trend with deepest ramifications for Russia's political order, economic development, and federal structure, as well as every other aspect of Russia's future, is the growing place of the constitution and its norms, as well as the laws born of it, in the operation of Russian society.

In each of the areas in which Russia continues to struggle, the law is playing a positive role in guiding the country toward stability and progress. No longer is the law simply about the constraints placed on one's personal liberty. No longer does consideration of the law consist of a cursory assessment of the letter of the law and how to get around it. No longer is the law separate and apart from the common man. Rather, the very operation of Russian society is increasingly being shaped by the law. As revealed daily in the Russian press, the spirit of the constitution is thus at the heart of discussions of Russia's relations with Chechnya, the president's health, and the balance of presidential and parliamentary power. A growing legal and political consciousness, one looking to the essence of constitutional, democratic processes, is increasingly Russia's guiding light. This altered consciousness, in the end, is the keystone of Russia's long-term transformation.

The increasingly functional work of the primary mouthpiece of the constitution, the Constitutional Court, demonstrates the increasingly salutary role of the law. Thus, in two recent conflicts between the president and parliament, the first over deputies' official immunity, which the court determined to be qualified, rather than the absolute immunity claimed by the parliament or the complete lack of immunity Yeltsin argued for, and the second over the scope of the authority of the president and parliament to determine the timetable for local elections, the court has firmly adhered to the law, ruling for the president and for the parliament as required not by political caprice, but by the law. Such basic issues of democratic governance are thus no longer left to the playground of heated political battle. Rather, they are increasingly seen as part of the special province of the law. Their resolution, once seen as best handled by the "political" process, is now considered a goal to which the courts are uniquely qualified to contribute. The continued increase in the number of complaints being filed in the courts by common citizens—addressing everything from contract disputes to defamation claims—is further evidence of the growing perception of the law as central to Russian economic, political, and social life.

It has been the suggestion herein that, ultimately, the legal consciousness of the Russian people, both elite and mass, will determine the future of Russia. Russian politics, by the very nature of its history and culture, if not by the very nature of politics itself, will eternally be characterized by heated dispute. Battles over the choice of one policy versus another thus continue to rage even in the most stable of polities such as the United States. Remember that the American government itself came to a halt in 1995 over such differences of opinion. The essence of American constitutionalism and of Russia's transformation, however, is that such conflict today is occurring within the bounds of the law, and that the law itself is playing a role in the resolution of such conflicts. This engagement of the law, as it becomes the norm, remains the best and greatest hope for Russia. No one can be sure whether inflation will remain low or whether Zhirinovsky may not rise again. A secure respect for law among the people of Russia, however, will make even the worse nightmare of Russian economics or politics an acceptable scenario. The rule of law, no matter what may come to pass, is Russia's ultimate protection. Should it persist, Russia's constitutional revolution will continue to press ahead.

New Haven, Connecticut
October 1996

BIBLIOGRAPHY

Interviews

(All interviews were conducted in Moscow and translated by the author, unless otherwise indicated.)

Ageev, Aleksandr. Head, Strategic Analysis Department, Ministry of Foreign Economic Affairs, 9 August 1993.

Ametistov, Ernst. Member, Russian Constitutional Court, 16 August 1993; 4 February 1994.

Antonov, Anatoly. Director general, Centre for Social Strategic Research, 13 August 1993.

Arzhannikov, Nikolai. Member, Russian Supreme Soviet, 5 August 1993.

Avakyam, Andrei. Department chairman, faculty of law, Moscow State University, 9 August 1993.

Baburin, Sergei. Member, Russian Supreme Soviet; president, National Salvation Front, 20 July 1993.

Bakhmin, Vyacheslav. Head, Directorate of International Humanitarian and Cultural Cooperation, 16 August 1993.

Barenboim, Peter. Vice president, Union of Advocates of the Commonwealth of Independent States, 3 February 1994.

Baturin, Yuri. Law and national security adviser to the Russian President, 11 August 1993.

Biryukov, Nikolai. Professor of philosophy, Moscow State Institute of International Relations. Presentation in English at Princeton University, 15 November 1993; interview at Princeton University, 18 November 1993.

Burlatski, Fyodor. President, Academy of Natural Sciences of Russia; former adviser to President Gorbachev, 14 August 1993; 1 February 1994.

Chernyaev, Anatoly. Adviser to the president, Gorbachev Foundation, 13 July 1993.

Dektyrov, Andrei. Professor of politics, Moscow State University; member, Moscow City Council, 16 August 1993.

Elderly taxi driver, Moscow, 4 February 1994.

Emerson, Caryl. Professor of Slavic languages and literature, Princeton University. Presentation in English at Princeton University, 3 March 1994.

Fedaseyev, Ivan. Secretary, Constitutional Commission of the Supreme Soviet, 13 August 1993.

Fedorov, Mikhail. Member of Federal Assembly (Duma), 1 February 1994.

Fyodorov, Yuri. Professor of politics, Moscow State Institute of International Relations, 17 July 1993.

Galovin, Andrei. Member, Russian Supreme Soviet; chairman, *Smena*–New Politics, 20 July 1993.

Glaziev, Sergei. Member of Federal Assembly (Duma); former minister for Foreign Economic Affairs, 2 February 1994.

Gorbachev, Mikhail. 17 August 1993.

Kartashkin, Vladimir. Professor of law, Institute of State and Law, 2 August 1993.

Khairov, Rustem. Deputy executive director, International Foundation for the Survival and Development of Humanity, 26 July 1993.

Klamkin, Igor. Director, Public Opinion Foundation, 5 August 1993; 4 February 1994.

Kovaldin, Yegor. Adviser to the president, Gorbachev Foundation; expert witness to the 1993 Constitutional Conference, 21 July 1993.

Kovalov, Sergei. Member, Russian Supreme Soviet, 5 August 1993.

Kudriavtsev, Vladimir. Vice president, Russian Academy of Sciences; academician of law, 17 August 1993; 31 January 1994.

Kurashvilli, Boris. Professor, Institute of State and Law, 24 July 1993.

Kutkovyets, Tatiana. Research fellow, Public Opinion Foundation, 27 July 1993.

Lafitski, Vladimir. Adviser to the Constitutional Commission of the Supreme Soviet, 11 August 1993; chief research fellow, Institute of Comparative Law, interview in English, 31 January 1994.

Lukasheva, Elena. Scholar of human-rights law, Institute of State and Law, 11 August 1993; 1 February 1994.

Malgin, Andrei. Editor, *Stolitsa,* 3 August 1993.

Marchenko, Mikhail. Vice rector, Moscow State University; professor of law, 31 January 1994.

Melville, Yuri. Professor of political science, Moscow State Institute of International Relations, 18 July 1993.

Migranyan, Andrannik. Member of Presidential Council. Interview in English, 4 February 1994.

Mishin, Avgust. Professor of constitutional law, Moscow State University, 14 August 1993.

Mossin, Mikhail. Student, Moscow State Institute of International Relations, 2 February 1994.

Murphy, Walter F. Professor of politics, Princeton University. Comments at presentation of Nikolai Biryukov, Princeton University, 15 November 1993.

Nikonov, Vyacheslav. Legal expert, International Reform Foundation, interview in English, 23 July 1993. Member of Federal Assembly (Duma), interview in English at Moscow Pizza Hut, 3 February 1994.

Olshanski, Dimitri. Chairman, Department of Political Psychology, Institute for Political Analysis. Interview in English, 7 August 1993; 2 February 1994.

Paen, E. A. Chairman, Presidential Working Group on National Politics, 28 January 1994.

Palazchenko, Pavel. Assistant to the president, Gorbachev Foundation, 20 July 1993.

Pastykov, Vladimir. Legal expert, Russian Supreme Soviet, 10 August 1993.

Pisigin, Valery. President, Society and Politics Association; former adviser to President Yeltsin, 27 July 1993.

Piskotin, Mikhail. Editor, *People's Deputy,* 6 August 1993.

Pugachov, Boris. Consultant, Constitutional Commission of the Supreme Soviet, 3 August 1993.

Rakitov, Anatoly. Chief, Analytic Centre of the Presidential Administration, 3 August 1993.

Ryabov, Andrei. Political scientist, Gorbachev Foundation, 26 July 1993.

Salmin, Aleksei. Director, Centre for Prognostic Programmes, Gorbachev Foundation, 27 July 1993.

Satarov, Giorgi. Senior adviser to President Yeltsin, 13 August 1993; 4 February 1994.

Schmemann, Serge. Moscow bureau chief, *New York Times,* 17 July 1993.

Shakhnazarov, Giorgi. Head, Political Science Department, Gorbachev Foundation, 14 July 1993; 3 February 1994.

Shakhrai, Sergei. Deputy prime minister, 6 August 1993.

Sharlet, Robert. Professor, Union College. Telephone interview in English, 16 June 1993.

Shuluzhenka, Yuri. Deputy director, Institute of State and Law, 2 August 1993.

Simonov, Aleksei. Director, Glasnost Institute; representative of Confederation of Journalists' Unions to Constitutional Conference, 30 July 1993.

Slussar, Anatoly A. Chief adviser to the president, Foreign Policy Association; member, Soviet Diplomatic Corps, 4 February 1994.

Smirnoff, Villiam. Secretary for political science, Institute of State and Law, 21 July 1993.

Sobakin, Vadim. Adviser to the chairman of the Constitutional Court, 4 August 1993.

Topornin, Boris. Director, Institute of State and Law; academician of law, 21 July 1993.

Topornin, Nikolai. Professor of constitutional law, Moscow State Institute of International Relations. Presentation in English (as part of a seminar on Russian constitutional issues), 27–28 July 1993.

Troyitski, Nikolai. Legal editor, *Megapolis-Express,* 20 July 1993.

Tsipko, Aleksandr. Head, Research Office, Gorbachev Foundation, 13 July 1993.

Tucker, Robert. Professor of politics, Princeton University. Comments at presentation of Nikolai Biryukov, Princeton University, 15 November 1993.

Vlasihin, Vasiili. Director, Department of Comparative Law, Institute of U.S. and Canadian Studies. Interview in English, 10 August 1993; 1 February 1994.

Yakhlakova, Tatyana V. Head, Politics Department, *Moscow News,* 7 August 1993.

Yakovlev, Aleksandr M. Legal adviser to the president, interview in English at his home, 14 August 1993; plenipotentiary representative of the president to the Federal Assembly, interview in English at his home, 5 February 1994.

Yakunin, Gleb. Member, Russian Supreme Soviet; Orthodox minister; presidential adviser, 20 July 1993.

Yegorov, Valeri. Scientific secretary, Russian Political Science Association, 2 February 1994.

Yusopovski, Aleksandr. Political analyst, *Smena*–New Politics, 10 August 1993.

Zavadskaya, Ludmila. Professor of law, Institute of State and Law; participant in 1993 Constitutional Conference, 5 August 1993.

Zorkin, Valery. Member, Russian Constitutional Court, 2 February 1994.

Books

Ajani, Gianmaria. "The Rise and Fall of the Law-Based State in the Experience of Russian Legal Scholarship: Foreign Patterns and Domestic Style," in Donald D. Barry, ed., *Toward the "Rule of Law" in Russia? Political and Legal Reform in the Transition Period*. Armonk, N.Y.: M. E. Sharpe, 1992.

Barber, Benjamin. *Strong Democracy: Participatory Politics for a New Age*. Berkeley and Los Angeles: University of California Press, 1987.

Barry, Donald D. Introduction to Donald D. Barry, ed., *Toward the "Rule of Law" in Russia? Political and Legal Reform in the Transition Period*. Armonk, N.Y.: M. E. Sharpe, 1992.

———. "The Quest for Judicial Independence," in Donald D. Barry, ed., *Toward the "Rule of Law" in Russia? Political and Legal Reform in the Transition Period*. Armonk, N.Y.: M. E. Sharpe, 1992.

Belyaeva, Nina, and Brad Roberts, eds. *After Perestroika: Democracy in the Soviet Union*. Washington, D.C.: Center for Strategic and International Studies, 1991.

Berdyaev, Nikolai. *The Fate of Russia*. Moscow: Soviet Writers Publishing House, 1990.

Berman, Harold J. *Justice in the USSR*. Cambridge: Harvard University Press, 1963.

———. "The Rule of Law and the Law-Based State *(Rechtsstaat)*," in Donald D. Barry, ed., *Toward the "Rule of Law" in Russia? Political and Legal Reform in the Transition Period*. Armonk, N.Y.: M. E. Sharpe, 1992.

Blaustein, Albert P., and Gisbert H. Flanz, eds. *Constitutions of the Countries of the World—Russian Federation Supplement*. Dobbs Ferry, N.Y.: Oceana Publications, 1993.

Bogdanor, V. "The Constitution and the Transition to Democracy," in W. E. Butler, ed., *Perestroika and the Rule of Law: Anglo-American and Soviet Perspectives*. London: I. B. Tauris, 1991.

Butler, W. E. Introduction to W. E. Butler, ed., *Perestroika and the Rule of Law: Anglo-American and Soviet Perspectives*. London: I. B. Tauris, 1991.

———. "Perestroika and the Rule of Law," in W. E. Butler, ed., *Perestroika and the*

Rule of Law: Anglo-American and Soviet Perspectives. London: I. B. Tauris, 1991.

Chalidze, Valery. *To Defend These Rights: Human Rights in the Soviet Union.* New York: Random House, 1974.

Custine, Marquis de. *The Empire of the Czar: A Journey Through Eternal Russia.* New York: Doubleday, 1989.

Elster, Jon. "The Necessity and Impossibility of Simultaneous Economic and Political Reform," in Douglas Greenberg, Stanley N. Katz, Melanie Beth Oliviero, and Steven C. Wheatley, eds., *Constitutionalism and Democracy: Transitions in the Contemporary World.* New York: Oxford University Press, 1993.

Entin, Vladimir L. "Law and Glasnost," in W. E. Butler, ed., *Perestroika and the Rule of Law: Anglo-American and Soviet Perspectives.* London: I. B. Tauris, 1991.

———. "Lawmaking Under Gorbachev Judged by the Standards of a Law-Based Society," in Donald D. Barry, ed., *Toward the "Rule of Law" in Russia? Political and Legal Reform in the Transition Period.* Armonk, N.Y.: M. E. Sharpe, 1992.

Faundez, Julio. "Constitutionalism: A Timely Revival," in Douglas Greenberg, Stanley N. Katz, Melanie Beth Oliviero, and Steven C. Wheatley, eds., *Constitutionalism and Democracy: Transitions in the Contemporary World.* New York: Oxford University Press, 1993.

Feofanov, Yuri. "Rejection of Justice," in Donald D. Barry, ed., *Toward the "Rule of Law" in Russia? Political and Legal Reform in the Transition Period.* Armonk, N.Y.: M. E. Sharpe, 1992.

Foster-Simons, Frances. "The Soviet Legislature: Gorbachev's 'School of Democracy,'" in Donald D. Barry, ed., *Toward the "Rule of Law" in Russia? Political and Legal Reform in the Transition Period.* Armonk, N.Y.: M. E. Sharpe, 1992.

Freeman, M. D. A. "The Rule of Law—Conservative, Liberal, Marxist and Neo-Marxist: Wherein Lies the Attraction?" in W. E. Butler, ed., *Perestroika and the Rule of Law: Anglo-American and Soviet Perspectives.* London: I. B. Tauris, 1991.

Ginsburgs, George. "Domestic Law and International Law: Importing Superior Standards," in Donald D. Barry, ed., *Toward the "Rule of Law" in Russia? Political and Legal Reform in the Transition Period.* Armonk, N.Y.: M. E. Sharpe, 1992.

Gogol, Nikolai. *Dead Souls,* George Reavey, trans.; George Gibian, ed. New York: W. W. Norton, 1985.

Handelman, Stephen. *Comrade Criminal: Russia's New Mafiya.* New Haven, Conn.: Yale University Press, 1995.

Hazard, John N. "The Evolution of the Soviet Constitution," in Donald D. Barry, ed., *Toward the "Rule of Law" in Russia? Political and Legal Reform in the Transition Period.* Armonk, N.Y.: M. E. Sharpe, 1992.

Huskey, Eugene. "The Administration of Justice: Courts, Procuracy, and Ministry of Justice," in Eugene Huskey, ed., *Executive Power and Soviet Politics: The Rise and Decline of the Soviet State.* Armonk, N.Y.: M. E. Sharpe, 1992.

———. "Executive-Legislative Relations," in Eugene Huskey, ed., *Executive Power and Soviet Politics: The Rise and Decline of the Soviet State*. Armonk, N.Y.: M. E. Sharpe, 1992.

———. "From Legal Nihilism to *Pravovoe Gosudarstvo*: Soviet Legal Development, 1917–1990," in Donald D. Barry, ed., *Toward the "Rule of Law" in Russia? Political and Legal Reform in the Transition Period*. Armonk, N.Y.: M. E. Sharpe, 1992.

Juviler, Peter H. *Revolutionary Justice and Order: Politics and Social Change in the USSR*. New York: Free Press, 1976.

———. "Russia Turned Upside Down," in Peter Juviler, Bertram Gross, Vladimir Kartashkin, and Elena Lukasheva, eds., *Human Rights for the 21st Century: Foundations for Responsible Hope*. Armonk, N.Y.: M. E. Sharpe, 1993.

Katz, Stanley N. *Constitutionalism in East Central Europe: Some Negative Lessons From the American Experience*. Providence, R.I.: Berghahn Books, 1994.

Kazimirchuk, V. P. "On Constitutional Supervision in the USSR," in W. E. Butler, ed., *Perestroika and the Rule of Law: Anglo-American and Soviet Perspectives*. London: I. B. Tauris, 1991.

Kolarska-Bobinska, Lena. "The Role of the State: Contradictions in the Transition to Democracy," in Douglas Greenberg, Stanley N. Katz, Melanie Beth Oliviero, and Steven C. Wheatley, eds., *Constitutionalism and Democracy: Transitions in the Contemporary World*. New York: Oxford University Press, 1993.

Koldaeva, N. P. "Separation of Powers in the USSR: Emerging Theory," in W. E. Butler, ed., *Perestroika and the Rule of Law: Anglo-American and Soviet Perspectives*. London: I. B. Tauris, 1991.

Livshits, R. Z. "Jus and Lex: Evolution of Views," in W. E. Butler, ed., *Perestroika and the Rule of Law: Anglo-American and Soviet Perspectives*. London: I. B. Tauris, 1991.

Migranyan, Andrannik. *Perestroika As Seen by a Political Scientist*. Moscow: Novosti, 1990.

Mishin, Avgust. "Constitutional Reform in the USSR," in Donald D. Barry, ed., *Toward the "Rule of Law" in Russia? Political and Legal Reform in the Transition Period*. Armonk, N.Y.: M. E. Sharpe, 1992.

Murphy, Walter F. "Constitutions, Constitutionalism, and Democracy," in Douglas Greenberg, Stanley N. Katz, Melanie Beth Oliviero, and Steven C. Wheatley, eds., *Constitutionalism and Democracy: Transitions in the Contemporary World*. New York: Oxford University Press, 1993.

Oda, Hiroshi. "The Law-Based State and the CPSU," in Donald D. Barry, ed., *Toward the "Rule of Law" in Russia? Political and Legal Reform in the Transition Period*. Armonk, N.Y.: M. E. Sharpe, 1992.

Okoth-Ogendo, H. W. O. "Constitutions Without Constitutionalism: Reflections on an African Political Paradox," in Douglas Greenberg, Stanley Katz, Melanie Beth Oliviero, and Steven C. Wheatley, eds., *Constitutionalism and Democracy: Transitions in the Contemporary World*. New York: Oxford University Press, 1993.

Petro, Nicolai. "Informal Politics and the Rule of Law," in Donald D. Barry, ed.,

Toward the "Rule of Law" in Russia? Political and Legal Reform in the Transition Period. Armonk, N.Y.: M. E. Sharpe, 1992.

Remington, Thomas F. "Parliamentary Government in the USSR," in Robert T. Huber and Donald R. Kelley, eds., *Perestroika-Era Politics.* Armonk: N.Y., M. E. Sharpe, 1991.

Rigby, T. H. "The Government in the Soviet Political System," in Eugene Huskey, ed., *Executive Power and Soviet Politics: The Rise and Decline of the Soviet State.* Armonk, N.Y.: M. E. Sharpe, 1992.

Ross, Cameron. "Party-State Relations," in Eugene Huskey, ed., *Executive Power and Soviet Politics: The Rise and Decline of the Soviet State.* Armonk, N.Y.: M. E. Sharpe, 1992.

Sajo, Andras, and Vera Losonci. "Rule by Law in East Central Europe: Is the Emperor's New Suit a Straightjacket?" in Douglas Greenberg, Stanley Katz, Melanie Beth Oliviero, and Steven C. Wheatley, eds., *Constitutionalism and Democracy: Transitions in the Contemporary World.* New York: Oxford University Press, 1993.

Savitsky, Valery. "What Kind of Court and Procuracy?" in Donald D. Barry, ed., *Toward the "Rule of Law" in Russia? Political and Legal Reform in the Transition Period.* Armonk, N.Y.: M. E. Sharpe, 1992.

Schmidt, Albert. "Soviet Legal Developments, 1917–1990," in Donald D. Barry, ed., *Toward the "Rule of Law" in Russia? Political and Legal Reform in the Transition Period.* Armonk, N.Y.: M. E. Sharpe, 1992.

Sergeyev, Viktor, and Nikolai Biryukov. *Russia's Road to Democracy: Parliament, Communism and Traditional Culture.* Hants, England: Edward Elgar, 1993.

Sharlet, Robert. "Citizen and State Under Gorbachev and Yelstin," in Stephen White, Alex Pravda, and Zvi Gitelman, eds., *Developments in Russian and Post-Soviet Politics.* Durham, N.C.: Duke University Press, 1994.

———. "The Fate of Individual Rights in the Age of Perestroika," in Donald D. Barry, ed., *Toward the "Rule of Law" in Russia? Political and Legal Reform in the Transition Period.* Armonk, N.Y.: M. E. Sharpe, 1992.

———. *The New Soviet Constitution of 1977.* Brunswick, Ohio: King's Court, 1978.

———. *Soviet Constitutional Crisis: From De-Stalinization to Disintegration.* Armonk, N.Y.: M. E. Sharpe, 1992.

Shelley, Louise I. "Legal Consciousness and the *Pravovoe Gosudarstvo*," in Donald D. Barry, ed., *Toward the "Rule of Law" in Russia? Political and Legal Reform in the Transition Period.* Armonk, N.Y.: M. E. Sharpe, 1992.

Urban, Michael. *More Power to the Soviets: The Democratic Revolution in the USSR.* Hants, England: Edward Elgar, 1990.

Vaksburg, Arkady. *The Soviet Mafia.* London: Weidenfeld F. Nicolson, 1991.

Van den Berg, Ger P. "Executive Power and the Concept of *Pravovoe Gosudarstvo*," in Donald D. Barry, ed., *Toward the "Rule of Law" in Russia? Political and Legal Reform in the Transition Period.* Armonk, N.Y.: M. E. Sharpe, 1992.

Wortman, Richard E. *The Development of Russian Legal Consciousness.* Chicago: University of Chicago Press, 1976.

Yakovlev, Aleksandr. *The Bear That Wouldn't Dance: Failed Attempts to Reform the Constitution of the Former Soviet Union.* Manitoba, Canada: Legal Research Institute of the University of Manitoba, 1992.

Journals and Magazines

Alekseev, Sergei. "*Kliucheviye zvenya Konstitutsiya*," *Russian Monitor* 2 (1993): 29–35.

"*Amerikanskaya model'*," *Konstitutsionnyi Vestnik* 14 (December 1992): 107–67.

Aslund, Anders. "Prospects of the New Russian Market Economy," *Problems of Post-Communism* 41 (Fall 1994): 16–21.

Bahry, Donna. "Society Transformed? Rethinking the Social Roots of Perestroika," *Slavic Review* 52 (Fall 1993): 512–54.

Bahry, Donna, and Lucan Way. "Citizen Activism in the Russian Transition," *Post-Soviet Affairs* 10 (October–December 1994): 330–66.

Barry, Donald D. "Amnesty Under the Russian Constitution: Evolution of the Provision and Its Use in February 1994," *Parker School Journal of East European Law* 1, no. 4 (1994): 437–61.

Belyaeva, Nina. "Russian Democracy," *Washington Quarterly* 16 (Spring 1993): 6–22.

———. "What Is Possible for NGOs in Russia: A Discussion of the Current Laws," *Interlegal Insert* (Spring 1993).

Blankenagel, Alexander. "Toward Constitutionalism in Russia," *East European Constitutional Review* 1 (Summer 1992): 25–28.

Bonner, Yelena. Speech at United States Capitol, *Journal of Democracy* 5 (July 1994): 137.

Brown, Archie. "The October Crisis of 1993: Context and Implications," *Post-Soviet Affairs* 9 (July–September 1993): 183–95.

Cohen, Ariel. "Crime Without Punishment," *Journal of Democracy* 6 (April 1995): 34–45.

Colton, Timothy J. "Superpresidentialism and Russia's Backward State," *Post-Soviet Affairs* 11 (April–June 1995): 144–48.

"Constitution Watch—Russia," *East European Constitutional Review* 3 (Spring 1994): 19–22.

"Constitution Watch—Russia," *East European Constitutional Review* 4 (Winter 1995): 23–30.

Davis, Newton. "Russian Bankruptcy and Enterprise Sell-Off: Creating a User-Friendly System," *Parker School Journal of East European Law* 2, no. 1 (1995): 59–76.

Diligenski, German. "*Konstitutsiya nikogda ni prinimaetsa v abstraktom prostranstve*," *Russian Commentary* (24 November 1993).

Fish, M. Steven. "Russia's Fourth Transition," *Journal of Democracy* 5 (July 1994): 31–42.

"*Gamil'ton*, Federalist 9," *Konstitutsionnyi Vestnik* 10 (February–March 1992): 128–34.

Goble, Paul A. "Chechnya and Its Consequences: A Preliminary Report," *Post-Soviet Affairs* 11 (January–March 1995): 23–27.

Hall, Stephen. "Privatization in Russia After July 1, 1994," *Parker School Journal of East European Law* 1, no. 4 (1994): 503–7.

Hazard, John N. "Is Russian Case Law Becoming Significant As a Source of Law?" *Parker School Journal of East European Law* 1, no. 1 (1994): 23–46.

———. "Russian Judicial Precedent Revisited," *Parker School Journal of East European Law* 1, no. 4 (1994): 471–77.

Hoffmann, Erik P. "Challenges to Viable Constitutionalism in Post-Soviet Russia," *Harriman Review* 7 (November 1994): 19–56.

Holland, William E. "Privatization in Russia," *Parker School Journal of East European Law* 1, no. 2 (1994): 275–80.

Holmes, Stephen. "Superpresidentialism and Its Problems," *East European Constitutional Review* 2, 3 (Fall 1993 and Winter 1994): 123–26.

Horton, Scott, and Mikhail Saakashvili. "The Stage Is Set for the Russian Securities Market," *Parker School Journal of East European Law* 2, no. 2 (1995): 245–56.

Hough, Jerry F. "Russia: On The Road to Thermidor," *Problems of Post-Communism* 41 (Fall 1994): 26–31.

———. "The Russian Election of 1993: Public Attitudes Toward Economic Reform and Democratization," *Post-Soviet Affairs* 10 (January–March 1994): 1–37.

Huskey, Eugene. "The State-Legal Administration and the Politics of Redundancy," *Post-Soviet Affairs* 11 (April–June 1995): 115–43.

Juviler, Peter. "Human Rights After Perestroika: Progress and Perils," *Harriman Institute Forum* 4 (June 1991): 1–10.

———. "The Soviet Declaration of Individual Rights: The Last Act of the Old Union," *Parker School Bulletin of Soviet and East European Law* 2, no. 8 (1991): 3–4.

Kistiakovski, Bogdan. "*Gosudarstvo pravovoe i sotsialisticheskoe,*" *Voprosy filosofi i psikhologi,* no. 5 (1906).

Konstitutsionnoe Soveshchanie (Constitutional Conference) (August 1993).

Konstitutsionnyi Vestnik, nos. 3–16 (October 1990–May 1993).

Lapidus, Gail W. "Two Years After the Collapse of the USSR: A Panel of Specialists," *Post-Soviet Affairs* 9 (October–December 1993): 281–313.

Lempert, David. "Changing Russian Political Culture in the 1990s: Parasites, Paradigms, and Perestroika," *Comparative Studies in Society and History* 35 (July 1993): 628–46.

———. "The Proposed Constitution of Ukraine: Continuity Under the Banner of Change," *Demokratizatsiya* 2 (Spring 1994): 268–96.

Lessig, Lawrence. Introduction to "Roundtable: Redesigning the Russian Court," *East European Constitutional Review* 3 (Summer–Fall 1994): 72–74.

Linden, Carl. "The Dialectics of Russian Politics," *Problems of Post-Communism* 42 (January–February 1995): 8–12.

Malia, Martin. "Russia's Democratic Future: Hope Against Hope," *Problems of Post-Communism* 41 (Fall 1994): 32–36.

Medvedev, Roy. "On Stalin and Stalinism: Historical Essays," *Znamya* 4 (1989).

Mikhailovskaia, Inga. "Constitutional Rights in Russian Public Opinion," *East European Constitutional Review* 4 (Winter 1995): 70–76.

————. "Why the Russian Public Will Support Reform," *East European Constitutional Review* 2, 3 (Fall 1993 and Winter 1994): 28–32.

Mikhailovskaia, Inga, and Evgenii Kuzminskii. "Making Sense of the Russian Elections," *East European Constitutional Review* 3 (Spring 1994): 59–64.

Millar, James R. "The Failure of Shock Therapy," *Problems of Post-Communism* 41 (Fall 1994): 21–25.

Monitor, nos. 1 and 2 (1992 and 1993).

Moore, Rita. "The Path to the New Russian Constitution," *Demokratizatsiya* 3 (Winter 1995): 44–60.

Paleev, Mikhail S. "The Establishment of an Independent Judiciary in Russia," *Parker School Journal of East European Law* 1, nos. 5–6 (1994): 647–61.

Pastykov, Vladimir. "'Noviye russkiye': payavleniye ideologii (II)," *Polis* 3 (1993): 15–26.

Pettibone, Peter J., and Juliette M. Passer-Muslin. "Russian Banking and Currency Regulations," *Parker School Journal of East European Law* 1, nos. 5–6 (1994): 709–17.

Radio Liberty Report on the Soviet Union, 8 March 1991.

Remnick, David. "The Exile Returns," *New Yorker* (14 February 1994): 64–83.

RIA/Novosti. *Constitutional Journal* (June–July 1993).

————. *Russian Commentary* (November 1993–January 1994).

Roeder, Philip. "Varieties of Post-Soviet Authoritarian Regimes," *Post-Soviet Affairs* 10 (January–March 1994): 61–101.

Rose, Richard. "Postcommunism and the Problem of Trust," *Journal of Democracy* 5 (July 1994): 18–30.

————. "Russia as an Hour-Glass Society: A Constitution Without Citizens," *East European Constitutional Review* 4 (Summer 1995): 34–42.

Sartori, Giovanni. "Constitutionalism: A Preliminary Discussion," *American Political Science Review* 56 (December 1962): 853–64.

Semler, Dwight. "The End of the First Russian Republic," *East European Constitutional Review* 2, 3 (Fall 1993 and Winter 1994): 107–14.

————. "Summer in Russia Brings No Real Political Progress; Federative Issues Dominate Constitutional Discussions," *East European Constitutional Review* 2 (Summer 1993): 20–23.

Sharlet, Robert. "The New Russian Constitution and Its Political Impact," *Problems of Post-Communism* 42 (January–February 1995): 3–7.

————. "The Prospects for Federalism in Russian Constitutional Politics," *Publius: The Journal of Federalism* 24 (Spring 1994): 115–27.

————. "Russia's 'Ethnic' Republics and Constitutional Politics," *Eurasian Reports* 3 (Winter 1993): 39–46.

————. "The Russian Constitutional Court: The First Term," *Post-Soviet Affairs* 9 (January–March 1993): 1–39.

————. "Russian Constitutional Crisis: Law and Politics Under Yel'tsin," *Post-Soviet Affairs* 9 (October–December 1993): 314–36.

Shelley, Louise I. "Organized Crime in the Former Soviet Union," *Problems of Post-Communism* 42 (January–February 1995): 56–60.

Slider, Darrell. "Privatization in Russia's Regions," *Post-Soviet Affairs* 10 (October–December 1994): 367–96.

Smith, Tanya. "The Violation of Basic Rights in the Russian Federation," *East European Constitutional Review* 3 (Summer–Fall 1994): 42–47.

Solomon, Peter. "The Limits of Legal Order in Post-Soviet Russia," *Post-Soviet Affairs* 11 (April–June 1995): 89–114.

Strashun, Boris. "*Kakoye gosudarstvo myi stroyim?*" *Russian Federation* (January 1994): 11–13.

Thornburgh, Richard. "The Soviet Union and the Rule of Law," *Foreign Affairs* 69 (Summer 1990): 13–27.

Thorson, Carla. "The Fate of the Communist Party in Russia," *RFE/RL Research Report* 1 (18 September 1992): 1–6.

Tolz, Vera, and Julia Wishnevsky. "Election Queries Make Russians Doubt Democratic Process," *RFE/RL Research Report* 3 (8 April 1994): 19–27.

Urban, Michael. "December 1993 As a Replication of Late-Soviet Electoral Practices," *Post-Soviet Affairs* 10 (April–June 1994): 127–58.

Vinton, Louisa. "Poland's 'Little Constitution' Clarifies Walesa's Power," *RFE/RL Research Report* 1 (4 September 1992): 19–21.

Walker, Edward W. "Designing Center-Region Relations in the New Russia," *East European Constitutional Review* 4 (Winter 1995): 54–60.

————. "Politics of Blame and Presidential Powers in Russia's New Constitution," *East European Constitutional Review* 2, 3 (Fall 1993 and Winter 1994): 116–19.

Yakovlev, Aleksandr. "To Build the Russian Federation," *Parker School Journal of East European Law* 1 (1994): 1–22.

Zielonka, Jan. "New Institutions in the Old East Bloc," *Journal of Democracy* 5 (April 1994): 87–104.

Newspapers

Afanasyev, Yuri N. "Russia's Vicious Circle," *New York Times,* 28 February 1994: A17.

Aksyonov, Vassily. "My Search for Russia's Revolution," *New York Times,* 22 November 1994: A23.

Andrews, James H. "Helping Law Come in from the Cold," *Christian Science Monitor,* 21 March 1994: 15.

Belyaeva, Nina. "Humanitarian Aid and Charity," *Interlegal Bulletin,* August 1993.

Dashkevich, Vladimir. "Plot and Counter-Plot," *Independent Newspaper from Russia,* 2, nos. 12–13, August 1991.

Dobbs, Michael. "Mobsters in Red Square," *Washington Post Book World,* 13 August 1995: 4.

Ericson, Joel M. "Russia Shows Life Signs Beyond Moscow," *New York Times* letter to the editor, 4 March 1994: A26.

Erlanger, Stephen. "If the Russians Can Talk Freely, What's to Write About?" *New York Times,* 29 May 1994, section 4: 3.

———. "Russia's New Dictatorship of Crime," *New York Times,* 15 May 1994, section 4: 3.

———. "Russian Battle: Stage Is Reset," *New York Times,* 2 March 1994: A10.

———. "Yeltsin Denounces Amnesty but Concedes to Parliament," *New York Times,* 5 March 1994: A5.

International Reform Foundation. "We Need a New Constitution, and It Must Be Adopted Without Haste," *Nezavisimaya Gazeta,* 7 December 1993.

Kinzer, Stephen. "Bitter Goodbye: Russians Leave Germany," *New York Times,* 4 March 1994: A1.

Mufson, Steven. "Chinese Movement Seeks Rule of Law to Keep Government in Check," *Washington Post,* 5 March 1995: A25.

Nixon, Richard. "Moscow, March '94: Chaos and Hope," *New York Times,* 25 March 1994: A29.

PostFactum Daily News, 11 December 1992.

"*Pravo i sila,*" *Moskovski Komsomolets,* 18 May 1991: 2.

Remnick, David. "'We Are Already in a State of Chaos'; Gorbachev, Beset by Deputies' Protests, Appeals to People for Peace," *Washington Post,* 19 December 1990: A1.

Satarov, Giorgi. "What Fate Lies in Store for the Parliament?" *Rossiiskiye Vesti,* 11 January 1994.

Schmemann, Serge. "Solzhenitsyn's 'Deepest Russia': Is It Still There?" *New York Times,* 30 May 1994: A2.

———. "Why Russians Can't Get Excited About a Constitution," *New York Times,* 14 November 1993, section 4: 5.

"School of Democracy," *Izvestiia,* 30 May 1989.

Simes, Dimitri. "Is Yeltsin Losing His Grip?" *New York Times,* 6 March 1994, section 4: 15.

Specter, Michael. "Climb in Russia's Death Rate Sets Off Population Implosion," *New York Times,* 6 March 1994: A1.

———. "May Day in Moscow: Remembrance of Soviet Past," *New York Times,* 2 May 1994: A11.

———. "Russia's Voters Turn Cranky," *New York Times,* 1 October 1995, section 4: 4.

———. "Soaring Unemployment Is Spreading Fear in Russia," *New York Times,* 8 May 1994: A3.

———. "Yeltsin Wins Peace Accord in Parliament," *New York Times,* 29 April 1994: A5.

———. "Yeltsin's Anti-Crime Decree Sets Off a Storm of Outrage," *New York Times,* 19 June 1994: A14.

Stankevich, Sergei. "Why I Will Vote Aye," *Rossiiskaya Gazeta,* 11 December 1993.

Stanley, Alessandra. "Oh, That Coup (Yawn); In the Land of Show Trials, Playing to an Empty House," *New York Times,* 26 June 1994, section 4: 5.

———. "Russia's New Rulers Govern, and Live, in Neo-Soviet Style," *New York Times,* 23 May 1995: A1, A8.

———. "Yeltsin Prods Government on Economy," *New York Times,* 11 June 1994: A3.

Stepanov, Andrei. "Grand Piano Lurking in Bush," *Moskovski Komsomolets,* 5 January 1994.

Tretyakov, Vitaly, in Stephen Erlanger, "Russian Battle: Stage Is Reset," *New York Times,* 2 March 1994: A10.

Trushkov, Viktor. "Russia Said Goodbye to Democracy, Curtailed As It Was," *Pravda,* 29 January 1994.

Vaksburg, Arkady. "*Kakim dolzhno byt' pravovoye gosudarstvo?*" *Literaturnaya Gazeta,* 8 June 1988.

Zharinov, Vladimir. "Yeltsin's Historical Period: Coming to an End," *Nezavisimaya Gazeta,* 25 January 1994.

Official Acts

Amnesty of 23 February 1994: Published in *Rossiiskaya Gazeta,* 26 February 1994, 5.

Civil Code of Russia: *Vedomosti RF,* no. 32, item 3301 (1994).

Committee for Constitutional Supervision. Decision of 13 September 1990 (nullification of Gorbachev demonstration decree), published in *Izvestiia,* 15 September 1990.

Concept of Judicial Reform: *Vedomosti RSFSR,* no. 30, item 1435 (1991).

Constitutional Court of the Russian Federation. Decision of 30 November 1992 (Communist Party case), published in *Izvestiia,* 16 December 1992.

Constitution of the Russian Federation (1993), published in "Text of the Draft Constitution," *Izvestiia,* 10 November 1993. Translation in *Current Digest of the Post-Soviet Press* 45 (8 December 1993): 4–16.

Constitution of the Soviet Union (1977). Translation in *Current Digest of the Soviet Press* 29 (9 November 1977): 1–13.

Constitution of the Union of Soviet Republics of Europe and Asia (Andrei Sakharov's draft constitution). Translation available in *FBIS, JPRS Report–Soviet Union: Political Affairs* (19 January 1990): 1–5.

Declaration of Individual Rights and Freedoms, published in *Izvestiia,* 7 September 1991.

"*Dogovor ob obshchestvennom soglasii*" (Treaty on Social Accord), published in *Izvestiia,* 30 April 1994: 4.

Executive Decrees of 21 September 1993 ("On the Step-by-Step Constitutional Reform of the Russian Federation") and 7 October 1993 ("On the Constitutional Court"): *Vedomosti RF,* no. 41, item 3921 (1993).

Law of 23 December 1989, on the Committee for Constitutional Supervision (enabling law): *Vedomosti SSR,* no. 29, item 572 (1989).

Law on Freedom of Conscience and Religious Organizations: *Vedomosti SSR*, no. 41, item 813 (1990).

Law on Habeas Corpus: *Vedomosti RSFSR*, no. 20, item 1084 (1992).

Law on Public Associations: *Vedomosti SSR*, no. 42, item 839 (1990).

Law on the Constitutional Court of 12 July 1994, published in *Rossiiskaya Gazeta*, 23 July 1994.

Law on the Press and Other Mass Media: *Vedomosti SSR*, no. 26, item 492 (1990).

Law on the Status of Judges in the Russian Federation, *Vedomosti RF*, no. 30, item 1792 (1992).

Law on the Status of Judges in the USSR: *Vedomosti SSR*, no. 9, item 223 (1989). Translation available in Jane Henderson, "Law on the Status of Judges in the USSR," *Review of Socialist Law*, no. 3 (1990): 305–38.

Official declaration of the opening of 1977 constitutional discussions, published in *Pravda*, 5 June 1977.

On Amendments and Additions to the RSFSR Constitution: *Vedomosti RSFSR*, no. 29, item 395 (1990).

On Amendments and Additions to the USSR Constitution (Fundamental Law), 1988 amendments: *Vedomosti SSR*, no. 49, item 727 (1988). Translation available in *Review of Socialist Law* 15, no. 1 (1989): 75–118.

On Elections of USSR People's Deputies, 1988 amendments: *Vedomosti SSR*, no. 49, item 727 (1988). Translation available in *Review of Socialist Law* 15, no. 1 (1989): 75–118.

O Sude ("On the Courts"): *Sobranie Uzakonenii 1917–1918*, no. 4, item 150.

Sobranie Zakonodatel'stva RF 1995, no. 18, item 1589; no. 19, item 1709.

"Texts of Declarations by 3 Republic Leaders," *New York Times*, 9 December 1991: A8; "Soviet Disarray: Accord on Commonwealth of Independent States," *New York Times*, 10 December 1991: A19.

Treaty on Social Accord, FBIS-SOV-94-083, 29 April 1994: 18.

Vedomosti RF, no. 33, item 1313 (1993).

Zakon o Konstitutsionnom Sude RSFSR (Law on the RSFSR Constitutional Court): *Vedomosti RSFSR*, no. 30, item 1017 (1991). Translation available in *FBIS– Soviet Union: Republic Affairs* (10 September 1992): 21–46.

Miscellaneous

Ametistov, Ernst. Comments at Mentor Group Conference on Russian Constitutional Affairs, 14–18 November 1994. Conference report, 75–90.

Bobotov, Sergei. Comments at Mentor Group Conference on Russian Constitutional Affairs, 14–18 November 1994. Conference report, 7–31.

Huskey, Eugene. "The Presidency in Russian Politics: A Study of the State-Legal Administration." Unpublished manuscript.

Juviler, Peter. Excerpts from draft of book in progress: "Human Rights and Democracy in Post-Soviet Systems: The Ordeal of Freedom."

Public Opinion Foundation's survey materials, 1992–93.

Rumyantsev, Oleg. Comments at Mentor Group Conference on Russian Constitutional Affairs, 14–18 November 1994. Conference report, 91–104.

———. Speech to the Supreme Soviet, 10 October 1991.

Staff of the Commission on Security and Cooperation in Europe. *Presidential Elections and Independence Referendums in the Baltic States, the Soviet Union and Successor States,* August 1992.

Vitrouk, Nikolas. Comments at Mentor Group Conference on Russian Constitutional Affairs, 14–18 November 1994. Conference report, 33–57.

Yakovlev, Aleksandr M. Speech at the Kremlin, 26 July 1993.

———. Unpublished manuscript on Russian constitutional reform.

Yeltsin, Boris. "State of the Union" address, Vremya television, 24 February 1994. Translation in *FBIS Daily Report: Central Eurasia* (24 February 1994).

"Yeltsin's Address on National Television," official Kremlin international news broadcast (available on LEXIS: News, Sovnws), 21 September 1993.

Youngstown Sheet and Tube Co. v. Sawyer, 343 U.S. 579 (1952).

INDEX

Agrarian Party, 77–78, 120, 177
agricultural reform, economic reform and, 181–82
Aizderdzis, Andrei, 142
Aleksandr I (Tsar), 13n.2
Aleksandr II (Tsar), 13, 97
Alekseev, Sergei, 13n.2, 14, 28, 55, 87n.169
Aleksei II (Patriarch), 66–67
All-Russian Referendum, 56
All-Union Referendum, 43
American Bar Association Central and East European Law Initiative, 162
Ametistov, Ernst (Justice), 66, 71–72, 86, 153–54, 165
amnesty, Russian political compromise and, 121–22, 201
Andropov, Yuri, 17, 110, 139n.120, 144–45
Anglo-American legal tradition, Russian judicial reform and, 160
apparatchiki: political corruption and, 148; resistance to Gorbachev's reforms from, 23
Armenian expatriates, 193
authority figures, Russian legal consciousness and, 105–6
autonomous republics. *See* ethnic republics

Baburin, Sergei, 54
Baklanov, Oleg, 38n.107
Baltic republics: economic reform in, 177–78; influence on Russia of, 194
Barannikov, Viktor, 140
Barenboim, Peter, 17

Bashkortostan, federalism and, 135–36
Baturin, Yuri, 43, 60
Belyaeva, Nina, 18, 137
Berdyaev, Nikolai, 104–5, 116
Berman, Harold J., 19, 19n.24
Biryukov, Nikolai, 20, 27, 52, 96, 110, 117, 216–17
Black Tuesday, 189
black-market enterprises, economic reforms and, 183
Bolshevik Revolution: court system under, 148; government perks abolished under, 146; legal consciousness and, 15–16, 37, 48, 96–98; November 1918 Decree of, 139
Bonner, Yelena, 217
Brezhnev, Leonid, 23, 38, 98; constitution of 1977 and, 16–17, 59–60, 75; corruption during regime of, 140, 145; law and order rhetoric of, 139n.120; legal consciousness under, 19, 69, 116; rhetoric of, 129
Buckley, William F., 58
bureaucracy: as alternative to courts, 164n.229; constitutionalism and, 201–2; constitutional restructuring under Gorbachev and, 23; reduction of corruption in, 140–48
Burlatski, Fyodor, 32–33, 44, 68, 167, 197
business interests: government regulation of, 186–87; judicial reform and, 158
Butler, William, 193
"Byelorussian coup," 42

Catherine II (Tsarina), 148

censorship, constitutional rhetoric and lifting of, 66, 71–72, 131n.83

Central Bank: rouble confiscation, 5, 158, 178, 188; Yerashenko's resignation from, 182–83

Central Electoral Commission, 74

Chechen-Ingushetia, Yeltsin's state of emergency decree in, 50n.12

Chechnya: Constitutional Court ruling on, 125, 150; constitutionalism and, 213; federalism and, 133, 135–39; human rights violations in, 131; Russian invasion of, 125n.50, 133, 139, 200–201; television coverage of, 132; war in, 167–68

Chernenko, Konstantin, 17, 129

Chernomyrdin, Viktor, 125, 144, 178, 189, 199, 202–3

Chicherin, Boris Nikolaevich, 14

Chubais, Anatoly, 179

Churbanov, Yuri, 145

citizen democracy, lack of, at Constitutional Conference, 58

citizenship, Russian concept of, 174

Civil Code of 1995, 158, 186

civil rights: Constitutional Court rulings on, 54, 84n.155, 150–51, 154–55, 173–75; development of Russian civil society and, 211–13; fragility of, under Yeltsin, 42–44

Clinton, Bill (President), 193–94

Code of Criminal Procedure, 159–60

Commission on Corruption, 145

Committee for Constitutional Supervision, 28–29, 80, 85n.161, 87n.169

Committee for the Economy, 42

Commonwealth of Independent States, 42, 44

Communist Academy, 15

Communist Party: attempted revival of Soviet Union and, 118–19; August coup against Gorbachev and, 40–41, 81–82; bureaucracy of, 202; Constitutional Court ruling on status of, 80–83, 151n.169, 207; economic reform and, 177; electoral victories of, 127; Gorbachev's reforms and, 18–19, 21, 23–24, 32–34; in mid-1990s, 32n.86; Russian legal consciousness and, 98,

104; Sakharov's reform of, 24–25; Slobodkin's draft constitution, 54–55; transfer of property holdings, 156; Yeltsin's banning of, 42; 1993 elections and, 77–78

compromise, Russian political culture and, 115–28

Concept of Judicial Reform, 162

Conciliation Commission, 201

Congress(es) of People's Deputies, 56; establishment of, 25–27; federalism and, 134; Gorbachev's reforms and, 27–37; lack of compromise and cooperation in, 117–19; size of, 34–35; televised sessions of, 27, 130; Yeltsin and, 24–25, 49–50

consensus and cooperation: constitutionalism and, 200–201; Russian political culture and, 115–28

Constitutional Arbitration Commission, 61

Constitutional Commission: civil society and, 211; Constitutional Conference compared with, 61; constitutional drafts and, 65, 68; early reforms of, 51–56; establishment of, 49; rhetoric of, 130; Zorkin as advisor to, 88n.174

Constitutional Conference of 1993, 7, 54, 56–62, 65, 104; draft revised by, 72–73; list of participants, 57n.42; Zhirinovsky's participation in, 119

Constitutional Court, 7, 56, 71, 78–90, 148–55; Communist Party status under Yeltsin, ruling on, 80–83; formation of, 50, 148–49; judicial powers of, 153–54, 156n.186; judicial reforms under, 206–7; political legacy of, 83–89, 164–65; property rights rulings, 187; salary benefits for justices of, 151n.169, 152; Tatarstan's independence referendum, 85, 87n.169; Yeltsin's police/internal security force merger overturned by, 79–80, 85

"Constitutional Game, The," 38

constitutionalism: August coup against Gorbachev and, 38–41, 81; Communist Party and development of, 32–33; compromise and cooperation and, 115–28; Constitutional Court and, 85–89, 149–55; corruption and, 139–48; cultural resistance to, in Russia, 2–10; early constitutional reforms and, 48–56; emerging paradigm of, 111–13; "evolution from below" model, 9, 103–8; federalism and, 133–39; future development of, in Russia, 4–10; future of, 210–17; under Gorbachev, 13, 23–37, 44–46, 99; government's impact on, 199–208; history of, in Russia, 3–8, 13–15; human rights and, 173–75; lower courts and, 155–65; mass media and, 131–32; masses vs. elites and, 108–11; public participation and support of, 197–98; rhetoric and development of, 17–22, 128–32; Russian Federation Constitution as reform measure, 47–48, 165–73; in Second Russian Republic, 93–94; western influences on, 190–95; *zakonost* (legalism) and, 37–39

Constitution of the Russian Federation, 62, 165–73, 208–9

Constitution of the Russian Republic, 129, 165

Constitution of the Union of Soviet Republics of Europe and Asia, 25

corruption, constitutionalism and, 139–48, 180, 183, 202, 214. *See also* organized crime

Council of Economic Advisers (Russia), 5

Council of Europe's Charter, 175

Court of Conscience, 148–49

courts, under Bolshevism, 16. *See also* Constitutional Court; People's Courts.

Covenant on Civil and Political Rights, 175

criminal activity, economic reform and, 179n.306, 183n.335, 183–86, 214

cultural values. *See* political culture

Custine, Marquis de, 10, 190

Daniel, Iulii, 37n.105, 41n.117

decentralization of economy, constitutionalism and, 179

Declaration of Individual Rights and Freedoms, 31, 43–44, 170–71

Declaration of Sovereignty (1990), 64, 104

Decree no. 1400, 66, 69–70

"Defenders of August," 39, 41

DeKlerk, F. W., 111

democratic institutions: absence of, in Russian political culture, 105–8, 118; cooperation and compromise in Russia and, 117–28; corruption and, 140–48; economic reform and, 183; federalism and, 138–39; interbranch relations, need for development of, 123–27; party politics and, 127–28; political change and economic reform under Gorbachev and, 21–22; western influence on, in Russia, 192

demokratizatsiya, legal system reforms and, 18–19

Den, 66

de-Stalinization, legal consciousness and, 98

dissent: Russian legal system and, 36–37; Russian political culture and, 115–17

Draft Constitution of the Russian Soviet Federated Socialist Republics, 54

Duma: grant of amnesty, 121–22; budget allocations for, 202; compromise and cooperation needed in, 117–28; Constitutional Court and, 149–50, 154; constitutional establishment of original, 14, 171; constitutionalism and, 203–5; corruption within, 140–45; economic reform and, 124, 204–5; Foreign Relations Committee, 124; judicial reforms and, 157–59; National Security Council and, 124–25; presidency and, 122–26; reduction of perks and privileges needed by, 146–48; Russian anti-crime measures and, 184–86; Russian Federation Constitution and, 167–68; Yeltsin's constitutional reforms and, 72–74, 77–78

Eastern Europe, Russian legal reforms and, 21

economic reform: constitutionalism and stability in, 175–89, 214–16; ethnic republics and, 133–34; under Gorbachev, 18–22, 29; judicial reform and, 158–59; political corruption and, 144–48; under Yeltsin, 50, 202–3

economic rights in Russia, 174–75, 187–88

elected officials, lack of, at Constitutional Conference, 58 elections: constitutional reform and, 73–78, 204–5, 215; corrupt campaign financing during, 142–43; Gorbachev's reform of, 26–30; party politics and, 127–28

elites: categorization of, 110n.61; constitutionalism and, 32–34, 50; coup against Gorbachev and, 38–40, 45–46; interaction through rhetoric with, 130; in organized crime, 143; regional republics and federalism and, 136–39; Russian Federation Constitution and, 169–70; Russian legal consciousness and, 96; vs. masses, constitutional reform and, 108–11

Entin, Vladimir, 129

Estonia, economic reform in, 178

ethnic republics, federalism and, 133–34. *See also specific republics*

European influence on Russian constitutionalism, 191–92

"evolution from below" model: emerging paradigm and, 111–13; federalism and, 137–39; masses vs. elites and, 108–11; Russian constitutionalism and, 9, 103–8

extremist politics, federalism and, 137–38

Faundez, Julio, 192

Federal Assembly, 170

Federal Bureau of Investigation (FBI), liaison office in Moscow, 192

Federal Organs of Power, 57

Federal Security Service, 125n.52

federalism: constitutionalism and, 133–39; constitutional reform and, 63–64

Federation Council, 64, 72, 77–78, 117n.13; budget allocations for, 202; compromise and cooperation from, 121, 124–26; federalism and, 136–39; nominations to Constitutional Court rejected by, 149–50; Russian Federation Constitution and, 170

Federation Treaty, 64–65, 73, 133n.90, 134

Fifth Extraordinary Congress of People's Deputies, 79

Finance Ministry, 42

First Congress of People's Deputies (1989), 27

fiscal policy, economic reform and, 181

foreign aid, Russian constitutionalism and, 194–95

Foreign Corrupt Practices Act, 184

foreign policy in Russia, constitutionalism and, 215

France's Fifth Republic, 167n.246

Fundamental Law of 1906, 14, 171

Fundamental Principles of Criminal Prosecution (1958), 16

Fyodorov, Boris, 127

Gaidar, Yegor, 77–78, 127, 193–94, 215

Galovin, Andrei, 53–55

Gerashenko, Viktor, 182–83

German Constitutional Court, 155, 160, 162n.219

German *Rechtsstaat*, 19

Germany, influence of, on Russian constitutionalism, 191

glasnost: legal system reforms linked to, 18–19, 22; legitimation of government through, 129

Gogol, Nikolai, 210n.52

Golushko, Nikolai, 122

Goodwill Games, 193

Gorbachev, Mikhail, 3, 7, 9; August coup against, 37–41; ban on demonstrations by, 29, 80, 101; Communist Party role in coup attempt, 40–41, 80–83; consolidation of power by, 35; constitutionalism under, 13, 17, 61–62, 99, 123, 203; corruption in regime of, 145; election of, as general secretary, 18n.21; elites and, 33, 109; judicial reforms of, 27–29, 160; legacy of, 46; legal consciousness under, 17–22, 42–46, 78, 98–101; move to right by, 34–35; political and economic reforms of, 23–37; power base of, 18–19; resignation of, 45; revolutionary ideology of, 105; Union Treaty and, 42–44

gospodstvo prava, 99

government subsidies, economic reform and, 181

Great Britain, parliamentary sovereignty and, 99

Great Caviar Scandal, 140

Gusinsky, Vladimir, 200–201

habeas corpus legislation, 160n.202
Hamilton, Alexander, 51
Hazard, John, 44
Helsinki Accords, Basket Three human
    rights principles, 190
High *Arbitrazh* Court, 206
Hoffmann, Erik, 50, 73, 120–22, 125–26,
    141, 155, 171–72, 177, 199, 214
human rights: constitutionalism and, 173–
    75, 213; courts' defense of, 207; exter-
    nal influences in Russia and, 190;
    Gorbachev's political reforms and, 31;
    property rights as component of, 187–
    88; rhetoric concerning, 131; Russian
    anti-crime measures and, 184–85
Hurricane Operation, 185
Huskey, Eugene, 147, 163, 202

Ilyushenko, Aleksei, 139
Imperial Russia: constitutionalism under,
    13–15, 48; development of legal con-
    sciousness and, 97
inflation, economic reform and, 178–82,
    189, 215
institutional decline: future of constitution-
    alism and, 7–8
intelligentsia, Russian constitutionalism
    and, 33
Internal Affairs Ministry, 42
internal passports (*propiski*) reforms of, 29
International Labor Organization, 154
Italy, corruption in, 141
Izvestiia, 74, 129

Jackson, Robert (Justice), 119
Japan, 160; corruption in, 141
judges, improved standards and qualifica-
    tions for, 162–65
Judicial Conference of the United States,
    206
judicial reforms: Constitutional Court and,
    84–89, 149–55; constitutionalism and,
    206–8; under Gorbachev, 27–29; im-
    proved standards and qualifications for
    justices and, 162–65; lower courts and,
    155–65; of Tsar Aleksandr II, 13, 97
jury trials, Russian judicial reform and,
    160–61
Justice Ministry, 161
Juviler, Peter, 46, 165, 170–71, 190, 214

Kalmykov, Yuri (Minister), 207n.34
Kazannik, Aleksei I., 122
Khasbulatov, Ruslan, 49, 51, 59, 66, 68,
    87, 121; Yeltsin's relations with, 49, 86
Kholodov, Dmitri, 145n.143
Khrushchev, Nikita, 38, 98
Kievan Rus, 118n.16
Kistiakovski, Bogdan, 112, 116
Kommunist, 95
Konstitutsionnyi Vestnik, 51
Korzhakov, Aleksandr (General), 200n.12
Kosygin, Aleksei, 38
Kovalov, Sergei, 131, 175
krai, federalism and, 133
Kryuchkov, Vladimir, 38
Kudriavtsev, Vladimir, 18, 20, 61n.64, 75–
    76; on corruption in government, 140;
    on federalism, 133; Russian legal con-
    sciousness and, 95–96, 100
Kurashvilli, Boris, 59

Lafitski, Vladimir, 50, 52, 68, 130, 143–
    44, 169
land ownership, rights to, 187–88
Latvia, 178
law-enforcement community: anti-crime
    activities of, 186; police/internal security
    force merger, 79–80, 85, 152; political
    corruption and, 145–46
Law on Amendments and Additions to the
    Constitution of the RSFSR, 78–79
Law on Freedom of Conscience and Reli-
    gious Organizations, 31
Law on Public Associations, 31, 212
Law on Referenda of 1990, 76, 205
Law on the Constitutional Court, 79,
    83n.150, 124, 149, 153
Law on the Presidency, 29–30
Law on the Press and Other Mass Media,
    31, 35
Law on the Status of Deputies, 125
Law on the Status of Judges, 27–28,
    162–63
League of Russian Cities, 135n.97
Lebed, Aleksandr (General), 138
legal consciousness: Constitutional Court
    and raising of, 85–89; constitutionalism
    and, 3–4, 9, 37; corruption and, 141–
    48; emerging paradigm for, 111–13;
    under Gorbachev, 17–22, 42–46,

legal consciousness: (*continued*) 98–99; influence of Soviet ideology on, 48; leadership's impact on, 198–208; masses vs. elites and, 108–11; People's Courts and judicial reform, 155–65; political stability and, 102; post-Soviet political reforms and, 100–101; public participation and support of, 198; rhetoric as tool for raising, 130–31; Russian Federation Constitution and, 170–73; weakness of, in Russia, 95–97; Western influence on, 190–95

legal education in Russia, 162–63

legal nihilism: under Bolsheviks, 15, 37; Russian Federation and, 47–48

legal system: Bolshevism and, 15; Constitutional Court and, 79–90; coup attempt against Gorbachev and, 39–41; Gorbachev's rhetoric concerning, 17–22; in nineteenth-century Russia, 13–14; post-Gorbachev constitutional reforms and, 49; professionalization of, in Russia, 161–63; Russian political culture and, 106–8; Russian suspicion of, 2; in Soviet Union, 15–16

legislative initiatives, legal consciousness and, 204–5

legitimacy of government: August coup as test of, 38–41; Constitutional Conference participants and, 58; corruption and, 142–48; federalism and, 138–39; legal consciousness and, 101–3; reduction of perks and privileges as enhancement of, 146–48; Yeltsin's constitutional reforms and, 69–78

Lempert, David, 100, 106–7, 128, 146, 169–70

Lenin (Vladimir Ilyich Ulyanov), 15–16, 105, 197–98

"Lenin head," as Bolshevik symbol, 112

Lezhnev, Mikhail, 142n.132

Liberal Democratic Party (LDP), 33n.89, 77–78, 177, 215

Linden, Carl, 138

Listyev, Vladislav, 185

Literaturnaya Gazeta, 32

Lithuania: economic reform in, 178; Gorbachev's actions in, 34–35

local arbitration courts, 159

Lukasheva, Elena, 43–44, 95–96, 135, 140, 169, 176

Lukin, Vladimir, 124

Malia, Martin, 180

Man and the Law, 132

Mandela, Nelson, 111

Mandelstam, Nadezhda, 105

Manifesto of 17 October 1905, 14, 171

Marbury v. Madison, 84n.156

Marchenko, Mikhail, 87

market economy, Russian constitutionalism and, 106n.48, 176–77, 188–89, 215–16

Markidonov, Sergei, 142n.132

Marshall, John (Chief Justice), 84n.156

Marx, Karl, 15, 19, 48, 164

masses: as "mystic unit" in Russian culture, 117; Russian political culture and, 105–8; vs. elites, constitutionalism and, 108–11

mass media: constitutionalism and, 210; constitutional rhetoric through, 131–32; coverage of corruption by, 143–44; on Yeltsin's anti-crime measures, 185–86

Mavrodi, Sergei, 142

Medvedev, Roy, 97n.10

Mezhkov, Yuri, 215

Migranyan, Andranik, 20–21, 69, 77, 166–67

Mishin, Avgust, 26, 31–32

Moscow News, 35

Moscow State Institute of International Relations, 10

Moskovski Komsomolets, 145n.143

mozhna concept, 98

Murphy, Walter, 216

National Education Program, 138

nationalism, federalism and, 138

National Salvation Front, 54, 84n.155

National Security Council, 124–25, 201n.7

NATO, Partnership for Peace program, 126n.56, 215

New Moscow Deputies, 27

Nezavisimaya Gazeta, 43

Nicholas II (Tsar), 13n.2, 14, 171

Nikonov, Vyacheslav, 7, 25, 45, 129,

156n.191; on Constitution of the Russian Federation, 165

Nineteenth All-Union Conference of the Communist Party, 24

Nobel Peace Prize, Sakharov's receipt of, 24

nomenklatura: masses vs. elites and, 23, 110; political corruption and, 148

nongovernmental bodies: constitutionalism and, 212; federalism and, 138

nyelza concept, 98

offshore assets, return to Russia of, 189n.368

Okoth-Ogendo, H. W. O., 209

Olshanski, Dimitri, 120

O'Neill, Tip, 49

Organization for Economic Cooperation, 191

organized crime: political corruption and, 141–48; privatization of economy and, 179n.306, 183n.335, 183–86

Orthodox Christianity, Russian constitutionalism and, 115–16, 209, 212–13

Ostankino, 185

ownership, economic reform and, 187–88

Paen, Emil, 126, 133

Pankratov, Vladimir, 185

parliament: attack by Yeltsin on, 66–72, 69n.95; constitutional drafts of early 1990s and, 51–56; constitutionalism and, 203–5, 208–9; coup attempt against Gorbachev and, 38–41; Gorbachev's political reforms and, 24–27, 30–37; murder of deputies in, 142; Russian Federation Constitution and, 167–68, 172n.278

participatory democracy: absence of, in Russian political culture, 105–8; masses vs. elites and, 108–11

partinost, Gorbachev's political reforms and, 32

partisan politics: court procedures and, 159–60; increased role in Russian political culture, 127–28, 210–11. *See also specific parties*

Partnership for Peace, 126n.56, 215

Pashukanis, E., 15

paternalism: human rights in Russia and, 174–75; Russian constitutional reform and, 61–62

Pavlov, Valentin, 38

People's Courts, 155–65

perestroika: federalism and, 137; historical roots of, 13–17; legal system reforms linked to, 18–22, 94, 107–8; Russian political culture and, 96. *See also* economic reform

Perm oblast, 136

Peter the Great, 105

Philadelphia Constitutional Convention, 60

Pisigin, Valery, 5

Pizza Hut, 147

Podgorny, Nikolai, 38

Poland, "little constitution" of, 126

political culture: bureaucracy and, 202; compromise and cooperation in, 115–28; constitutionalism in Russia and, 2–10, 115–28; corruption in government and, 140–48; economic reforms and, 182–86; "evolution from below" model of constitutionalism and, 103–8; federalism and, 133–39; human rights in Russia and, 173–75; judicial reform and, 163–65; legal consciousness, 37–38, 95–98; legitimacy of government and legal consciousness, 101–3; masses vs. elites and, 108–11; new paradigm in post-Soviet Russia, 111–13; parliamentary government and, 203–5; rhetoric's role in, 128–32; role of Duma in, 117–28; Russian Federation Constitution, 166–73

political dissidents. *See* dissent

Poltoranin, Mikhail, 143, 145

"polymerization," of Russian legal and political culture, 96

Ponomaryev, Gennady, 185

Popov, Gavriil, 144

power, law as, in Communist Russia, 98

Pravda, 42, 59–60, 75, 132, 169

pravovoe gosudarstvo (law-based state): Gorbachev's embrace of, 24, 39, 98–99; history of, 13–17; legal consciousness and, 18–22, 96–97, 111–13

pravovoe soznaniye, 98–99

presidency: constitutionalism and, 62n.68, 66–78, 198–203; in Constitution of the Russian Federation, 165–66; cooperation and compromise between Duma and, 121–28; Gorbachev's creation of, 29–30
Presidential Working Group, 54
price reforms, economic reform and, 182–83
prime ministers, cooperation with Duma and, 125–26
privatization: organized crime and, 143; Russian economic reforms and, 179–82, 187–89
privileges, necessity for reduction in, 146–47
procurators, political power of, 156
professionalization of Russia's legal system, 161–63; western contacts for, 192–93
propaganda, constitutionalism in Russian and, 130
property rights, legalization of, 187–88
Provisional Government of 1917, 112
public demonstrations: August coup against Gorbachev and, 39; Gorbachev's ban on, 29, 80, 101; judicial reform and, 163–64
public opinion: Constitutional Conference and, 56–57; on Constitutional Court, 88n.171; constitutional reform and, 55, 171–73, 213; coup attempt against Gorbachev and, 39–41; on economic reform, 216; human rights in Russia and, 173–75; impact of corruption on, 143–44; on organized crime, 184n.340, 185–86; of parliamentary representatives, 118n.20
Pugo, Boris, 38
Putnam, Robert, 212

Quayle, Dan (Vice-president), 162

Racketeer Influenced Corrupt Organizations (RICO) Act (U.S.), 185
"Refusenik," 82
religion, constitutionalism in Russia and, 96, 209
republics: federalism and sovereignty in,

133–36; opposition to constitutional reform from, 63–78
"revolution from above" model, Russian constitutionalism and, 9, 105–8
revolutionary ideology, Russian legal consciousness and, 104–8
rhetoric of law: constitutionalism and, 128–32; government corruption and, 143
Rigby, T. H., 15
Rousseau, Jean-Jacques, 106
Ruble, Blair, 139
Rumyantsev, Oleg, 51–52, 55, 65, 81n.145, 88n.174, 169–70; on constitutional reform, 126, 204, 210; on Russia's political culture, 90, 104
Russian Civil War (1918–21), 183
Russian Constitution of 1978, 49–51
Russian Federation: adoption of draft constitution and, 62–78; background to, 47–48; Constitutional Conference and, 56–62; Constitutional Court of, 78–90; Constitution of, 165–73, 208–10; early constitutional debates of, 48–56; economic reforms in, 178–89
Russian Republic, Declaration of Sovereignty (1990), 104
Russian School of Private Law, 158n.195
Russian Securities and Exchange Commission, 186n.353
Russian Socialist Federated Soviet Republic, 15
Russia's Choice party, 77
Russia's Road to Democracy: Parliament, Communism and Traditional Culture, 96
Russo-Japanese War, 14
Rutskoi, Aleksandr, 66, 68, 87, 121, 138; anti-corruption campaign of, 143, 145
Rybkin, Ivan, 120, 124, 125, 144, 203

Sakharov, Andrei, 24–26, 30, 33n.88, 115, 217
samizdat (underground journals), 41n.117
Sartori, Giovanni, 208
Satarov, Giorgi, 69, 125, 168
Second Russian Congress, Constitutional Court created by, 78–79
Second Russian Republic: birth of, 4, 78
Segodnya, 66n.84, 200–201

separation of powers: Constitutional
   Court rulings based on, 79–80, 84, 153;
   in Constitution of the Russian Federation, 165–67; Gorbachev's political reforms and, 30–37; interbranch relations,
   need for development of, 123–26; political reform in post-Soviet Russia and,
   121–28, 208; presidency and Duma,
   compromise and cooperation between,
   122–28; Russian legal consciousness
   and, 99
Sergeyev, Viktor, 20, 27, 96, 110, 117
"shadow businesses," corruption and, 142
Shakhnazarov, Giorgi, 43–44, 70
Shakhrai, Sergei, 55, 57–58, 122
Sharlet, Robert, 6–7, 69n.95, 78, 94, 108;
   on constitutional reform, 165; on corruption, 144–45
Shumeiko, Vladimir, 75, 124–25, 143, 145
Simonov, Aleksei, 104
Siniavsky, Andrei, 37n.105, 41n.117
600 Seconds, 132
Skorochkin, Sergei, 142
Slavic republics, Union Treaty negotiations
   and, 42–43
Slobodkin, Yuri, 55, 59
small business, rights awareness in,
   187n.356
Smena-New Politics faction, 53
Smolentsev, Yevgeny A., 164
Sobchak, Anatoly, 54–55
Sobyanin, Aleksandr, 74
"social contract democracy," 106
Socialist Revolutionaries, 151
sociopolitical system, masses vs. elites and,
   110
Solzhenitsyn, Aleksandr, 47, 97
Soros, George, 191
South Africa, political reform in, 111
sovershenstvo zakona, 116
Sovetskaya Rossiya, 66
Soviet Constitution of 1924, 26
Soviet Constitution of 1977, 165n.235
Soviet Peace Committee, 10
Soviet Union: attempted revival of, 118–
   19; constitutionalism in, 151, 212–13;
   corruption in, 139–40; legal system un-
   der, 15–17, 47–48, 97–99; People's
   Courts in, 156; political legacy of, 94,
   104, 121; Russian Federation parallels

with, 47–48; Yeltsin's dismantling of,
   42–45, 101
special license plates, for government officials, 146
Speransky, Mikhail, 13n.2
Stalin, Josef: bureaucracy of, 23; constitution of 1936, 15, 60, 76, 112; legal system under, 15–16, 30, 37; purges of,
   68–69, 184; revolutionary ideology of,
   105
stare decisis, Constitutional Court and,
   153–54
Starodubtsev, Vassily, 38n.107
State Committee for the State of Emergency (GKChP), 38
State Council, formation of, 42
State Legal Administration, 130, 201n.17,
   206
Stepashin, Sergei, 125n.52
Stolitsa, 87
Subjects of the Federation, 57, 63
"superpresidentialism": in Constitution of
   Russian Federation, 166
Supreme Court of Russia, 149n.160, 153,
   161, 164, 206
Supreme Soviet: Chechen-Ingushetia decree
   and, 50n.12; Constitutional Conference
   and, 61; constitutionalism and, 51–52,
   65, 118; elections of 1993 and, 146;
   establishment of, 25–26; Gorbachev's
   reforms and, 34–37; Human Rights
   Committee, 131; Yeltsin's disbanding of,
   66–68, 101; Yeltsin's restructuring of,
   42
Sweden, constitutional comparisons with
   Russia, 113

Tartarstan: federalism and, 135–36; inde-
   pendence referendum of, 85, 87n.169
"telephone justice," 156, 163
television: constitutionalism and, 130–32;
   Soviet elections on, 27
Thornburgh, Richard, 192
Tizyakov, Aleksandr, 38n.107
Tocqueville, Alexis de, 10, 160, 188
Tolstoy, Leo, 97
Treaty of Union (1922), 64
Treaty on Social Accord, 124, 136, 170,
   201, 215
Tretyakov, Vitaly, 202–3

trickle-down reform efforts: Russian political culture and, 105–8

Tucker, Robert, 47, 108

Tumanov, Vladimir (Justice), 89n.177, 152–53

Ukraine: economic collapse of, 176–79; independence referendum in, 44

unemployment, economic reform and, 179–80

Union of Advocates of the USSR, 161

Union Treaty, renegotiation of, 42–46

unitarism, and constitutional reform, 73–78

United States Constitution, Russian interest in, 51–52, 54–55, 60, 76, 167n.250, 172, 191–92, 208

United States Supreme Court: Constitutional Court compared with, 84, 165; Russian political culture and, 119

Universal Declaration of Human Rights, 154, 170–71

Urals Republic, 135

Urban, Michael, 74

utopianism, Soviet legal system and, 15

Uzbekistan, anti-crime measures in, 185

Vaksburg, Arkady, 212

verhovenstvo prava (supremacy of law), 19, 37

verhovenstvo zakonov (supremacy of laws), 37

violence, economic reform and, 184

Vitrouk, Nikolas (Justice), 84, 89–90

Voschanov, Pavel, 140

voucher program, economic reform and, 189

Vyshinsky, Andrei, 15

"war of laws," in Constitution of the Russian Federation, 166

western capital investment, economic reform and, 182

western influences on constitutionalism, 190–95, 209–10

women, as People's Court judges, 156

Yakovlev, Aleksandr, 34, 44, 60–62, 70; on judicial procedure, 159; on Russian legal consciousness, 95, 100, 112; on Russian political culture, 123, 128

Yakovlev, Venyamin F., 192

Yakunin, Gleb, 197

Yanayev, Gennady, 38

Yasnaya Polnya, 97n.8

Yavlinsky, Grigory, 127

Yazov, Dimitri, 38

Yegorov, Nikolai, 125n.52

Yeltsin, Boris, 5; acceptance of Duma's amnesty decision, 122; adoption of constitution of, 62–78; anti-crime legislation, 184–85, 199; anti-democratic moves of, 41–45, 68–78, 121–24; Chechnya and, 57, 125n.50, 133, 139, 168, 200–201; Clinton and, 193–94; Communist Party suspended by, 80–83; Constitutional Conference and, 56–62; Constitutional Court and decrees of, 79, 89, 149, 151–52, 156; constitutionalism and, 49–56, 198–203; cooperation and compromise needed by, 117, 121–28, 200–201; corruption in regime of, 140–47; economic reforms of, 178–89, 202–3; election of, 30, 49; executive decree powers of, 199–200; executives ousted by, 199; federalism under, 133–39; Gorbachev coup opposed by, 39–41; health status of, 7; human rights activism and, 175n.288; Khasbulatov's relations with, 49, 86; legal consciousness under, 99–101; merger of Constitutional and Russian Supreme Courts, 149n.160; National Salvation Front ban of, 84n.155; New Moscow Deputies and, 27; nominations to Constitutional Court, 149–50; police/internal security force merger, 79–80, 85, 152; post-coup arrests and bans, 41–42; revolutionary ideology of, 105; rhetoric of, 129–30; Russian Federation Constitution and, 166–68; Russian School of Private Law created by, 158n.195; self-granted emergency powers of, 87; United States support for, 193–95; use of force by, 67–69

Yerin, Viktor, 125n.52

Young Communists (Komsomol), 26

Youngstown Sheet and Tube Co. v. Sawyer, 119

Yugoslavia, Russian policy regarding, 126n.56

zakonost (legalism): August coup against Gorbachev and, 41; economic reforms and, 186–87; political dissidents and, 37, 41n.117; Russian culture of, 37–38, 97

Zavadskaya, Ludmila, 60

Zemskie Sobori, 118

Zhirinovsky, Vladimir, 7, 33n.89, 60, 77, 119; constitutionalism and, 199, 214–15; federalism and, 138; Russian anti-crime measures and, 185

Zorkin, Valery, 1, 66, 76, 127n.64; Constitutional Court and, 80–81, 85–90, 151–52, 152n.173; on democracy in Russia, 123